"A breath of spring to the troubled heart. Don't miss this uplifting collection of stories that will lift your soul and stretch your faith."

Ed Hindson, Ph.D.
Dean of the Institute of Biblical Studies
Liberty University

"These stories can bring a touch of healing to both those who have suffered some terrible tragedy, as well as to those who must watch others suffer."

Archibald D. Hart, Ph.D.
Professor of Psychology
Fuller Theological Seminary

"As a counselor, I highly recommend it to my colleagues and to anyone who struggles with the concept of hope. The theme of hope as both a noun and a verb is well articulated from the preface to the last page of the book."

Jane Lynne Stockinger, BSN, MSW
Christian Counseling Center
Grand Rapids, Michigan

Hope Grows in Winter

Hope Grows in Winter

INSPIRING REAL-LIFE STORIES OF
HOW HOPE CHANGES LIVES

WOODROW KROLL &
GEORGE D. MILLER III
GENERAL EDITORS

kregel
PUBLICATIONS

Grand Rapids, MI 49501

Hope Grows in Winter: Inspiring Real-Life Stories of How Hope Changes Lives

Published by Kregel Publications, a division of Kregel, Inc., P.O. Box 2607, Grand Rapids, MI 49501. For more information about Kregel Publications, visit our web site: www.kregel.com

Cover photo: PhotoDisc

Library of Congress Cataloging-in-Publication Data
Hope grows in winter: inspiring real-life stories of how hope changes lives / [edited] by Woodrow Kroll and George Miller III
    p.   cm.
  Includes bibliographical references.
  1. Hope—Religious aspects—Christianity. I. Kroll, Woodrow Michael
BV4638 .H66   2000   248.8'6–dc21   00-032702
                                        CIP

ISBN 0-8254-3062-3

Printed in the United States of America

1 2 3 4 5 / 04 03 02 01 00

Contents

Contributors

Bill Boulet, B.A.
Senior Pastor, Heritage Baptist Church, Lakeland, Fla.
Board: Practical Bible College

Donald Hall, Ed.D.
Vice President, Practical Bible College, Binghamton, N.Y.
Graduate: Practical Bible College

Ron Hawkins, Ed.D.
Dean, College of Arts and Sciences,
Liberty University, Lynchburg, Va.
Graduate: Practical Bible College

Charles F. (Chick) Kiloski, D.D.
Senior Pastor, First Baptist Church, Altoona, Pa.
Graduate: Practical Bible College

Woodrow Kroll, Th.D.
President and Senior Bible Teacher,
Back to the Bible, Lincoln, Neb.
Former President: Practical Bible College

Robert Lightner, Th.D.
Professor of Systematic Theology Emeritus,
Dallas Theological Seminary, Dallas, Tex.
Adjunct Professor: Practical Bible College

R. Peter Mason, D.Min.
Executive Director, Conservative Baptist Association Northeast,
Oneonta, N.Y.
Adjunct Professor: Practical Bible College

Don McNeal, B.A.
Assistant Pastor, New Testament Baptist Church, Miami, Fla.
Adjunct Professor: Practical Bible College

Carol Miller, M.D.
Physician, Obstetrics and Gynecology, Binghamton, N.Y.
Board: Practical Bible College

George Miller III, Ed.D.
President, Practical Bible College, Binghamton, N.Y.
Graduate: Practical Bible College

Gil Parker, D.Min.
Vice President, Practical Bible College, Binghamton, N.Y.
Graduate: Practical Bible College

Michael Peck, D.Min.
Senior Pastor, Central Baptist Church, Binghamton, N.Y.
Graduate: Practical Bible College

Dino Pedrone, D.Min.
Senior Pastor, New Testament Baptist Church, Miami, Fla.
Board: Practical Bible College

Bill Pepper
Senior Pastor, Grace Bible Church, Altoona, Pa.
Graduate: Practical Bible College

Preface

SEVERAL YEARS AGO I learned what it means that hope grows in winter. I suppose I already knew, but I had somewhat of a "winter experience" that imbedded in my mind forever the fact that, when life blows its coldest chill, that's when hope grows its strongest.

I was making plans to travel to India to preach in churches large and small, even in fields and on river banks. My travels required a visa, so my wife and I applied. Linda's visa came back in a matter of days; mine did not. I called the Indian Embassy in Washington, D.C. and they told me not to worry. "It's probably just some snafu somewhere. It will come." Weeks went by. No visa. I called again, and again I was assured, "We're just waiting for clearance. There's no problem. Just be patient." Patience was becoming my middle name.

As the time for our departure drew near, I again faxed the embassy to see what was holding up my visa. Return fax: "Don't worry. It's almost complete. Maybe tomorrow." Tomorrow came and went with no visa.

Finally, it was the day we were to leave and I still had no visa. In desperation I called the embassy again. At 9 A.M. all was well. The visa would be waiting for me at the airport in New York. By 10 things had changed. No visa was coming. My hopes were dashed. Around 11:15, my pleadings by phone again secured the promise that the visa would be issued and everything would be okay. Hope soared. But by noon I received the final word: No visa. No explanation was given. My hope was buried beneath the cold snow.

Hope is a tricky thing and sometimes can be cruel. It's when our lives are covered with winter's deep chill that hope seems to die. That's what had happened to me. But while my hope was being buried by circumstances, I learned a valuable lesson. Hope is not what you do; hope is what you have. Hope is a noun. Hope doesn't die in winter, hope grows in winter. It's the most difficult circumstances of life, the winter seasons of life, that give rise to the strongest hope.

A year later I obtained a visa, flew halfway around the world, and enjoyed some of the most productive preaching ministry I've ever experienced. But that whole episode taught me something: Because hope is a noun, hope grows, even in winter.

That's what this book is all about—growing hope in the winter seasons of life. Making hope a concrete possession every day, not just when the sun is shining and the south winds are warm. Your life can be lived with the reality of hope, not just the prospect of hope.

Hope as a Noun

In the Hebrew Old Testament as well as the Greek New Testament, hope is a prominent word. It is used both as a noun and a verb, as it is in English. There are more than a dozen Hebrew words translated *hope*, and even though they look and sound very different in Hebrew, they are all remarkably similar in meaning.

When Bible translators attempt to accurately translate words with multiple meanings, they look for the context to give them some help. As a result, these Bible scholars have translated *hope* far more frequently as a noun than as a verb. In fact, the ratio is 3:1. In the New Testament the story is much the same.

What makes hope so concrete in the Bible? It is because hope is not something we grasp at in the warmth of summer, only to have it dashed in the bitter winter seasons of life; hope is something we possess in all seasons of life. That's why the New Testament writers especially speak about what we have when we have hope. For example, we have:

Hope of resurrection	Acts 23:6
Hope of the promise	Acts 26:6
Hope of Israel	Acts 28:20
Hope of glory	Romans 5:2; Colossians 1:27
Hope of righteousness	Galatians 5:5
Hope of your calling	Ephesians 1:18; 4:4
Hope laid up in heaven	Colossians 1:5
Hope of the gospel	Colossians 1:23
Hope of salvation	1 Thessalonians 5:8
Hope of eternal life	Titus 1:2
Hope set before us	Hebrews 6:18

In each case, hope is a very tangible thing. It is something we have, not something we do. We even have a blessed hope (Titus 2:13), a better hope (Heb. 7:19) and a living hope (1 Peter 1:3)—all nouns. Because we know hope is a present possession, we can rest in hope (Acts 2:26) and rejoice in hope (Rom. 5:2; 12:12). In fact, in my favorite expression of the concreteness of hope, the prophet Zechariah says that God's people are "prisoners of hope" (Zech. 9:12). If you're going to be a captive, that's the best kind to be!

Stories of Hope

The Bible is filled with great stories of hope. Who can forget the three Hebrew children in the fiery furnace? The flames may have been hot, but this was definitely a winter season of life for Shadrach, Meshach, and Abed-nego. They were going through the toughest, most chilling experience of their lives. There didn't seem to be any hope for them to survive. And yet, when King Nebuchadnezzar took a peak into the furnace, he observed, "Look . . . I see four men loose, walking in the midst of the fire; and they are not hurt, and the form of the fourth is like the Son of God" (Dan. 3:25). Hope grew in the winter season.

And what about when King Darius asked Daniel after a night in the lions' den, "Has your God, whom you serve continually, been able to deliver you from the lions?" (Dan. 6:20). That was Daniel's winter experience. The king posed the question hoping that Daniel would somehow still be alive. It was a verb, something Darius was doing. Daniel's response, however, was a noun, something God had done. "My God sent His angel and shut the lions' mouths, so that they have not hurt me . . ." (Dan. 6:22). Again, hope grew in the winter experience of Daniel's life.

Perhaps there is no greater story of hope in the Bible than when the women came to the tomb seeking Jesus that first resurrection Sunday morning. It was the darkest time of their lives—the winter of their existence. They came doing the verb thing; they left with the noun thing. They hoped to find someone to roll away the stone. They left with the concrete hope that Jesus is alive. Hope grew in the winter of Christ's days and nights in a dark tomb.

But not all the good stories of hope occur in the Scriptures. Some are stories of everyday life today. God is still the God of hope. Hope in the concrete, not hope in the abstract. Hope that grows in the winter of life, the toughest season of all to have hope.

Real-Life Stories of Hope

More than two years ago, Dr. George Miller III and Dr. Donald Hall came to visit me at my home in Nebraska. Dr. Hall was the academic dean at Practical Bible College of Binghamton, New York, and Dr. Miller was the president. George and I share much in common, for that's the position I held before coming to Back to the Bible.

Practical was founded in 1900 by evangelist John A. Davis. For its entire history, the campus has been perched on a knoll overlooking the Susquehanna River in the southern tier of New York State. Also throughout its history, the college has prepared men and women for vocational ministry. And since the year 2000 marks the one-hundredth anniversary of PBC, George and Don came to me with an idea.

So many men and women who have been associated with Practical over the years have seen hope grow in the winter experiences of their lives. So many have served in out of the way places, with little or no recognition. So many have held on to hope as a noun rather than watch it escape as a verb. Their idea was to encourage all of you who may be wondering if hope is dead or alive in your life, with stories of those whose lives have been changed by hope. They asked me to compile those touching stories.

In the pages that follow you will read stories from real-life people—all of them friends of mine—who discovered that hope grows in winter. For them, hope is a noun. Each author will tell his or her own story of hope. And each of them enjoys a three-fold bond with the other authors. Like the proverbial three-fold cord, that bond cannot be broken. First, each has a dynamic relationship with God through a personal relationship with Jesus Christ. Second, each author has experienced a winter season in life and yet hope grew during that season. And third, each one is associated with Practical Bible College—as a graduate, a member of the faculty, a member of the board, or some other close relationship.

In many respects, *Hope Grows in Winter* is our tribute to the one hundred years that Practical has been used of God to prepare men and women for global impact. It is our tribute to hope. It is our way of saying that for this college, hope was never just a verb; hope has always been a noun.

As you read these inspiring stories, my prayer for you is that of Paul for the Romans: "Now may the God of hope fill you with all joy and peace in believing, that you may abound in hope by the power of the Holy Spirit" (Rom. 15:13). Remember, when life deals you a cold wintry blast, hope grows in winter.

WOODROW KROLL
Lincoln, Nebraska

Bouncing Back from Disappointment

Don McNeaſ

HOPE IS SOMETIMES ELUSIVE. It's hard to hold onto, especially through frustration and failure. Although I've had my share of success, I've also had an equal share of disappointment. The most visible took place in Pasadena, California, at Super Bowl XVII.

I remember it as if it were yesterday. But I don't remember it from the secluded safety of the stands, tucked away among the hundred thousand screaming fans at this annual rite of pro football. Nor do I remember it as one of the millions watching on TV from their favorite easy chair. I remember it from the football field.

My Greatest Disappointment

On that field, I missed a tackle on John Riggins. As a result, my team, the Miami Dolphins, lost the Super Bowl. That moment stands out as my greatest disappointment; I can't believe that I didn't bring him down. In fact, every time I see the replay I still think that I'm going to make the tackle. Even today, I can close my eyes and see the play unfold with startling clarity.

This was my first Super Bowl and the game was an intense battle from the beginning. The Washington Redskins and the Dolphins were evenly matched. The Redskins boasted one of the finest defenses in the NFL, and a daunting offense. In the Dolphins lineup were some of the best players ever to step on a football field, plus we carried a legacy. Ours was the only NFL franchise that had accomplished a perfect season—the memory of the 1972 Miami Dolphins was part of who we were. So players from both teams came onto the gridiron with a "We are the best!" mind-set. Both teams fervently expected to win.

Fourth and One

The pivotal moment of the game came early in the fourth quarter. The Dolphins were ahead. It was a fourth-down play and the Redskins needed one yard for a first down. If we stopped them, there was a good chance we could take hold of the momentum and go on to win the game.

About ten minutes remained as the Redskins broke from their huddle. I just knew we were going to stop them. I slipped as I changed direction while following a receiver who was in motion. Then they snapped the ball. For some reason, every one of our players was blocked except me. I drew a bead on the backfield. This stop was mine to make and mine alone. I steamed untouched across the line of scrimmage toward Riggins, as if he were waiting for me. I remember every thought: *I am going to make this tackle! . . . This is going to be a five-yard loss. . . . We're going to win the Super Bowl.*

I hit him hard, so hard that he had to go down. But he didn't. *Come on guys, where are you?* I thought as I held onto his jersey. I can visualize that moment today in slow motion, as I lost my grip and started to slide down. Grasping his fishnet jersey in one hand, I felt the material under my fingernails. Just as determined to get free as I was to hold him, Riggins was pushing my head down with his right hand. His powerful legs churned. Then the last vestige of hope faded as he tore away from my fingers, and I lost my grip. John raced away for the go-ahead touchdown. We would never catch up. The Redskins won Super Bowl XVII, 27 to 17.

Even now, words fail to describe my feelings of disappointment. I had let my teammates down. I had let my coaches down. I had let our fans down. And I had let myself down. To make matters worse, millions of people across the world had seen it. Millions. Everybody knew I failed. My family, my coaches, and my teammates did not blame me for losing the game. With time I learned not to blame myself. In fact, this most embarrassing disappointment has become the source of my greatest opportunity to share God's Word. What was a hopeless failure turned out to be a hopeful change in my life.

Just Go Through It

Of course I'm not the first to encounter deep waters. I think about another team who faced water as far as the eye could see. The sea blocked their way forward. They could go to the north or south along the coast and eventually get around the sea. Without a doubt, their enemies would catch them if they tried to run down the shoreline. The leader heard fear-filled voices of his people as they wondered what was to become of them. *What do I do now?* he may have thought. *It seems fruitless to try to go up the coast. How did I get us in this situation anyway?* Once again his gaze returned to the waters of the Red Sea. *If we only had some way to cross the sea, then we could get away.*

Suddenly God brought hope to a hopeless situation. Moses heard God instruct him to lift his staff high in the air and stretch it out over the Red Sea. As Moses obeyed God, a most awesome event occurred. While the armies of Pharaoh remained confused by the dark clouds God had placed behind the children of Israel, a mighty wind blew upon the waters of the sea. As the wind blew through the night, it parted the waters and dried out the muddy bottom so that God's children had a path to the far shore.

But the path to deliverance still seemed as frightening as anything they had yet encountered. More than one Israelite must have quaked while walking between the towering walls of water. Many must have thought, *What if the water comes crashing down? What if the winds stop blowing? We will all drown!*

They did cross the Red Sea, though, by the path that God provided, and they were delivered from captivity.

As I read the story of the Red Sea, I remember the words of my father: "Never go around a problem; just go through it." That is what the children of Israel did. They went right through the problem as God provided the way.

God's provision for the Israelites has run through my mind at every trial. And it has provided the hope to enable me to bounce back from those disappointments.

Second Timothy 1:7 says, "For God has not given us a spirit of fear, but of power and of love and of a sound mind." The Greek word the apostle Paul chose, which we translate "fear," means the "spirit of cowardice." God does not give us a spirit of cowardice and hesitation; He provides us with a spirit of confidence and hope. This Scripture served as my anchor after my Super Bowl failure and it continues to steady me whenever I am tempted to lose hope now. It does not matter what disappointments I experience, God provides an active hope within me so that I can, in the words of my dad, "Just go through it."

God Prepares Us for Disappointments

Someone once said that the easiest way to see God's will for your life is to look at it in retrospect, as through a rearview mirror. It's much easier to see His movement in our lives when we reflect on the journey behind us than when we try to predict what He plans for the future. Looking back, we often see clearly how something that did not make sense at the time has proven to be essential. During the times that do not make sense, hope makes it possible to demonstrate a vibrant faith in God. Oswald Chambers put it this way: "Faith is the deliberate confidence in the character of God whose ways you may not understand at the time."[1]

Through his life, my father showed me that we must never allow life to dictate our choices. We must take responsibility for our own decisions. When we do, God will sustain us. I learned that this is true as I grew up with ten brothers and sisters in the small town of Atmore, Alabama. The most significant event in my early life was the death of my mother when I was six years old. I clearly remember the night my father and one of my older sisters took her to the hospital, but she did not come home. Although people urged my father to split up the family, so others could help raise the children, he was adamant that he would keep us together as a family. He did just that. We had a lot of hardship because we were poor. We lived on a small farm and all of us worked hard just to make it.

I knew that my mother was a Christian, but it was not until I was ten years old, four years after her death, that I dealt with the issue of eternal life.

My oldest sister, Eunice, was visiting the family. My mother's death continued to trouble me, and I asked Eunice, "Where did Mom go when she died?" In response, my sister explained the salvation story to me, and in simple faith I asked Jesus to come into my heart and life as Savior.

We can never overestimate the power of love in a Christian family. Although my mother had gone on to heaven, each of us kids remained faithful to one another, just as my father remained faithful to us. Watching my family survive those difficult years, I first saw hope in action. That hope became ingrained in my spiritual and emotional being. I have never doubted that I could overcome any obstacle. In no small part, this is due to the hope that took root and grew during my early life.

My life is not very different from the lives of other Christians. Job says, "Yet man is born to trouble, as the sparks fly upward" (Job 5:7). God uses our hardships to mold us for His work. For example, one of my teammates on the Miami Dolphins lost his young daughter in a drowning accident. A cousin of mine, who was playing for the Houston Oilers, lost his life when he overdosed on drugs. A young couple in our church experienced unimaginable tragedy when their four-year-old son accidentally shot to death his two-year-old brother. A promising marriage ended in early divorce for the daughter of a good friend.

Heartaches are inevitable; they are the season of winter for our spirits. But we must have hope if we are to overcome them without becoming bitter or defeated. Only through the presence and power of God, can that hope grow even in winter. God uses all of our experiences to foster that growth.

A friend at church once commented, "Don, it must be really tough for a professional athlete to live a Christian life." The statement threw me for a minute, and I looked at him as if he'd gone crazy. "It's not hard at all," I said, "if you know what you believe in before you become an athlete. But I guess it would be very difficult if I had not settled the issue."

My friend's comment reinforced the decision I had made long before I played for the Miami Dolphins—to place God first in my life. Once I made this decision, I constantly experienced the presence and power of the Holy Spirit, even during my difficult childhood. It's this presence of the Holy Spirit that makes hope so enduring. My goal became "Lord, use my life!" Once I made this commitment to Him, everything else, even disappointment, became His tool for making me what He needed me to be.

Public Disappointments

All of us face an almost infinite variety of disappointments, some public, some private, some personal. Public disappointments are those times when we fail in the eyes of others. Looking back, I believe that God used all of my experiences to prepare me for my great public disappointment—that missed tackle in the Super Bowl. He produced in me an active hope that truly is a noun, not a passive hope that remains a verb.

But not all public disappointments happen before the cameras. A marriage that dissolves in divorce is a public disappointment. For many Christians, getting a divorce means feeling the scorn—real or imagined—of other Christians. Often divorced people live with a feeling of unending sorrow. They "failed" in this most sacred of trusts—to live "happily ever after." It can be a crushing burden if faced without hope.

Not graduating at the top of the class can be a public disappointment. It means not only being personally disappointed, but also feeling the disappointment of parents as well. Starting a business on sheer determination, only to discover that the cash to continue is not available, can be a great public disappointment. You have failed, and others have reason to be disappointed in you. Or your spouse is disappointed in you because you just can't seem to get this parenting thing right.

Five of the most powerful words in the English language are, "I am disappointed in you." When used appropriately, such words goad us into correcting flawed behavior and give needed chastisement. When used unfairly, they can scar forever and render hope ineffective. Usually the latter is the case.

In team sports, the approval of teammates is very important. Because I stayed in contact with my former team members, the need for their approval continued after I retired. So I felt let down when a former teammate expressed disappointment in me that I had chosen to enter the ministry.

"Don, why in the world would you want to do that?" he asked. "You can't make any money working for God." Although he has since come to be more supportive, his initial response remains somewhat painful. I was excited to be answering God's call, and my former teammate's disappointment deflated me. Yet God gave me a hope in my calling, which made it possible to deal positively with this friend's lack of understanding.

Disappointment in Yourself

There are times when we become disappointed in ourselves because of what takes place in the public eye. Missing a tackle in a crucial game, before millions, was like that. That event was more traumatic than it might seem, simply because of the extreme competitive atmosphere of professional sports. Athletes are measured only by their achievements during the game. Every professional football player wants to be on the field every play, in on every down. Those who don't hunger for playing time, won't last long in the National Football League.

There came a time in my professional career when I was relegated to playing only in specific situations or on third downs. I had to adjust to spending more time on the sidelines than on the field. That was tough. Even though my contribution to the team was still deemed to be important, I felt like a failure. Family and friends came to the games to see me play, not to see me stand on the sidelines. At that temptation to give up hope, I had to find a way to channel my feelings into something positive. So I took up a new challenge to be an encouragement to my fellow defensive backs.

I made a deliberate decision to speak a word of encouragement to my teammates every time they took the field: "Come on Liffort, you can do it! Focus, concentrate, make the play! We can win this game, guys!" I was determined to be a source of positive energy and enthusiasm. Being forced to stand on the sidelines and to cheer others on turned out to be one of the most important spiritual lessons I ever learned. It is vitally important to actively and verbally support our Christian brothers and sisters, especially during those times when God may be using them in a more visible or prominent role than the place where He is using us. It is just this spirit of unity that is taught throughout the New Testament. The Lord extolled the early church, and us today, to be the body of Christ in its truest sense.

Letting Family Down

A friend and his family recently traveled to Orlando to see his niece play in a volleyball tournament. Bob and Anita and their two children, Heather and Will, were excited to have the chance to see Crystal play and to spend time with her parents, Tom and Sherry.

A high school senior, Crystal was playing at a very competitive level of club volleyball. College scouts often attend these club tournaments to seek players for their schools. In fact, the purpose of many of the tournaments is more to demonstrate the skills of the players than to determine the best team.

Crystal's mom and dad believed in her and had invested in her volleyball career, hoping that she would have the opportunity to win a college scholarship. An excellent player, she was featured in local newspapers as early as her sophomore year. Stories highlighting her team-leading number of kills were common. But her skills developed to a higher level once she became involved with club ball, and this would be the first time Bob and his family could see her play.

Much to everyone's disappointment, however, Crystal did not get to play much. The regular coach could not make the trip, and the inexperienced assistant coach made very few substitutions. As disappointed as her family was, Crystal was even more disappointed. She said to her mom, "I hope Uncle Bob doesn't think I'm a bad player because I'm not getting to play."

To the contrary, Bob never thought of her as anything but an excellent player. He knew that Crystal had received multiple scholarship offers to play college volleyball. And yet she felt extreme disappointment because she was not able to play when Uncle Bob and Aunt Anita and the kids were there to watch.

Life is filled with disappointments like that, many of them public. Through no fault of our own, we are often stuck on the sidelines, just when we want to show others what we can do. This does not mean that we are failures; it means we are being given an opportunity to strengthen our hope. As Job said, "Though He slay me, yet will I trust Him" (Job 13:15). Public disappointments can be God's tools to build hope.

More Disappointment

I have been forced to build hope through a variety of public disappointments, in and apart from my NFL career. One of the most significant experiences of my ministry was just such a disappointment.

While our church was between pastors and searching for God's man, I was asked to serve as the youth pastor. God has given me a very special burden for young people in America, and this seemed like the ideal position for me. But when our new pastor arrived, one of the first staff members he added was a youth pastor, and I was asked to accept the responsibility for (are you ready for this?) the *children's* programs. Big NFL defensive back in charge of the children's ministry. It kind of blew my mind.

My first thought was, *What did I do wrong?* The children's ministry felt like such a demotion. I had great dreams for our youth ministry and to turn over those responsibilities was one of the toughest tests of just how concrete my hope really was. Why? Because I thought it would communicate to others in the church that I was not cutting it as the youth pastor. While I was assured this was not the case, and though God used this circumstance to effect His will in my life, the disappointment was severe nevertheless.

Advice and Covenants

How did I get beyond this disappointment? Not easily! I was extremely tempted to find a ministry in another church. I had no doubt that I could find another position because I still had some name recognition. But I knew God did not want me to leave our church. I was convinced of that. So I did two things: First, I remembered my covenant to God, that I wanted Him to use my life. I restated it in this simple prayer: "Dear God, I am Your man. I will do what You want me to do. Period." Second, I again remembered my dad's advice on how to handle adversity: "Just go through it."

The best way to live with public disappointments is to remember that we are in the family of God. I have always been known as a "team player," and in God's family the team is the church. Therefore, whatever I chose to do I had to do it with unflagging devotion to my family—my church. I had to make us all look good in the eyes of our Father.

Also, in order to bounce back, you must find some of "His appointments" among your disappointments. I cannot adequately describe the satisfaction and contentment that God has allowed me to experience through working with young children. Serving as a children's pastor has brought to life the words of Jesus: "Suffer the little children. . . . Lest ye be like a little child. . . ." I was confronted with the reality of the extraordinary love and value Christ placed on children. If they are this important to our Savior, how come it took me so long to see how important the ministry to children is for the kingdom?

His Appointments

The position as children's pastor was God's appointment for me. And when I now think of that period I am warmed by many memories, but two stand out. The first is of the Bible Times Marketplace, an alternative Halloween program we stage each year. We transform our school gymnasium into a Bible-times village and marketplace complete with petting corral, pottery makers, storytellers, a well, and musical instruments. We all share the excitement and a sense of camaraderie as we plan, build the village, conduct the event, tear down afterward, and clean up the mess. It is as rewarding as any national championship game I ever played.

The other event is the annual Easter Egg hunt, including the "resurrection eggs" we use to tell the Easter story. It has immeasurable impact for the kingdom on the lives of our most valuable responsibility—our children.

Was it disappointing to be "demoted" to the children's ministry? Was it hard to accept that God's hand was in my life, even during this time of angst? You bet it was! But it was also a time to show the Enemy that I would not wilt under the pressure of disappointment and uncertainty. I would not give in to the spirit of fear during times of battle, and neither should you. You and I must take great joy in the struggle, while seeing each lesson learned as the precursor for ultimate success. This will never happen without an active hope, hope that is solid and always present.

Private Disappointments

As difficult as public disappointments may be, private ones can be even more destructive to one's grasp of hope. Private disappointments come in two kinds. The first is when others fail your expectations—when someone you really admire lets you down. The second comes when your dreams and desires are not fulfilled.

Let Down by Those You Look Up To

We all face our share of letdowns. The resignation of the pastor who first brought me to New Testament Baptist Church was such an experience. I had such confidence in him, and it was traumatic to see him fail and leave. In one sense, when we experience deep private disappointment we lose a little of our naiveté, and that's not all bad. But with it we may lose a lot of hope, and that's not good.

I also recall a high school teammate who possessed exceptional ability and talent. Yet he wouldn't make the commitment necessary to develop his talent. He was like many Christians who have potential to change the world for Christ, yet they lack the heart to be completely sold out to God. It is easy to become disappointed in them and write them off. But we must remain hopeful that God will get ahold of these Christians and use them in a mighty way.

Personal Betrayal

Another type of private disappointment is when someone we trust takes advantage of us. On a couple of occasions during my professional career, people I knew and trusted took advantage of me for money. More than the monetary loss, I was hurt by the disappointment that someone had misled me or had not failed to keep a promise.

On one occasion, I agreed to become a partner with a man I thought was honorable. I invested a modest sum of money to secure a hair salon. We were to share equally in the business responsibilities and income. But he failed to fulfill his end of the deal, and I was left with all of the responsibility.

I was a professional football player. What did I know about running a salon? In time I was able to sell the business, and the employees did not suffer undue hardship. I am not even sure I lost money on the deal. But my high hopes for a different sort of professional relationship were unrealized by a personal betrayal, an act that is more painful than the loss of money.

I often think of the parable of the landowner who established a vineyard in a foreign land. When it came time to reap the harvest, the people he put in charge treated him poorly. At first, they beat the servants he sent to collect, then they killed the servants sent to collect, and eventually they killed his son, whom he sent to collect (Matt. 21:33-44).

Why would the landowner have any sort of hope that they would give him and his son respect in light of the disappointments of their past actions? Because of "uncommon hope," that's why. God instills in us a hope that is supernatural, that empowers us to believe when all the evidence points to doubt. We must believe that God will touch hearts and change lives, even in those who have taken advantage of us. That is rock-solid hope to touch and feel, not just to believe in.

When Dreams Are Dashed

A second type of private disappointment is that of unfulfilled dreams and expectations. From 1976 to 1980 I played four years at defensive back for the University of Alabama without suffering a serious injury. I was blessed with a remarkable career, including back-to-back national championships (1978 and 1979), most valuable player awards, and all-American honors. I had the privilege of playing for Bear Bryant, perhaps the greatest collegiate football coach of all time. I was co-captain with Tony Nathan, another athlete who went on to play professional football. In fact, Tony and I played together for the Dolphins and were both inducted into the University of Alabama Sports Hall of Fame.

I thoroughly expected that my professional career would be equally blessed. I visualized being on a Super Bowl champion team, playing in the pro-bowl, winning most valuable player awards. I hoped that one day I might be inducted into the NFL Hall of Fame. None of this was to be, for I began to sustain injuries almost immediately after joining the NFL.

In 1980, I was the Dolphins first-round draft choice, and I eagerly reported to training camp, where I would play for yet another famous coach—Don Shula. I worked hard in training camp and won a starting job in the defensive backfield. My dreams were on the way to fruition. Then, after starting thirteen games as a rookie, I broke my wrist and tore ligaments in my thumb, ending my rookie season before the playoffs even started.

Fifteen games into the next season, I broke my right forearm and had to have surgery. I was able to come back for the playoffs that year, with a cast on my arm. Although we lost in the first round of the playoffs, I felt like I had triumphed simply by being on the field.

The next two years were even worse. I missed all of my third season because of a ruptured Achilles tendon. The fourth season I spent four weeks on injured reserve with a knee injury. I was injury-free no more.

Keeping Hope Alive

I never doubted that I would play again. Through all of the disappointments, all of the pain, all of the rehabilitation, I constantly visualized myself on the field making the key plays. I possessed hope in the concrete, not in the abstract.

I did play six more years with the Dolphins, including a second Super Bowl. We played the San Francisco 49ers in Super Bowl XIX and lost 38 to 16. I was never named to the pro-bowl, nor did I receive an

MVP award. I will never be inducted into the NFL Hall of Fame. I live with these very real disappointments. I now know that God used these circumstances to allow me to better serve the kingdom.

Most of us enter adult life with great dreams for success—a happy marriage, a fulfilling career, a healthy financial portfolio. But we soon face reality: some of our youthful dreams may go unrealized. What sustains us during the times of honest acceptance? Only one thing. Hope.

In my case, I thought I had left behind the private disappointments of unfulfilled expectations with my football career. I was on to my new career, my calling from God. Things would be different now.

The first time I spoke from the pulpit was a Wednesday night service. I was to bring the message, and I prepared hard. I knew I was ready. I was pumped and couldn't wait to get out there and just do it. Yet when I stepped up to the pulpit, I experienced strange and unaccustomed behavior. My hands shook, and I could barely speak. It's true what they say—the fear of speaking in public can be the number-one fear in the world. It certainly happened to me. After a couple of minutes, I turned to the pastor and let him know that I could not continue. Then I sat down. What a bitter disappointment I was to everyone, including myself!

It seemed as if God could never make a preacher out of me. It just wasn't going to happen. Little did I realize what God had in store for me. Because I had learned to cling to hope during all of my injuries, I did not lose hope that I could become a preacher.

My private disappointment in myself was matched by the public embarrassment I felt about letting down my pastor and my church. They did not see it that way, of course. In fact, everyone encouraged me to continue and I have. The combination of their belief in me and my hope in God kept me going.

Never Lose Hope

Any Christian can be sustained by hope in God. God is never done with our lives. We must never lose hope. He will provide someone to believe in you, and He will enable you to do anything He calls you to do. Just keep hope.

I know that's what John Mark must have done. Remember him? On Paul's first missionary journey he was accompanied by Barnabas and John Mark, an inexperienced young defensive-back type, full of enthusiasm and promise. And yet after the trio set sail from Paphos on the Island of Cyprus and docked at Pamphylia, the region of the southern coast of modern Turkey, John decided to return home to Jerusalem. No explanation. No warning. No reason. He just left (Acts 13:13).

When it came time for Paul and Barnabas to set out on their second missionary journey, Barnabas again wanted to take his young relative, John Mark. Paul refused. Bite me once, shame on you. Bite me twice, shame on me. "But Paul insisted that they should not take with them the one who had departed from them in Pamphylia, and had not gone with them to the work" (Acts 15:38). So strong was the difference of opinion that Barnabas took John Mark and sailed to Cyprus for ministry. Paul took Silas and journeyed overland to Asia Minor.

Although there is no mention of Paul and Mark working together after that incident, in the last epistle he wrote, Paul begged his associate, Timothy, "Get Mark and bring him with you, for he is useful to me for ministry" (2 Tim. 4:11). Even disappointments can turn out to be "His appointments" when you hold on to hope.

I have had disappointments and heartaches, as well as blessings. Through it all, hope has sustained me. Hope makes up the core of my being, and I am grateful to those who have helped shape the Don McNeal who now serves his Lord.

I talked with a reporter from *USA Today* prior to Super Bowl XIX about missing the tackle on John Riggins two years earlier:

"For two years, I've been watching that play. Friends have told me that every time they see it, they always hope that I'll make the play. But I'm glad I was there in the Super Bowl, and I'm glad we've got the opportunity to go back and play for the world championship one more time—and this time the outcome is gonna be different."[2]

The outcome wasn't different. This time we lost to the 49ers. But while my team lost a football game, I never lost hope. God is now using my experiences with disappointment to minister to others who have experienced disappointments.

That's just what Paul said would happen: "Blessed be the God and Father of our Lord Jesus Christ, the Father of mercies and God of all comfort, who comforts us in all our tribulation, that we may be able to comfort those who are in any trouble, with the comfort with which we ourselves are comforted by God. For as the sufferings of Christ abound in us, so our consolation also abounds through Christ" (2 Cor. 1:3–5). I have been buoyed by hope so that I may buoy the hopes of others. I could never have my current ministry had it not been for the grace of God in allowing me to miss that one tackle, viewed by millions around the world (and by me) as a disappointment. That day was the longest winter day of my life, but hope grows in winter. I'm living proof.

Because of my disappointment at being "demoted" to children's pastor, I am now able to reach out to young people beyond the walls of our church in ways that, as a youth pastor, I could never have dreamed. God knew what He was doing after all. Now I travel all across America with Sports World, an organization of former professional athletes who are Christians. Each month we share our testimonies with thousands of young people. A big part of my message to them is the message of hope.

Do you think that a high profile disappointment like missing that tackle makes me more credible when speaking to these kids? You bet it does! Nearly every young person with whom I speak can relate to disappointment. God is using my life as a source of encouragement and hope for others. My charge is that hope is what the Christian has, not what the Christian does. So hang on to the hope that will get you through life's greatest disappointments.

Chapter Notes

1. Quoted in George Sweeting, *Who Said That?* (Chicago: Moody, 1994), 190.
2. Gary Mihoces, "McNeal Replays Riggins' TD Run Many Times Over," *USA Today*, 8 January 1985.

Surviving the Death of a Child

Donald Hall

A CHRISTIAN SHOULD BE ABLE to survive the death of a child. Missionaries and pastors, especially, should be able to survive in a spiritually triumphant manner. That's what one would think. I wish I could say that my wife, Betty, and I survived triumphantly, but we didn't, at least not at first. We were totally unprepared for the emotional roller coaster we would ride following the death of our son, Dan. Eventually we did triumph, but it wasn't automatic and it didn't happen without a struggle.

Yes, as Christians and as missionaries, we knew the truth of God's Word, that we were to "sorrow not, even as others which have no hope" (1 Thess. 4:13 KJV). While we had hope based upon the Bible, that hope was often clouded by our discouragement, questions, anger, and bitterness. But let me start at the beginning.

Betty and I met in the summer of 1951. She was fun to be around, spirited, loved the Lord, and was beautiful. I fell in love instantly. I knew she came from a rock solid Christian family. I thought, *She has to be engaged, or have a steady boyfriend.* I couldn't believe my good fortune when I learned that such a wonderful person was unattached.

By February we were engaged, and on September 13, 1952, we were married. If Dr. Laura had been around in those days, she probably would have said, "This isn't going to work." But it did!

I knew God wanted me to be a missionary. After Ruth Stull, a missionary to Peru, spoke at the Montrose Bible Conference, God spoke to my heart in a distinct way and confirmed His call with Isaiah 30:21: "This is the way, walk in it." At Practical Bible Training School (now Practical Bible College), God burdened my heart for Africa. Although I didn't know it, God had been preparing Betty for Christian service as well. When we became acquainted, she had the same burden for Africa.

Thirteen months after our wedding, all support and passage money was in hand. We boarded a freighter and were on our way to Lagos, Nigeria.

A Defining Day

Our twin boys, Daniel Gay and Dean Wheeler, were born in Nigeria during our first term in West Africa. We considered twins to be a special blessing from God. Family and friends at home rejoiced with us when the twins were born, and because they were born in Africa, they were something of a curiosity.

After our first furlough, we returned to Nigeria and went immediately to Hausa language school in Kano. We had been there only three months and were doing well when someone noticed in our personnel file that I had worked in sales for an American automobile manufacturer. We were asked to consider moving to Accra, Ghana, where I would be a field representative for *The African Challenge* magazine. Although we had our hearts set on evangelism and church planting in Hausa country, we agreed to move.

The African Challenge was Africa's leading Christian magazine. Published monthly, it was a culturally relevant, powerful, appealing tool of evangelism and Bible study. The magazine was sold in schools, on city streets, and in bookstores, both religious and secular. In Ghana we joined Eric and Doreen Bowley in the capital city of Accra. We were to assist in the office and to travel throughout Ghana recruiting circulation, particularly among high school students.

The twins celebrated their fourth birthday that June in Accra. In August we discovered that Betty was pregnant again. She would give birth to our daughter, Nancy. Life was good. We were young, strong, and healthy. God had given us wonderful coworkers. We had two beautiful children and a third on the way. The circulation of *The African Challenge* was growing monthly, and we were involved in a vital and rewarding ministry.

Final Good-bye

One evening in mid-September, Dan was feeling a bit ill. We were not overly concerned. There was no fever, no headache. That meant no evidence of malaria. When we awoke the next morning, he appeared pale and acted listless, but he did not seem any worse. It was likely an upset stomach.

That morning a bulldozer was working in the street just outside *The African Challenge* compound. I said, "Dan, do you want Daddy to take you out to see the bulldozer?" That seemed to him like a splendid idea, so Betty wrapped him in his little blanket and I carried him out to see the bulldozer at work. After a few minutes we came back upstairs for breakfast.

That day I had several schools to visit in the Accra area where the headmasters served as *African Challenge* distribution agents. I told Betty I would be home for lunch and kissed her and the twins good-bye. That kiss was the last time I saw Dan alive—the last time I talked with him and heard him laugh.

Through the morning, Dan became much more ill. Betty called school after school and asked, "Is Don Hall there?" Each time the reply was the same: "He just left."

On the way home I stopped at the post office to collect our mail. We had a lot of magazine mail, plus several air mail letters from America. Normally, I would have read the letters from home on the spot, but that day I did not.

As I drove into our compound, Betty met me at the bottom of

the steps. She said, "Dan is unconscious, and I can't get him to wake up!"

We left Dean in the care of a missionary guest, and I gathered Dan in my arms and raced toward the car. Betty cradled his limp body as I drove insanely, blaring the horn all the way to the hospital.

The road was narrow and bumpy. A drainage ditch ran along one side, mango and palm trees were scattered along the other. Cars and trucks clogged the road. They seemed to be crawling. I swerved back and forth, threading my way through traffic. It's a miracle I didn't hit any bicyclists or pedestrians along the road. We made what was normally a fifteen-minute drive in half that time.

We rushed into the reception room screaming, "We have to see the doctor right away! Our child is unconscious, and we can't get him to wake up." The Ghanaian receptionist said, "The doctor is with a patient, but I'll check with him." We followed her and rushed in even before the other patient had left. We laid Dan on the doctor's examining table. He put his stethoscope on our son's tiny chest and listened. Then he looked up and said, "I'm sorry, but I'm afraid he's gone."

How could he be gone? Less than a day earlier he had been a healthy, happy child. That morning he was talking and laughing, hugging and kissing us. How could he be gone?

After comforting us, the British doctor explained how a death was handled in West Africa. There were no undertakers; embalming was out of the question. Dan would have to be buried that day. There would be an autopsy to determine the cause of death, and then a death certificate would be issued at a downtown government office. We would have to locate a carpenter to build a coffin. And we'd have to secure a cemetery plot and have a grave dug. We also had to notify friends in Accra and cable our parents in America and the mission office in Nigeria.

It was 11:30 A.M. when we left the doctor's office. It all had to be done by sunset, at 6:30 P.M. Our grief was masked by a flurry of activity. Even our dearest friends, Eric and Doreen, could not help. They had left several days before for vacation in northern Nigeria. We had never faced anything like this before, nor had we expected to.

The Sound of Red Earth

God's people rallied around us. That afternoon missionary friends from every mission organization in the city gathered to console us. As I looked after some needed arrangements, Betty looked after others. Our friends did the rest. Not only were there no funeral homes; there were no floral shops. But that doesn't mean there were no flowers. One of our friends arranged for the wife of the chief justice of the nation's supreme court to make a floral wreath from roses in her garden. By 5 P.M. we were at the cemetery.

Lee Ireland, a Baptist missionary friend who later died in an automobile crash in Ghana, used his station wagon as a hearse. He and another missionary carried Dan's coffin to the grave. How our Sudan Interior Mission (SIM) district superintendent managed to catch a flight from Lagos, Nigeria, to Accra on such short notice, we'll never know, but we were encouraged by Douglas Blunt's arrival in time to assist with the funeral. Jay Hostetler, a Mennonite missionary, brought a short message from Psalm 23, a passage our twins, Dan and Dean, had memorized. The coffin was lowered into the grave. We lingered until the gravediggers arrived. As we left, we could hear the red earth of Africa pummel down on our precious son's tiny coffin.

As the blazing sun sank into the sky, it seemed impossible: Just that morning Dan was alive. He had been sick but was filled with his usual zest for living. Now he was dead and in his grave. Betty and I clung to each other, and we both clung to the promises of God. We did not know how difficult the days ahead would be.

After returning from the hospital, the first and most difficult thing was explaining to Dean why Dan was not with us. How do you explain death to a four-year-old? From conception, Dan and Dean had always been side by side. They were identical. For the first time, one of their voices was silent.

We had no pastor to help us through this traumatic time. There were no parents present to console us. We were just a young missionary couple, bewildered and dazed. No books on how to survive the death of a child were available in a bookstore or library in West Africa. We had no knowledge of the stages of grief, nor any idea of what to expect. We were cast totally upon God in our struggle to cope.

Recently, we asked Dean, now an adult, "What did you feel that day when we came back from the hospital without Dan? Were you afraid? Did you think that if your parents couldn't save Dan, maybe they couldn't protect you?" He said, "I just believed what you told me, that Dan had gone to be with Jesus." Then he went on to say, "But I remember you and Mom standing in the rain at the bottom of the steps holding each other and crying, and I wondered why you were crying."

Searching for Answers

In those days Africa was considered to lie at the end of the world. Frequently it still was called "the Dark Continent," a place of mystery and intrigue that was definitely a world away. Parents and loved ones could not just hop on a jet to be with us. Missionaries did not go home on "compassionate leave" for a couple of weeks or a month. Unless a medical condition made it imperative to leave, each missionary was there for the duration of the four-year term.

Questions

Almost immediately after the funeral, questions flooded our minds: *Should we ever have come to this place? Would this have happened if we'd stayed in Nigeria? Should we even have come back to Africa at all?* The aura of death attached itself to our home. At every doorway, through every window, we imagined hearing Dan's little voice.

Foremost in our minds was the thought of fleeing this place of doom. To be "back home in America" became an increasingly tempting prospect. Back home there is no malaria. Back home there are large modern hospitals that give excellent medical care. Back home our parents and loved ones live. We began to picture America as a paradise. Should we stay or go? In our confused state of mind, we imagined that in America four-year-old children do not die, certainly not of cerebral malaria.

Then one day we received a letter from one of Betty's relatives whose young child had been killed. The child was playing in the driveway right behind the car. A family member, not realizing the child was there, put the car in reverse and ran over her. This heartbreaking tragedy had taken place in America.

Some Conclusions

Slowly, four concepts took shape in our thinking:

1. We were in Africa because we had responded to the call of God. This was not our choice; it was His. Like Isaiah of old we had said, "Here am I, send me" and God had accepted our offer. We couldn't just up and leave in hard times.
2. Bad things happen everywhere, not just in Africa. We could not run away from pain and problems that sin had brought to all of our world. God had placed us in Africa. If we left, we wouldn't be running *to the shelter* of home; we'd be running *from the shelter* of God (Ps. 91:1-4).
3. The safest place to be is in the center of God's will. "To walk out of His will is to walk into nowhere," said C. S. Lewis.[1] There is no joy, no peace, no hope apart from the middle of God's will, even if life there can be painful. Someone said that the will of God will never lead you where the grace of God cannot keep you. We now know that's true.
4. If we ran home, where would we run to when bad things happened there, and when would we ever stop running? If hope is a noun, it's a noun you have all the time; running doesn't help. It's a noun in Africa as surely as it is in America. We would stay put and draw on the hope that was God's strong gift to us.

Some who hear our story might say, "For twenty-eight-year-old parents, these people were really naïve if it took the death of a child to teach them these four obvious things." Maybe we were naïve, and maybe we were immature, but we began to believe that hope grows in winter.

Searching for the "Good"

In the years since the death of our son, Betty and I have experienced the death of parents, cousins, some aunts and uncles, and even a sibling. It is still difficult to know just what to say to another person who has lost a friend or loved one. We fear saying something inappropriate or trite. The hundreds of letters and sympathy cards sent to us meant a great deal. And none of them seemed trite.

However, one Scripture verse seemed to be overused, Romans 8:28: "And we know that all things work together for good to those who love God, to those who are the called according to His purpose." We heard this verse quoted often by well-meaning friends, frequently with the reminder that it was "still in the Book." At one point I said to Betty, "If I hear Romans 8:28 quoted one more time, I'm going to be sick." That may sound irreverent, but Betty and I were searching frantically to find the good in Dan's death. Frankly, we could find none. Betty has since confided her secret thoughts during this time: *I don't want to be pregnant; I don't want another baby. God will take it, too.* But God is too good to be unkind. Little did we realize that a very special baby, Nancy, would come into our lives and what comfort she would bring to our aching and troubled hearts.

Our mission was very considerate. They suggested that we travel to the SIM hospital in Jos, Nigeria, for medical checkups and then take a month's vacation at the mission's retreat center in Miango.

We flew from Accra to Lagos in an old prop plane, for which it took an hour just to get all four stubborn engines firing. It accommodated only twenty passengers, one engine for every five passengers! In my sorrow and gloom I thought, *Lord, just let this plane go down. Then we all can be together in heaven.*

We arrived safely, however, at Miango. Situated in a rural area nearly five thousand feet above sea level, Miango enjoys an ideally moderate climate. Miango Rest Home is near two extinct volcanoes. Also nearby is Mount Sanderson, which is unofficially named for a pioneer missionary. Because missionaries from Great Britain founded the rest home, it has a kind of Old World ambiance, a sense that time has stopped. The delicate scent of the frangipani and bougainvillea mingle with the heavy scent of cashew blossoms. With the palm fronds rustling in the cool night breeze and drums beating in distant villages, the sights, sounds, and scents of Africa became a salve that soothed our pain.

A Breakthrough in the Cemetery

At Jos and Miango we made friends with fellow SIM missionaries we had never met. One day Joe Swanson, an SIM pilot, and his wife,

Lois, invited us to lunch. They were easy to be around and we were able to relax in their home. We talked about Dan and his death. They listened silently, and on occasion sadly said, "We understand." Betty and I acknowledged their sympathy, but we wondered how they could possibly understand.

At Miango was Kent Academy, a "missionary kid" boarding school of three hundred students. Next to the academy was the beautiful stone Kirk Chapel, and a cemetery. Strolling through the cemetery, Betty and I saw markers remembering many missionaries and a great number of children. We spied one for a father and his son who had been on holiday at Miango. Swimming in a nearby river the boy had drowned. The father drowned as well as he attempted to save his child. Another grave was for a missionary who had been bitten by a rabid dog.

Then one marker caught our eye. It was unlike the others because it was made of North American granite and was professionally engraved. We stood transfixed, not by the marker, but by the name inscribed on it. Here lay the body of twelve-year-old Barbara Swanson, daughter of Joe and Lois Swanson. Our hearts broke for them. Indeed they did understand. For the first time since Dan had died, we were able to focus on someone else's sorrow. It was a breakthrough. We noticed the graves of children of Ian and June Hay, another family we knew, and we could hurt for them as well. We were not alone. We were beginning to realize that our mission was a loving, supportive, and—most of all—an understanding family. We were comforted, but other stages of grief awaited us.

Anger

Following the death of a child, spouses often blame one another, and it is not uncommon for a marriage to end in divorce. Thank God, that was not our experience. We depended on each other for love, comfort, and support. But that does not mean that we entirely escaped the blame syndrome.

My Muslim acquaintances in West Africa would say, "Allah has willed it." Western Christians believe in the sovereignty of God, but we are also influenced by rationalism. We have to know reasons, and we seek to affix blame. But Western rationalism is no more a Christian way of thinking than is Eastern fatalism.

My need to find someone or something to blame originated not only in my broken heart but also in my culturally influenced worldview. In his little booklet, *Grief,* Haddon Robinson expressed so well this need to blame: "Hostility often rises to the surface. People become angry at life, death, God, or even the person who had died. Of course, it is difficult to express anger and hostility toward these things."

I was much more guilty of laying blame than was Betty, and my blame was totally irrational. As Robinson says, "So often mourners look for a scapegoat."[2] My scapegoat was our mission. After all the kindness the mission had shown us and after all the love and under-standing individual missionaries had demonstrated to us, I blamed the mission. I didn't blame any particular missionaries; I blamed the organization. I blamed the whole idea of missions. The anger had a deeper root, but it took a while for me to find out what it was. I could not admit it at first, but I was angry with God.

I had always been taught reverence for God. I could never have doubled up my fist and shaken it in God's face. I wouldn't say, "I'm angry with you, God!" But I was. Charles Sell, in his booklet, *Grief's Healing Process,* said, "Anger, like fear, is a common grief response we need to learn to keep in our grip. Anger can break out in any direc-tion—at the doctors, at circumstances, at God." Sell says further, "Anger is best handled by bringing it into honest light. It needs to be admit-ted to avoid its negative effects. 'In your anger do not sin,' said Paul. It may be embarrassing and painful to admit that we are angry with God, others, or even the one who has gone. But this realism will bring anger out into the open where it can be managed."[3]

I wish I had known that when my son died. In my heart I felt that, since God could have prevented Dan's death, He arbitrarily let him die. Worse, He wouldn't tell me why Dan had to die. I was angry.

Bitterness

Following our holiday in Nigeria, we returned to Ghana for a few months. The mission agreed that we should return to Nigeria and resume our studies at the Hausa Language School. Betty and Dean went on ahead to our mission hospital in Jos because our baby was due at any time. I arrived a few days before the birth of our daughter,

Nancy. Later we all went to Kano and resumed language study. The jagged edges of our lives began to smooth out, but underneath the surface I was seething with anger and blame.

And there was something else. It takes real courage for friends to be vulnerable enough to confront one another. Two letters arrived at almost the same time from friends who did just that. A pastor friend from my Bible college days and our sister-in-law, Roberta, asked virtually the same question: "Don, why are you so bitter?"

This came as a total surprise. I was completely unaware of the anger and bitterness that was slipping to the surface in my daily conversation, and especially in my letters. I would not care to read any of those letters today, and I pray that they have been forgotten by their recipients. But why the bitterness? Grief counselors today know what Betty and I did not. We were taken by surprise as each stage of the grieving process overtook us. Only in retrospect have we been able to identify these stages. We did not know that, as Sell and Robinson have pointed out, anger must be admitted and dealt with. If it is not, hope dies—and hope is too precious to allow to die.

Anger denied or incorrectly handled leads to bitterness. This bitterness is a diabolical poison that sickens the entire person—body, spirit, soul, and mind. It destroys its host instead of its enemy.

God's Word warns about bitterness. Hebrews 12:15 cautions us to beware "lest any root of bitterness springing up cause trouble." This verse penetrated deep into my soul to convict me. I did not realize that I was bitter; I did not want to be bitter; but I was bitter. God, however, began a real work in my heart, convicting me that bitterness was a sin and driving me to my knees to confess. At that point, I began the ascent from the winter of our experience. I had discovered in my heart that hope really is a noun—something you have, not something you do. The birth of hope was the beginning of my recovery. Understandably, it had a healthy effect upon Betty. There was still a way to go, but the journey had begun.

One Lingering Question

Although we had gotten beyond our anger and slain the demon of bitterness, nagging questions lingered: Why? Why did God permit my little boy to die? Why me? Hadn't I given my life and my family to serve God in a distant land? Hadn't I sacrificed enough? Why did this happen?

I admire people who can apply their theology to this kind of situation and make it stick. Betty and I couldn't. The loss of our dear son was Teflon against our theology. There are those who say, "A sovereign God permitted this, He is all loving and all wise, and I accept this and that's the end of the matter." I knew this as well as the next person, but it wasn't easy to accept. I believed my theology about God, but I also wanted some answers. I wanted to know why our son had to die. It seemed so unfair. I explored every possible reason, but I still could not find the answer to "Why?"

Finally, I realized the futility of asking the question. I came to realize that, while on this earth, I likely would never receive an answer. I would never know the reason why. And then a strange thing happened. I yielded to God. I gave up. I simply prayed, "Lord I don't know why Dan had to die, and it's okay if you don't tell me. I'm going to stop asking why. I will wait until I get to heaven and then, if I still want to know, I will ask you." I find it hard to believe, and I can't explain it, but yielding to God settled it. I had perfect peace. I never asked why again. Betty was to find her peace later on but in another way.

Learning to Thank God

After we completed language school, I was asked to manage the business department at mission field headquarters in the city of Jos. Betty's assignment was to work in the office of the mission's doctor at the SIM hospital. In fact, we lived next door to the doctor and the hospital. As it turned out, being so close to the mission hospital was part of God's plan for us.

Betty was again pregnant, but five months into her pregnancy complications developed. The doctor discovered that she had a large ovarian cyst and surgery would be required. Dean was in first grade and Nancy was not quite one year old. Not only did Betty work at the hospital, but she now was a surgical patient there, which made me chief cook, bottle washer, and diaper-changer at home.

After her surgery, as Betty was coming out of the anesthetic, she began to cry. Later, her physician, Dr. Roger Troup, talked to her about it. He said it was a somewhat unusual reaction and asked her if something was troubling her. While I had given vent to my sorrow with bitterness and anger, Betty, in many ways, was still struggling, for she had decided to simply live with her feelings of loss.

Can You Thank God?

She shared her heart with Dr. Troup. He told her it was not enough to be willing to accept sadness and sorrow. To latch on to hope, she had to thank God for what He had permitted. What a strange concept—thanking God for taking our young son, trusting God to such an extent that even though we didn't have the answers, we did have the hope. Betty says, "It took me about two years, but I finally had peace in my heart." My wife, too, discovered that hope is a noun. And when you have hope, you can thank God even for the things you can't explain.

Haddon Robinson quotes George Matheson's touching prayer:

> My God, I have never thanked Thee for my thorns. I have thanked Thee a thousand times for my roses, but not once for my thorns. I have been looking forward to a world where I shall get compensation for my cross: but I have never thought of my cross as itself a present glory. Teach me the glory of my cross: teach me the value of my thorn. Shew me that I have climbed to Thee by the path of pain. Shew me that my tears have made my rainbow.[4]

A few months later a new baby came into our lives. Natalie was a happy, beautiful gift from God. Although our little Natalie had an extended hospital stay, life seemed to return to normal.

God Wasn't Finished with Us

That September, two years after Dan died, Dean came down with measles and chicken pox simultaneously. We knew he was seriously ill when we discovered that he could not stand upright or walk. Dr. Troup admitted him immediately and found that he also had developed pneumonia. A type of encephalitis developed as a complication of the measles, and he lapsed into a coma. Our immediate thought was, "O dear God. Please don't take another one."

We were tortured by thoughts of all the terrible things that can result from measles—blindness, deafness, and mental retardation quickly came to mind. One of the doctors stopped by Dean's room one day and asked, "How long has he been in a coma?" "Eight days," I said. He said nothing in response, but shook his head and walked out. That evening I related this to Dr. Troup, and I said, "The other doctor feels that it is hopeless." Dr. Troup said, "Then he has reckoned without God."

As Betty and I prayed, we begged, "Dear God, please don't take Dean from us also." That was the wrong prayer. So, too, was the prayer, "Lord, please don't let him live only to be a blind, deaf, retarded child." God was working in our hearts, and He was teaching us about hope. Finally we prayed, "Lord, do whatever You wish, for You are our only hope. We have learned to trust You. May Your will be done."

The Afflicted God

One of Dean's nurses at the hospital shared a verse of Scripture to encourage us. It was Isaiah 63:9: "In all their affliction He was afflicted, and the Angel of His Presence saved them." What could this possibly mean to us? Simply this. God's people in Isaiah's time were afflicted. We, Don and Betty, and our son Dean, were afflicted. And the God of heaven is afflicted when His people are afflicted. Our God was feeling our pain just as we were. He, too, was afflicted with sorrow and acquainted with grief. But He also is the provider of hope and saves His people out of their affliction. This gave us great comfort and enduring hope as we clung to this promise of God with all of our might.

One night as we were keeping our vigil at Dean's bedside, Dr. Troup came in. He said, "I have consulted with other doctors. I have gone to the medical books. I have done everything I know to do." Then he prayed something like this, "I ask you, Lord Jesus, the Great Physician, to come into this hospital room and take over. I have done all I can." Later that night Dr. Troup was awakened by a new idea. He immediately tried it, and it worked.

After eleven days, Dean began to come out of the coma. We clung to that precious hope that he would live. I took a toy car and moved it back and forth in front of him and his eyes followed it. Praise God, he wasn't blind! And it soon became apparent, he wasn't deaf. However, he could not talk, and he could not walk. Dr. Troup said he would have to learn these things over again. So he babbled like a baby and crept like an infant across the floor on his hands and knees. But God was so good and once again proved that He is the God of hope. Strangely, God began to work in our little boy's life and soon he was talking and walking. It wasn't long until he was back in school.

Prisoners of Hope

One might wonder if, after a term like that, we ever returned to Africa? Yes, we returned for two more terms with our children, teaching at a Bible college and seminary. They were wonderfully productive terms. And as an added measure of God's goodness, He allowed Betty and me to return in 1991 for an additional term to start a graduate school at the Evangelical Church of West Africa seminary in Jos, Nigeria. This, we agree, was the best term ever.

Dean served the Lord in Africa for several years with his wife, Peggy, and their children, Jason and Robbie, first as a missionary pilot and mechanic with SIM in Niger and later in Nigeria at a boarding school. Now at home in America, Dean continues to work in aviation.

Nancy and her husband, John DeValve, and their children, Daniel and Suzanne, are doing pioneer evangelism and church planting with SIM among the Songhai people in western Niger.

Natalie and her husband, Duane Wilkins, and their children, Alesha, Erika, and Jeremiah, are with the Association of Baptists for World Evangelism. They work in pioneer evangelism and church planting among the Wolof people of The Gambia, West Africa.

Our family is living proof that God can make you a survivor and give you hope. And when you hold tightly to that hope, He gives you the desires of your heart.

A fourth-century Christian named Basil wrote the following to a family who had lost a young son:

> We have not been bereft of the child
> but we have given him back to the Lender.
> Nor has his life been destroyed,
> but merely transformed for the better.
> Earth has not covered our beloved one,
> but heaven has received him.
> Let us abide a brief space
> and we shall be with him whose loss we mourn.[5]

More Than Survival

But this story is about more than surviving the death of a child. I have shared these painful memories with the hope that others who have lost a child of any age will be encouraged with hope. While at first we struggled more than survived, we experienced a measure of victory. We came to a greater appreciation for life and to savor it more fully. Through it all, we were welded together as a family. Betty and I became closer as a couple, and we came to a depth of peace and surrender to the will of God that we might not otherwise have known.

But above all was the hope. There was always the hope. One of the lessons we learned from the death of our young son and the near-death of his twin brother is that you cannot live without hope. Hope enabled us to walk away from a grave while the red earth of Africa covered our precious child. Hope tells us that we will see him again. Hope promises the Resurrection. We were sustained by the hope that we have not seen our Dan for the final time. We know the answer to Job's question, "If a man dies, shall he live again?" (Job 14:14). The answer is yes.

Hope enabled us to stand by the bed of our seriously ill child, who had been in a coma for days and whose survival was doubtful. Hope—the hope that only the God of hope can give—kept us clinging to that bedside. It enabled us to go on, to pray expectantly, and yet allowed us to trust explicitly. This hope is centered only in God.

While facing these traumas of our missionary service in Africa, in many ways we felt as if we were prisoners of our situation. We felt we were prisoners of distance and solitude and despair. But we weren't. What we've discovered by being survivors is that we were, as the prophet Zechariah says, "prisoners of hope" (9:12). I don't think we could have survived if God had not taken us captive and made us prisoners of hope. I don't think you can either.

Chapter Notes

1. C. S. Lewis, *Perelandra*, in *The Essential C. S. Lewis*, ed. Lyle W. Dorsett (New York: Collier, Macmillan, 1988), 222.
2. Haddon Robinson, *Grief* (Grand Rapids: Zondervan, 1974), 14.
3. Charles M. Sell, *Grief's Healing Process* (Portland, Ore.: Multnomah, 1984), 14.
4. Robinson, *Grief*, 26.
5. Quoted in a prayer letter from SIM missionary Soula Isch (Toronto, Canada, SIM, 1999).

Finding Hope in Forgiveness

Robert Lightner

July 1, 1992, WAS A NORMAL DAY at the Tarrant County Courthouse in Fort Worth, Texas. Prosecutors and defense attorneys all expected to win their cases. No one anticipated witnessing a blood bath.

At about 10 A.M., George Douglas Lott walked into the fourth-floor courtroom of the Second Court of Appeals. Neatly dressed and with briefcase in hand, Lott found a seat and settled in. After a few minutes, Lott quietly opened his briefcase. He pulled out a 9 mm semiautomatic handgun and fired randomly.

In a few minutes, Chris Marshall, 41, a Tarrant County assistant district attorney, lay dead. A Mr. Conder and appellate judges John Hill and Clyde Ashworth were seriously wounded. John Edwards, thirty-three, a Dallas attorney, ran from the room when the shooting began. The gunman reloaded, chased John into a stairwell, and shot him dead.

Needless to say, a lot of hopes and dreams were shattered that day.

George Lott had done what commentators at WFAA-TV called a "horrible, horrible thing." Could the families of Chris Marshall and John Edwards ever look into Lott's face without hatred? Could anyone find hope in forgiveness?

Forgiveness is vital to the human condition. We humans cannot relate to God without forgiveness. This is because God is sinless, and we are not. But it is equally true that we cannot successfully relate to each other as humans without forgiveness. No human relationship exists very long without tension. Conflict, inflicted pain, misunderstanding, alienation, and hurt feelings are parts of life. If you aren't experiencing one or more of these now, likely they are just around the corner.

The need to find hope in forgiveness was most dramatically demonstrated to me in the case of George Lott. His trial was brief because Lott, a University of Texas law school graduate and former lawyer, insisted on defending himself. I was serving as interim pastor at Calvary Presbyterian Church in Fort Worth. Nancy Lott, his mother, was an active member there. She was in church the morning the headlines announced the decision of the Amarillo jury that her son should die by lethal injection. It took the jury only about an hour to convict him on February 12, 1993.

It was through Nancy that I came to be George's friend. Twice I spoke with him in the Fort Worth jail before the trial. He and I sat together in a small, heavily guarded room and talked. George never denied doing what he was accused of or that he was in his right mind when he did it. George also assured me that, despite his horrible crime, he had genuinely trusted Jesus Christ as his personal Savior years before.

One day George confided to me the events that led up to the courtroom killings. He had just gone through a divorce, and the court in another state had awarded custody of his young son to his former wife. He insisted that the court and jury were prejudiced against him. No one would listen to him. George took out his anger and bitterness on innocent people who represented the justice system that, in George's mind, had let him down. If anyone ever had need of forgiveness, it was George.

The Meaning of Forgiveness

What does it mean when someone says, "I forgive you"? What, in fact, is forgiveness all about? The Bible provides the answers.

Seven words in the Bible convey the concept of forgiveness. Three appear in the Old Testament and four in the New Testament. The Hebrew Old Testament words are translated "to cover," "to bear," or "to take away," and "to pardon." Three of the Greek New Testament words mean "to put away" something, suggesting the idea of disregarding something. One of the New Testament words, *charizesthai,* is used only by Luke and Paul and always with the sense of forgiving sins (2 Cor. 2:7; Eph. 4:32; Col. 3:13). *Charizesthai* contains as a component the word that is translated "grace" in English. Its Pauline occurrences are in contexts in which the apostle exhorts those in the church to extend grace and forgiveness to those who have wronged or offended.

Forgiveness Misunderstood

The concept of forgiveness is not found in most religions. The Hindu, for example, know much about morality and devotion but Hinduism does not make provision for forgiveness. Among the religions, only the God of the Bible completely forgives sins. Our God is the God of hope. He brings hope to the hopeless and help to the helpless. You don't find that kind of god in other religions, but you will find that God in the Bible.

The biblical doctrine of forgiveness is often misunderstood because God's forgiveness is confused with human forgiveness. The two must be kept distinct. God's gracious work of forgiveness is indeed a costly gift. The Lord Jesus Christ, the most costly gift heaven had, gave Himself as the Sacrifice, the substitution, for human sin. His sacrifice met every demand of the heavenly Father. Sinners who trust Jesus as Savior are forgiven, but only after they place their faith in the finished work of Christ. When we express this kind of faith, the result is hope. It is faith in Jesus Christ as Savior that provides hope in this life and hope beyond the grave.

By contrast, human forgiveness simply remits or cancels a penalty or charge. Perfection and complete satisfaction are not required in order to attain human forgiveness. They are not even possible, because none of us is perfect.

Thus, there are four categories related to forgiveness—God's forgiveness of sinners, our forgiveness of each other, the consequences of unforgiveness, and our forgiveness of ourselves. There is hope in finding forgiveness, just as there is hope in forgiving others, but that hope must come from God, just as forgiveness must meet the standards of God.

God's Forgiveness

The way God forgives sinners is unique. No one else can forgive in this way, and all who have received the true, holy, and living God's forgiveness receive His concrete hope.

Forgiveness in Salvation

An illustration will help explain what it means to be forgiven by God in salvation.

Imagine that your next door neighbor, Bill Maguire, has accumulated a large debt. He has been spending freely, to the credit limit set for each of his credit cards. He's been living dangerously close to the edge for some time. Then Bill loses his job. Where will he get the money to pay his mountain of bills? Which ones will have to go unpaid? What will Bill do? What can he do? With his family needs, including unexpected medical and dental expenses, there is no way that Bill can pay the large debt he owes. Creditors threaten legal action against him, but your neighbor is at a loss for a solution. He cannot pay. It is hopeless.

One day you hear the dog barking outside. You inch back the curtain at the kitchen window to see the mailman putting something in Bill's mailbox. It must be another threat from the credit card companies. No sooner has the mailman left than Bill appears at the door. His face is drawn and worried as he retrieves the mail. You see him reluctantly open the letter. And then you see something you have never seen before. Bill jumps straight up into the air and lets out a holler that can be heard down the block. Worried and not a little curious, you make your way over to Bill's front porch.

"Bill, are you all right?" you ask. "All right?" Bill replies, "I've never been better." He gives you a hug and shoves the letter into your face. "Read this," Bill urges excitedly. There is the statement giving the total amount that Bill has owed, but something has been added. Stamped in red ink across the statement are the words "Paid in Full." As it turns out, someone else paid the total amount that your neighbor owed. His debts are entirely forgiven. The companies he has owed can no longer hold Bill's debts against him. Someone else has satisfied every demand. Bill is free, totally out of debt.

That is what Jesus Christ did when He died on the cross. He paid our debt. Of course, you can, and many do, reject God's offer of forgiveness. God's payment of a sinner's debt must be accepted or the debt is not canceled. In other words, God, in Christ, made provision for the forgiveness of sin, but that payment must be appropriated by faith. Otherwise, the debt is still owed.

Paul declares that a person's sin is forgiven when he or she trusts the Savior. Paul assured the Roman Christians that "all have sinned and fall short of the glory of God" (Rom. 3:23). To be "justified," or declared righteous, he said is a gift by His grace "through the redemption which is in Christ Jesus" (v. 24). He is the One "whom God displayed publicly as a propitiation in His blood through faith. This was to demonstrate His righteousness, because in the forbearance of God He passed over the sins previously committed" (v. 25 NASB).

In Ephesians 1:7 Paul pointed out that our redemption is "according to the riches of His grace," and all of this wealth is what generates authentic hope. Note that God forgives us in salvation *according to* His riches, not *out of* His riches. There is a huge difference. Suppose Microsoft computer pioneer Bill Gates, said to be the most wealthy man in the world, found that you are in great financial distress. You are about to lose your home, your car, your business—everything of value. Out of the goodness of his heart, Bill Gates sends you a check for $5,000. That would be wonderful, and you would surely be very grateful to him. But he would have given this gift to you *out of* his riches. It would not be a large gift when seen within the perspective of his entire wealth. It would not be commensurate or in keeping with his riches. If he had given you $5 million, the gift would have come closer to being *according to* his riches.

God the Father's great forgiveness to us through Christ His Son was according to, and not simply out of, the abundance of His riches. The one condition for getting this gracious divine forgiveness, this hope, is to have faith in Christ alone as Savior. There can be no other way to receive hope than God's way in Christ. It is God's grace-gift to the believing sinner. The payment Christ made is transferred to— put to the account of—all who receive it by faith. We have been forgiven of all our trespasses and suddenly what seemed to be hopeless—the prospect of being forgiven—is now a reality. God gives us hope because only He can forgive our sins.

Forgiveness for Service

God's forgiveness of the sinner results in salvation and secures an eternal *relationship* with God. His ongoing forgiving the sins of those who have trusted Christ as Savior results in the restoration of *fellowship* with Him, so that there can be effective service for Him.

The great foundational truth concerning sin is that a believer's salvation encompasses the forgiveness of all his or her trespasses— past, present, and future (John 3:18; 5:24; Rom. 8:1; Col. 2:13.) By confession the Christian is forgiven and restored to fellowship (1 John 1:9). Were it not for Christ's finished work on the cross and His present intercession in heaven, the least sin would result in the believer's banishment from God's presence and in the believer's eternal ruin.[1]

First John 1:9-10 makes it clear that a believer will not receive the forgiveness of his or her sins without confessing them to God. To confess sin means to agree with God that something is, in fact, sin. Confession is not necessarily begging God to forgive or even feeling terribly remorseful. Rather, it means to view the sin as God does—an offense against Him and something that requires payment. John R. W. Stott said of this text that "God will both *forgive us our sins and . . . cleanse us from all unrighteousness.* In the first phrase sin is a debt, which He remits and in the second a stain which He removes. In both He is said to be *faithful and just* [righteous]."[2]

But once we have received forgiveness from God, either as a sinner for the ultimate penalty for our sin or as a believer for the sins we have committed against the God who loves us, we are still faced with the need to receive forgiveness from others and—perhaps even more difficult—to extend forgiveness to others. If you possess the hope that comes from having your sins forgiven by God, how do you gain the hope that comes with forgiving the sins of others? Again, the Bible has the answer.

Forgiving Others

It is seldom easy to forgive someone who has wronged us. The words "I forgive you" are easy to say but not easy to mean.

Martha Edwards is the widow of John Edwards, the attorney killed by George Lott. She was left without a loving husband to help raise three small boys. Martha Edwards told me she has forgiven Lott. That wasn't easy to say, and I'm sure it wasn't easy to do. It took time for her to reach the point where she could forgive her husband's murderer. At first she lived with the despair that results from hopelessness. Eventually forgiveness replaced her anger and bitterness. Martha said that when she forgave, she discovered hope again, hope that she and her three boys could go on with their lives. Forgiveness did not bring her husband back, but it did free her from the bondage of bitterness and give her the gift of hope.

Not many of us have been grieved as was Martha Edwards, but other wrongs are very real and exceedingly painful, whether involving the actions of a spouse, a child, a betraying friend or someone who promised to love forever and then reneged on the vow. One can endure a lifetime of pain without bringing closure to hostilities against those who have disappointed and betrayed. It takes courage to do what my friend Martha Edwards did—enjoy the freedom of forgiveness and rekindle hope in your heart and life.

Steps to Forgiveness

Three steps are necessary for forgiving: (1) Face the facts—acknowledge the wrongdoing and then reaffirm love; (2) release the past; and (3) forgive the wrongdoer as soon as he or she repents. If we fail to take any one of these steps, we not only fail to forgive but we also fail to rise out of the quagmire of hopelessness that engulfs those who have been hurt. If we take all three steps, they lead to hope.

Face the Facts

The road to forgiveness begins with the acknowledgment that the offense was committed. It is perfectly normal to see the other party as the offender, the guilty one. And the other person may, in fact, be primarily responsible. George Lott was guilty of killing John Edwards; he admitted it, and Martha Edwards knew it. This was indeed a one-sided injustice. But God helped Martha to the place of forgiveness. Lott pulled the trigger. John Edwards died. Martha Edwards forgave.

Such obvious one-sided injustices, however, are rare in relationships. We occasionally witness one-way violations in which one person is obviously the offender and the other is offended. But when pain exists in relationships within families, friendships, at work, or in other communities, it is rare indeed when more than one party did not contribute to the difficulty. It generally takes two to generate a hurt.[3]

Thus, if we are to find hope in forgiveness, we must accept that nothing is to be gained by pointing the finger of blame. We must be willing to see our own culpability. We must do this sincerely and not merely to expedite an end to disagreement. Further, we must neither tone down the seriousness of the problem nor put a guilt trip on the other person. In talking with the other person, we should simply accept our share in the problem rather than bring up the other party's share. It's not as much fun as assigning blame, but it generates a more lasting hope.

Tony, an account executive at a big New York firm, and Susan, who worked part-time at an art gallery, had been married fifteen years. They were an upwardly mobile couple with divergent interests. Tony moved up in the company, until his salary reached what he once considered to be the stratosphere. But he was consumed by his work, easily spending ten and twelve hours a day at the office.

Susan wanted Tony to share her passion for art, but he didn't. She found both meaning and solace in her appreciation of what she saw around her every day at the gallery. Because of similar interests, she also related well to those who came into the gallery.

Tony and Susan didn't know they were growing apart. No infidelity was involved, at least not physically, but they were headed for trouble. Their discontent came to a head one spring night after Tony had promised Susan that he "absolutely, positively, would be at the gallery for a showing." At 8 P.M. he had not arrived. Susan was embarrassed and hurt. After everyone left, she went home and filled her pillow with tears. Tony arrived home and walked into an intergalactic battle. There was name-calling, abusive language, threats, and counter threats. Such phrases as "It's not my fault" and "You think of nobody but yourself" were launched in an all-out offensive.

Each of them had a legitimate point of view. Tony tried to explain that a client had flown in from out of town unexpectedly, and he was trapped at the office. He had tried to call, but Susan had turned off her cell phone so it wouldn't disturb the showing. Susan responded that Tony had made a promise and failed to live up to it. Susan never had clients just drop into town and could not appreciate Tony's dilemma.

Whenever an injustice has been done, we feel a need to somehow bring justice to the situation. Susan sought to legitimize her feelings, and she wanted to hurt Tony as he had hurt her. To Susan, that was justice. To Tony, justice meant justifying his actions. Neither perceived justice as trying to understand the other's position.

Reaffirm Love

The healing begins only when we stop placing blame and admit that poor choices were made on both sides. But we often feel that pointing a finger or acting as though a problem does not exist will make everything all right. The first step toward forgiveness is acknowledging joint wrongdoing, not establishing blame. It is far better to simply admit and agree that wrongs were committed by both parties.

Tony finally realized how much this event had meant to Susan. He stopped, collected his thoughts, and agreed that his absence had broken his wife's heart. He apologized. Susan knew that, though his thoughts were often on business, Tony truly loved her and he would have kept his promise had not circumstances intervened. Susan eventually came to the point in her healing when she could apologize. They hugged each other and began to lay the groundwork for the next gallery showing, which Tony would definitely attend.

Nowhere in Scripture are we exhorted to love only certain people. Instead we are often told to love one another without restrictions or limitations. Thus, no matter how badly we have been hurt we must value the wrongdoer as a person God loves. God brought Martha Edwards to that place.

If we are to find hope in forgiveness, we must learn to truly love the wrongdoer with the kind of love that God has. Pain often occurs in our day-to-day relationships, but when love connects the parties, communication and trust can be reestablished. David Augsburger makes this point:

> Love makes it possible for us to see, think, feel, want and act differently toward another again; but love becomes possible as all of these elements are exercised in responding positively toward the other once more. . . . When caring, trusting relationships are broken by a perceived wrongdoing, the loving relationship begins again with changing how I see you. This is the most available, more possible and usually effective point for moving back toward loving another once more.[4]

When we love others—even those who have wronged us—as we love ourselves, we show our love for God (Matt. 22:37-39). Everyone must be viewed as equally precious in God's sight. We must not draw lines to define how far our love will go. Did Jesus draw limits on His love (John 15:9-14)?

Release the Past

We often hang on to past resentments because our anger has not yet been satisfied. Even when the past seems to be fading, we try to keep it in our grasp. We want our demands met and we want to get even. When such attitudes prevail, we will not be able to give or to experience forgiveness. The past cannot be undone. The unchangeable cannot be changed. We cannot turn time backward. Cruel, hurtful words cannot be returned, any more than can the husbands and fathers killed by George Lott. What God would have us do instead is what the Spirit exhorted the Hebrew Christians to do: "Let us press on to maturity" (Heb. 6:1 NASB). If we hold back and hold on to our grudges we cannot move toward reconciliation.

Since the past cannot be changed or undone, we must give up our demands related to the past. Best as we can, we must let the past go. Augsburger expressed it so well:

> Forgiveness is willingly accepting the other on the basis of our loving and leveling, of our caring and confronting, agreeing to be genuine with each other here, now and in the future. Forgiveness is being willing to let it be with the best that we can achieve now and move on into the future without repressing my own spontaneous response to you or seeking to restrict yours.[5]

Forgetting past injustices does not necessarily mean wiping them out of our minds. That's likely not possible. It does mean letting go of the hurt, releasing it to God, and moving on toward completeness in Christ. You can't forgive and forget, but you can forgive and forsake. Don't beat yourself up for remembering, for not doing what you can't do; hold yourself accountable for doing what you must do.

There is hope in forgiving others, but not if we cling tightly to the hurt they've caused us. Martha Edwards could never forget what George Lott did to her husband, but she could forgive him and let go. The only hope she had to restore sanity to her broken world was the hope of forgiveness. If you are still holding on to the hurt after you have forgiven, take a second look at whether or not you have really forgiven the one who hurt you. There is hope in forgiveness; there is nothing but pain in unforgiveness. Therein lies the choice.

Facing the Future

Reaching out to the future may make us fearful, but it must be done in order for forgiveness to be meaningful and for hope to be restored. Reaching out gives us freedom to forgive. It shows the offending party that we are extending trust, we are giving the relationship another chance. Forgiveness gave Martha Edwards an opportunity to be strengthened in her faith and to grow in her likeness to Christ.

When Paul wrote to the Philippian Christians, he was not dealing with the issue of forgiveness. However, he did relate to his readers how he viewed his own life as a believer. What he said illustrates what we have just said about the past, the present, and the future. The apostle said he was *forgetting his past,* both as an educated Jew and as a persecutor of Christians (Phil. 3:4–7). Then he *affirmed what was true in the present*—Christ Jesus was his Lord and he was found in Him (vv. 8–10). Third, Paul said he was *reaching out to the future.* He had not yet attained, was not yet perfect, but was pressing on to what was ahead (vv. 12–16).

The same apostle reviewed the same three steps for the Corinthian believers in 2 Corinthians 5:11–21. Here too he wrote of what was past, what he had in Christ, and his responsibility in the future.

Facing the future involves three things—repentance of the wrongs done, reconciliation with the one who offended us, and restoration of a right relationship with that person.

Repentance

Repentance means owning up to what has been done and expressing the desire to change. Repentance is central to forgiving and being forgiven. In fact, without repentance there can be no true restoration. If one does not express repentance, how can the slate be wiped clean? We can turn over our hurt to God and forsake it, but the relationship cannot be restored until whatever severed the relationship is acknowledged.

Some insist that "unconditional forgiveness" should be extended, even if there is no repentance. In this view, forgiveness is said to lead to repentance. I believe this approach confuses unconditional love with unconditional forgiveness. The two are not the same.

"Forgiveness" that is not based on repentance leaves justice and integrity unresolved and glosses over the original issue. On the other hand, when repentance is followed by forgiveness, there can be true restoration and trust for the future. We can hope again. In all instances of forgiveness there must be trust, which shows we care enough to risk the future.

Reconciliation

Reconciliation is the hardest step in achieving the hope that comes from forgiveness. But until reconciliation occurs, we can never have hope. Thus, the hope of restoring relationships rests on reconciliation. Even in the case of George Lott, reconciliation was achieved.

I visited George in Huntsville Prison three times after his conviction. The last visit was on September 19, 1994, at 12:19 A.M. George seemed very glad to see me on the day of his execution. He touched the inside of the glass and I touched the outside—our way of shaking hands. He did most of the talking—still terribly upset with the judicial system. I watched when George took his last breath. His mother and sister, Pam, did not wish to witness the execution, but he had asked that I watch him die. All hope in this life was gone for George, but despite the crimes he had committed, George's hope of seeing Jesus was realized because George trusted in Him. Jesus forgave George all his sins. Reconciliation with God was achieved.

Restoration

Lott's unforgiving spirit led to bitterness and that led to murder and great harm to innocent people. I am happy to say, though, that in the end, just before he was strapped on the gurney to die, George was broken and remorseful for what he had done. His unforgiving spirit seemed to be gone, and so was the bitterness.

Martha Edwards was undoubtedly devastated by her loss and hurt. John was dead. She alone was totally responsible for rearing their three young boys, and she struggled. Plunged into the deep night of winter, relief came to this dear wife and mother when she honestly said, "I forgive the one who killed John." Hope was alive. It had grown. It was real. Now she could be the mother her boys needed. She could again be effective in her love and service for God. She was given extra emotional and physical strength to carry on with what she and John had covenanted before the Lord to do. Restoration was achieved.

Keeping hope alive is crucial when you are faced with overwhelming pain. A situation viewed as hopeless will be hopeless. But with the tiniest flicker of hope, there can be a blaze of forgiveness and restoration. Forgiveness keeps hope alive.

Chapter Notes

1. Merrill F. Unger, *Unger's Bible Dictionary* (Chicago: Moody, 1957), 377.
2. John R. W. Stott, *The Epistles of John* (Grand Rapids: Eerdmans, 1974), 77.
3. David Augsburger, *Caring Enough to Forgive* (Ventura, Calif.: Regal, 1981), 10.
4. Ibid., 34, 36.
5. Ibid., 54.

F • O • U • R

Hope for Loving
Hard-to-Love People

Michael Peck

DEPARTURE GATE 27 AT THE Buffalo International Airport was filling up. Glancing up from my newspaper, I studied the people with whom I would be flying to Jacksonville, Florida. They seemed to be in good spirits, and the prospects of Florida sunshine produced pleasant conversations. Then, suddenly, the scenario changed. All eyes shifted to the check-in desk. There a passenger argued in a loud voice.

"Don't tell me this shoulder bag is too big to fit in the overhead bin. I always take this with me," bellowed the passenger.

"Sir, I'm sorry. You've got it stuffed too full. It will not fit. We'll have to check it, and you can claim it with your luggage in Jacksonville."

"I will not. I'm taking it on board with me, and you can't stop me. I'll hold it on my lap if I have to."

"Sir, airline regulations do not permit passengers to hold items on their laps during takeoff and landing," the gate attendant said politely but with determination.

Unconvinced the passenger screamed, "I want to talk to a supervisor. You have no authority to stop me from carrying my luggage onto that plane."

By now everyone in the departure lounge was watching. All eyes focused on the fracas. Most felt sorry for the airline employee and disgust for the arrogant passenger. The airline could have nominated him their P. P. D. ("Problem Passenger of the Day"). His behavior surely qualified him. We couldn't wait for the supervisor to arrive, to see what would happen.

Hard-to-Love People

Is it my imagination, or are people more outspoken and demanding today? It is not that sweet and generous people cannot still be found—the kind gentleman who insists you go first at the grocery checkout, the honest lady who noticed your misplaced wallet on the pharmacy counter and returned it to you. And there are people like you and me who would never dream of being difficult. But it just seems that such stressful modern settings as flying on crowded airplanes bring out the worst in some people.

You don't have to fly the unfriendly skies to struggle with hard-to-love people. There is also the obnoxious coworker and the loudmouth on the bowling team. Hard-to-love persons can even be found at church or at the Bible study. It's possible that a hard-to-love person resides in your home. Things aren't going well with an elderly parent who has moved in. Your mate has become set in his or her ways and refuses to make the compromises that have made your marriage work. The most difficult people in your life right now may be children. You'd like to send them to Camp Anywhere—for the next couple of years.

Is there hope for peaceful coexistence with your hard-to-love person, or hope that the hard-to-love will become not-hard-to-love? Is there any hope for you? Yes, there is hope, because God is a God of hope. He will help you deal with difficult people. I know. He helped me and gave me hope.

Hope in God. That's what David did when surrounded by people who deliberately made life difficult. God's hope is far more than wishful thinking. Wishful thinking would make those difficult people just go away or change their personalities magically. It doesn't work that way, partly because God uses hard-to-love people to teach us valuable lessons.

The obnoxious passenger at the airport was told by the supervisor, "Either check your luggage or you will not be flying with us today." The man checked his baggage but continued his abusive muttering. His displeasure never eased; it rarely does for hard-to-love people. He was difficult for the next eleven hundred miles. I know because I sat in row 13. Guess who sat in row 12.

Hope Gets You Through Life

The hope that believers express in God is far greater than wishful thinking. It centers around the character of God. It assures us of His interest in His people. Biblical hope gives us confidence because we know our sovereign God deeply cares about us and is in control even of our most difficult situations.

If you embrace this kind of hope in God, it will revolutionize the way you think. Prolific author and popular speaker Barbara Johnson says, "Hope is the essential ingredient to make it through life. It is the anchor of the soul. The Lord is good to those who hope in Him. If your hope is gone, it can be rekindled."[1]

Since none of us is free from difficult people, we all have to learn how to handle them. That's where the hope comes in. What hope is there if you are living with or working with a hard-to-love person? What can you do?

Here's what I've learned.

Prepare for Hard-to-Love People

We are coming to one of those "good news/bad news" situations. The apostle Paul warned believers in 2 Timothy 3:1 that bad times were coming. Then, in verses two through five he described difficult people—nineteen things hard-to-love people do to make the times perilous (vv. 2–5). He concluded in verse five: "From such people turn away!" Paul's words are certainly descriptive of the times. The bad news is, most of us will encounter difficult people. Their numbers are growing, and not just in the unfriendly skies. They are every- where, including the church and at home.

This is no time for self-pity. When King David of Israel was surrounded by his enemies and people who made life difficult, God encouraged David with hope. Armed with hope instead of pity, the king responded with a little self-talk: "Why are you cast down, O my soul? And why are you disquieted within me? Hope in God, for I shall yet praise Him for the help of His countenance" (Ps. 42:5). When you encounter hard-to-love people, don't focus on yourself. Focus on them and how you can help them and love them. You won't always be appreciated, but then Christians have never been fully appreciated in this world. Jesus said, "If the world hates you, you know that it hated Me before it hated you" (John 15:18). So don't expect hard-to-love people to make any effort to become easy-to-love.

But that's where the good news comes. Even though difficult people are not prone to try to be less difficult, God gives us hope. Hope is what we have, not just what we do. Hope is a noun. God really is in control, and He has a wise master plan for your life, including how to love hard-to-love people. I pray you will see what follows as God's way of breaking into your regular programming with a good news bulletin.

You Are Not Alone

It is nice to know that we are not alone in dealing with difficult people, and that is not a case of misery loving company. It is a blessing to know that others have gone through the same things you are now experiencing. Even the Bible chronicles a remarkable succession of hard-to-love people. Difficult people have always surrounded God's children.

Old Testament People

Abel had his Cain (Gen. 4:8). Imagine having a brother who was willing to kill you.

Abraham must have been deeply hurt by his selfish nephew Lot (13:11). He gave Lot the opportunity to travel, to increase his herds, to be somebody. And in return, Lot chose the best land for himself. Even after Abraham rescued him from the powerful Chedorlaomer, there was no hint of gratitude from this hard-to-love nephew.

Consider Joseph. His brothers hated him and wanted to kill him. Failing that, they sold him into slavery (37:20). Potiphar's wife hated him because she couldn't seduce him and ruined his reputation (39:12). Joseph was forced to endure two years of false imprisonment because the butler forgot about him after promising to help (40:23). How many hard-to-love people must one person endure?

Throughout the first twelve chapters of Exodus, Moses endured the arrogant Pharaoh, the mightiest man in the world, who lied to him and ridiculed his God. For the next forty years, Moses endured the largest crowd of complainers in recorded history. They threatened to stone him and on several occasions got up a party to select a new leader and return to Egypt.

The list of biblical figures who had to endure hard-to-love people includes Esau, Hagar, Joshua, David, Jeremiah, Daniel, the three Hebrew children, Nehemiah, and a host of others. Almost every patriarch, poet, and prophet in the Old Testament encountered difficult people.

New Testament People

The Lord Jesus encountered difficult people throughout His life. Almost everybody Jesus encountered was, at times, hard to love. Some of them were hard to love all the time. Christ constantly faced the opposition of the religious leaders of His day (Matt. 22:15, 23). Lawyers came to test Him (v. 35). His disciples disappointed Him (Luke 22:45). Judas betrayed Him (Mark 14:43–45). Peter denied Him (John 18:27). The soldiers abused Him (Matt. 27:27–31). The crowds taunted Him (Luke 23:35). And many of His own people rejected Him (John 1:11). Jesus was surrounded with hard-to-love people. If you want to learn how to deal with people like this, He's your best teacher.

Jesus' disciples didn't fare better. Certainly the early apostles faced hard-to-love people. In 2 Corinthians 11:13, 24–26, Paul relates his encounters with difficult people. He tells how he suffered from robbers, from those who stoned him, from those who whipped him, and from his own countrymen, as well as from the Gentiles. Even his close friends and compatriots were not always easy to love. John Mark abandoned him on the first missionary journey (Acts 13:13). Barnabas and Paul had a falling-out on the second journey (15:37–40). Demas forsook him when he was in a Roman prison (2 Tim. 4:9–10).

Even the kindly and gentle apostle John had his Diotrephes, who loved preeminence (3 John 9). It's evident that hard-to-love people are found everywhere. Your experience may not be pleasant; but you can be certain of one thing—you are not alone. That's the good news when you're dealing with difficult people.

Not a Unique Experience

You are not an explorer in the new and uncharted territory of the hard-to-love. There may be times when you think that no one else has ever faced a problem child like yours, but God says that isn't so. First Corinthians 10:13 reminds us, "No temptation has overtaken you except such as is common to man." The phrase *common to man* is translated from the Greek word *anthropinos*, which means "after the manner of a human, or things belonging to humankind."

In the example of a hard-to-love child, you never dreamed that one born to you or adopted into your family could break your heart as has this child. It may have become hard even to be in the same room with the child. How do you feel? Are you angry? Do you feel shame or isolation? How about hopeless? That's pretty common with hard-to-love people. But you're not in a hopeless situation. God is the God of hope, and there are other people who understand what you're going through. In fact, I understand.

God was gracious to my wife, Karen, and me. He gave us two sons, Jeremy and Jeffrey. Jeffrey was a very special little boy. He had multiple physical problems, and we were told he couldn't possibly live. But in His grace, God gave Jeffrey to us for a lot longer than anyone anticipated. Though his health was always tenuous, we loved him and he clung to life for four years. Then Jeffrey died. Jeffrey was easy to love, and we still miss him dearly. But God did not rob us of joy when Jeffrey was no longer in our home; He simply allowed us to transfer that love and joy to others.

In addition to our biological sons, Karen and I adopted eight children and raised another fifteen foster children who were not eligible for adoption. While most of our children have loved us and appreciated our home, a few seemed dedicated to making our lives miserable. That's how we learned to look to God for hope in loving.

One of those was Peter (not his real name). He came to us at age seven and remained in our family until he was sixteen. We also adopted his older brother and older sister. These three children were hard to place, and of all our adopted children, these three chose to leave us and return to their biological roots. All three have since told us that they regret their decisions. Unfortunately, current laws permit adopted children to decide at age sixteen where and with whom they want to live. None of our other adopted children walked out of our lives, so Peter and his siblings' decisions were indeed a new and painful experience.

While still living with us, Peter and his older brother manifested typical sibling rivalry. Often they would be mad at each other one minute and best friends the next. Peter never mistreated his older sister; most of his mistreatment was directed at our biological son Jeremy. As hard as Jeremy tried to love him and care for him, Peter continually rejected Jeremy's love and hurt him.

As a family we worked hard not to show favoritism or partiality. Jeremy was older than Peter, and with his age came more privileges. We allowed Jeremy to stay up later, he had a driver's license, and he was extended the privileges given to a responsible teen. Peter would have had those same privileges at the appropriate time. But Peter resented Jeremy and often tried to embarrass him in public places like the bus or school. Peter often tried to embarrass us as well, telling private family matters to others in Jeremy's presence. Also, Peter frequently stole from Jeremy or purposefully destroyed his things. Sometimes he would go through Jeremy's things, just to let him know someone had been there. Other times specific items would come up missing. Jeremy couldn't leave anything unattended. Peter often stole and tried to sell or give to others Jeremy's coin collection, baseball collection, pocketknife collection, money, and even his clothes. Peter did everything he could to get Jeremy to hate him. As I saw Jeremy being hurt, it became harder than ever for me to love Peter. I needed help, God's help. It's not natural to love hard-to-love people. It is fortunate that the God who gives hope also gives help.

God Can Teach You

Hard-to-love people are some of God's best instructors, and He often uses them to teach us things we couldn't learn any other way. God does not waste time or experiences. He knows what He's doing. In His own sovereign way, He has allowed a difficult person to come into your life. Embrace the experience. God often uses difficult people to teach His most valuable lessons.

Think again of Joseph. The wicked brothers ignored his pleading and sold him to the Ishmaelites (Gen. 37:28). It was a painful time for Joseph, yet silently and incredibly, God used the brothers to provide free transportation to the land over which Joseph would eventually become ruler. And the story gets better. God used the gentle Joseph to save the world, including his own family of ungrateful brothers, from famine. That's not irony; that's God.

Think of Paul. He reported to the believers in Philippi the serious problems he was experiencing during his imprisonment. In spite of these problems, God used difficult people to achieve two great accomplishments in Paul's life. First, Philippians 1:12–14 records that special doors of opportunity were opened to Paul through his imprisonment. Hard-to-love people had treated Paul abominably, but God taught the apostle how to use that treatment to further the gospel. Second, fearful believers were fortified and empowered to become bold in their witness as a result of observing the shoddy treatment of Paul.

No one is foolish enough to suppose that Paul enjoyed his treatment at the hands of hard-to-love people or in prison, but no one can deny that he rejoiced in the good things that happened as a result. He learned not to let difficult people or situations get him down. He looked for the fingerprints of God on his life, even on the hard-to-love in his life.

Because of the difficulties that our son Peter brought into our lives, Karen and I learned love and patience through perseverance. We learned not to allow one difficult child to destroy our ministry with the other children.

At one point, God led me to minister in a new town. It was Peter's chance to start afresh with new friends, new school, new surroundings.

He made friends quickly with our new neighbor's son. It looked as though things were going to turn around and that Peter was making some wise choices in his life. Then one day the neighbors called me to come to their home. They had a list of things that were missing, several items just since Peter's last visit. It was the most humiliating moment of my life. I am a pastor; my kids are not supposed to do things like that. In my embarrassment, I decided I should resign from my church. After all, Paul said, "If a man does not know how to rule his own house, how will he take care of the church of God?" (1 Tim. 3:5). But the elders of my church wouldn't hear of it. Our oldest adopted daughter, who loves the Lord and is raising her family for Christ, said, "Papa, when you think of resigning because of Peter, think about staying in the ministry because of the rest of us. We ought to be proof of your ministry." Our daughter held Karen and me in her arms and together we cried. God had taught me that sometimes we allow a difficult child to capture all our attention, and we forget about those trophies of God's grace in our family.

As incredible as it may seem, it's actually good news when God allows a difficult person to come into your life. In the hands of God, he or she can be a great tool of instruction in your own spiritual growth. That may be hard to believe now, but give it time. Like Tough Times 101, nobody enjoys the classes, but everyone benefits from them.

You have to be able to see the good news that often lies hidden under the difficulties caused by hard-to-love people. But this doesn't come naturally. It's an acquired skill. Consider keeping a journal. List the things that God teaches you through your hard-to-love person. Let the Holy Spirit probe your attitude. What are the main lessons you are learning in God's classroom? And just as important, list ways in which you can use these lessons to help others. Maybe even keep a list of others who need your help. Who knows? Your difficult person may be God's way of opening a whole new opportunity of ministry for you. God doesn't give that opportunity to everyone. Grab hold of it with joy.

Christ Shares the Hurt

When you live or work with difficult people, you may think that everyone around you is oblivious to what you're going through. They seem to be blind to the problems your hard-to-love person is causing. But rarely are your difficulties lost on others. Hard-to-love people are also hard to miss. Others know when you deal kindly with hard-to-love people. And most importantly, Jesus knows, and He shares the hurt caused by difficult people.

Paul spoke with heartfelt conviction when he expressed his desire "that I may know Him and the power of His resurrection, and the fellowship of His sufferings, being conformed to His death" (Phil. 3:10). Whenever a believer has the opportunity to share a deeper, more intimate companionship with Christ, that's good news. But as in Paul's case, that fellowship is often born through suffering. Is it the desire of your heart to enjoy more intimate fellowship with Christ? Do you want to know your Savior in a deeper, more firsthand way? If you do, there's no better way than the fellowship of His sufferings. It is a hidden treasure.

Peter taught me many lessons. God used him to remind me of the unconditional love (not necessarily unconditional approval) that my heavenly Father has for me. How many times have I failed the Lord and hurt Him? I shudder to count them. Still He loves me unconditionally. His demonstration of love for me is the way He instructs me to love Peter. God also used Peter to remind me of His great concern for me. The writer of Hebrews indicates that Christ knows exactly how we feel and He cares (Heb. 4:14–15). He invites us to find the resources for coping with that hard-to-love person at the very base of His throne (v. 16). In the hard times, when Peter's behavior was unacceptable and his future with us was in jeopardy, our hearts were breaking. But that's when the personal fellowship and blessing of Christ became something I would never trade away.

Oswald Chambers wrote, "Why shouldn't we experience heartbreak? Through those doorways God is opening up ways of fellowship with His Son. Most of us collapse at the first grip of pain. We sit down at the door of God's purpose and enter a slow death through self-pity."[2] But by the grace of God, you can abandon your self-pity and enter into the greatest joy imaginable. The sweetest fellowship known comes to the believer who shares with Christ in suffering. I wouldn't have known that had it not been for Peter.

A sweet lady who had been through many severe difficulties said, "When it comes to trials, I'm learning not to ask, 'Why me?' Rather I'm saying, 'Why not me?'" That kind of attitude opens the door for intimate fellowship with Christ. The good news is that Christ wants to share these experiences with you and He does so through your hard-to-love person. Besides, sharing in Christ's sufferings also means sharing in His glory. That not only gives you patience, it gives you hope.

Opportunity for Impact

On the beautiful grassy slopes overlooking the Sea of Galilee, Christ preached the greatest sermon in human history. It is recorded in Matthew chapters five through seven. We often refer to it as the Sermon on the Mount. Jesus both expounded scriptural precepts and made practical applications. One of the points He emphasized concerned the role of light in the world. Light penetrates the darkness. That's not headline news, but if you are walking home on a dark night, the penetrating light on the front porch is a welcome sight indeed.

The Lord Jesus explained our role as light in the world: "You are the light of the world. A city that is set on a hill cannot be hidden. . . . Let your light so shine before men, that they may see your good works and glorify your Father in heaven" (Matt. 5:14, 16). He specifically chose the word *shine*. He did not use the word *twinkle*. We are not called to flicker for Jesus. We are not even supposed to flash for Him. The believer is to shine.

The goal of shining is to focus light on the Lord and magnify Him. When Christians live biblically, in ways that clearly indicate we belong to Christ, the light of our good works penetrates the darkness of sin and wickedness. Our observers (and there are many) are not able to ignore the Christian lifestyle. And it's how we have impact in the office, at school, in the church, or at home. Even hard-to-love people can't ignore our light.

Light that is fully shining penetrates the darkness and turns the spotlight on the Lord God. This is what the apostle Peter had in mind when he said, "But sanctify the Lord God in your hearts, and always be ready to give a defense to everyone who asks you a reason for the hope that is in you, with meekness and fear" (1 Peter 3:15). Hope is the confident conviction of who God is and what He can do. It is the hope that all believers possess. As we live out that hope, we reflect the true light of John 8:12. This hope fosters a lifestyle that penetrates the shallow, empty lives of hard-to-love people. When we live in hope, we give hope to the difficult.

The Limits of Responsibility

It's not hard to spot a frustrated Christian. Simply look for someone who has taken on the responsibility for somebody else's actions. The frustration will be as unmistakable as it is debilitating. Watch the parent who carries profound guilt for the way an adult child acts. Keep alert for the wife who is trying to play the part of the Holy Spirit in convicting her husband. Observe the one in every crowd whose self-appointed mission is to control and convict others. Frankly, it's good news that we do not have the authority or the ability to change people.

Remember the apostle Peter and the Lord on the resurrection side of Calvary? In John 21, we find Peter fishing in a boat. Jesus calls to him, "Come and eat breakfast" (v. 12). Type-A Peter is given several opportunities to publicly state his love for Christ, and each time he is instructed to feed God's people. Finally Christ tells Peter, "Follow Me" (John 21:19). It was a never-to-be-forgotten moment in the life of Peter. He turned, saw John nearby, and asked, "But Lord, what about this man?" (v. 21). That was the wrong question. The lesson Peter was about to learn would be heavy but liberating. Peter was responsible for himself, not for John. Still, Jesus responded with balance and stunning tenderness. He stated, "What is that to you? You follow Me" (v. 22).

You may have been a controlling kind of person for many years. When it comes to ordering things and people, you have managed fairly well. Now suddenly there is a person in your life who is hard to control, let alone love. You have made the shocking discovery that you cannot change his or her behavior. That may be disappointing but don't let it defeat you. You may not have great success in controlling the life of your hard-to-love person, but neither are you responsible for his or her actions.

Prepare yourself to deal with hard-to-love people. Rest and rejoice in the good news of God's hope. Do all that is required of you in loving them, guiding them, confronting them, and even reprimanding them. But do not fret over what you cannot change. Recognize that you do not fully control them but you do have significant impact on them. Let God's hope be the cornerstone of your life. Do what God enables you to do in molding and shaping them, but don't fret when they make decisions that reflect poorly on your love. God can even use this to better your life. When you are committed to living in hope, you'll find a silver frame around the silhouette of every hard-to-love person.

Now that you've got your mind straight, and you've prepared to deal with your hard-to-love person, it's time to take the next step. God has graciously provided several wonderful tools to help you cope with your difficult person.

The Tools

Surely a caring and sovereign God has provided the means for us not to crack under the pressures of dealing with hard-to-love people. God has promised to provide for our needs (Phil. 4:19). As a wise and loving Father, God has planned and provided everything essential for His children. His tools are available because of the settled certainty, the hope we have in Christ. The question, then, is not *Has God provided us with tools to cope?* Rather, the question is *Are we using the tools we already possess in Christ?* You'll find a list of them in Paul's letter to the Colossians.

Prayer

> For this reason we also, since the day we heard it, do not cease to pray for you, and to ask that you may be filled with the knowledge of His will in all wisdom and spiritual understanding. (Col. 1:9)

One of the greatest tools you possess is the privilege of prayer. God invites us to talk with Him on a regular basis. Prayer is the privilege of a redeemed people, and it is the one tool Satan fears the most in our struggle to love hard-to-love people. Come before the Father and pray for your difficult person. Do that consistently. Ask God to bring your difficult person to the place of blessing. Pray for a change of heart and attitude in his or her life. And while you're at it, pray for a change of heart and attitude in your own life. God has good things in store for those who pray. We miss profound blessings when we do not.

Love

> But above all these things put on love, which is the bond of perfection. (Col. 3:14)

In your mind's eye you see the face of that difficult person, and you remember the last time he or she hurt you. You've read this verse, and you're tempted to close the book. Certainly you cannot be expected to love a difficult person. After all, that person is hard to love. You are not perfect; he or she is not perfect. How can your bond of love be perfect? A war builds within you. On one hand, you are convinced that your hard-to-love person is so unlovable that no one would blame you for excluding him or her from your love. On the other hand, you know how undeserving you are of God's love, and that's a problem for your argument. The tension rises as you try to excuse yourself from loving unconditionally while personally enjoying the unconditional love of God.

Maybe you can identify with Tevye, the impoverished Jewish milkman in *Fiddler on the Roof*.[3] Remember the struggles and self-imposed arguments he went through? You can almost hear him stubbornly shout, *"Never!"* Then a moment later, he meekly says, "But on the other hand . . . " Is that how you're feeling about loving that hard-to-love person? *"Never!* But on the other hand . . ."

The love described in Colossians 3:14 is not a feeling—it is a fact based on hope. Remember, hope is what the believer already has. Because you have hope, the Holy Spirit wants to grow this love in your life (Gal. 5:22–23). It is not something you will manufacture; it is something you will discover. When you decide to seek the well-being of the hard-to-love person in your life, you discover something incredible: God will help you to love the unlovable. He will give you a capacity to love, a capacity you never experienced before.

This doesn't mean you approve of the hard-to-love person's actions. It does mean you unconditionally love them through the love God gives you. When Peter caused deep conflict and hurt to our family, I was concerned about him, but I was just as concerned about Jeremy. What if the mean things Peter did to Jeremy caused hatred and bitterness in Jeremy's heart? What if Jeremy had such a bad experience as a child that he would never want to be around children as an adult. What if Peter's attitude scarred Jeremy and drove him from the Lord? These were genuine fears because Peter caused a lot of disruption in Jeremy's life. It was hard not only for me to love Peter, it was hard for everybody in our family. That was especially true for Jeremy because he wanted so badly a brother to share things with. When God was pleased to take Jeffrey home at such a young age, Peter did not seem like a good substitute.

Yet there is not only hope for that hard-to-love person in your life; there is hope, too, for those who love the hard to love. The Lord actually used Peter to prepare Jeremy for future ministry. Today Jeremy and his wife, Christina, serve the Lord at Baptist Children's Home and care for many "Peters" daily. Jeremy received on-the-job training as a boy. God used what we all saw as a disruptive influence to mold Jeremy's life for ministry. That's a miracle of God's grace, and it proves that when we have hope, we have everything we need. Hope is tangible. You can reach out and grab it.

The love you have for hard-to-love people is not a feeling you must create. It is not a warmth you must possess. It is not even a friendship you must establish. It is based in the hope that God gives you. It's God-love, not human-love, because it's God's hope. He is the God of hope, and when you latch onto that hope, God will use it as a basis for amazing things. He will love that unlovely person through you. So the love you have for a hard-to-love person is a choice based in a noun—*hope*.

Peace

> And let the peace of God rule in your hearts, to which also you were called in one body; and be thankful. (Col. 3:15)

The peace of God is a precious tool He gives to the believer. Like hope, it's a possession not a feeling. The word translated *peace* is *eirene,* meaning the absence of strife. This peace is a quiet tranquillity that will not be ruffled by adversity or disturbed by fear.

I'm not saying that Christians are unaffected by hurtful situations or difficult people, for we are. Believers through the centuries have walked through deep water and profound adversity. Only God knows the number of tears shed by His dear children in their extremity. When you wait years for news of your missionary husband's fate in the wilds of Columbia, you are affected by it. When you learn your son or daughter has been unfaithful to his or her spouse, you are affected by it. When the news leaks that your pastor had a "secret" life before he came to your church, you are affected by it. When you lose your dearest friend on earth, you are affected by it. However, because of the hope that believers possess, the peace of God, which passes all understanding, not to mention all explanation, is readily available.

Imagine the pain Horatio G. Spafford experienced. All four of his daughters drowned in a great sea disaster. Not one of his children was saved. The profundity of his grief would be hard to describe. And yet you have sung his sweet hymn of hope many times—*It Is Well with My Soul.* The next time you sing,

> When peace, like a river, attendeth my way,
>   When sorrows like sea-billows roll;
> Whatever my lot, thou hast taught me say,
>   It is well, it is well with my soul.

know for sure that you too can have this same peace and hope. They are the possessions of the redeemed. We already have those resources; we only need to draw on them.

You do not have to live in a world of apprehension or dread because of your hard-to-love person. God greatly desires to rule with peace in your heart. Probably you will never stand on deck of a ship as Spafford did, and pass near the spot where your children died but, thank God, the same peace that was available to the hymn writer is available to you. Peace that arises from hope is as tangible as is the hope.

The Word

> Let the word of Christ dwell in you richly in all wisdom. (Col. 3:16)

You've probably chuckled at the quip, "After everything else has failed, read the directions." Why does that silly statement demonstrate such truth? Why do we try so hard, spend so much energy, and make such a mess of things before we read and follow God's directions?

God's Word is not to be a mere visitor in the life of a Christian. Paul used the word *dwell* to describe the Word of God in the life of the believer. Dwelling gives the idea of being at home or residing. The Scripture is not a rare visitor that comes to call for a short time after a long absence. Rather, the Bible must consistently be a daily part of our lives. It is to dwell in us.

You are not prepared to face a hard-to-love person until you have met with the Lord and allowed Him to speak to you through His Word. Paul reminded Timothy that God's inspired Scripture would be "profitable for *doctrine*, for *reproof*, for *correction*, for *instruction* in righteousness, that the man of God may be complete, thoroughly equipped for every good work" (2 Tim. 3:16–17, emphasis added). As you deal with your difficult person, discover how these four uses of Scripture work together to prepare you for the task.

Doctrine

Doctrine is what the Bible teaches, the truth found in its pages. The Bible is the best place I know to find guidance on how to deal with difficult people. To calm agitated situations, God's Word directs us to answer softly when spoken to harshly (Prov. 15:1). Paul warned the Ephesian believers to speak the truth in love (4:15). That's good advice for us too. Often when we deal with a difficult person, we either become silent or we say too much. We need balance, and we need God's love as the glue that holds our relationship together. If God's Word is dwelling in us, we will heed its teachings—its *doctrine*—and the words we say will be acceptable in God's sight (Ps. 19:14).

Reproof

Reproof carries the idea of bringing change through conviction. The Word of God powerfully confronts sin, brings conviction, and results in change. But before we confront others with the obvious sins in their lives, we must surrender to the careful scrutiny of Christ's reproof in Matthew 7:3–4: "And why do you look at the speck in your brother's eye, but do not consider the plank in your own eye? Or how can you say to your brother, 'Let me remove the speck from your eye'; and look, a plank is in your own eye?" What we may consider to be a major difficulty in another's life may actually be a speck compared to our plank. Because of the hope we possess, God's reproof will profoundly affect the way we deal with a difficult person.

Correction

Every parent can identify with *correction. Correction* means "to straighten again." Children are wonderful; but they can clutter a room like a Kansas tornado. How many times have you found it necessary to straighten the house after your children or grandchildren go ballistic? God's residing Word straightens the disorder in our lives. When we apply the Bible properly, the operation of correction may not be pleasant at first, but it will be well worthwhile in the completion.

How does correction operate? It depends on the situation. When Paul encouraged the early church to use the correcting power of God's Word, he urged, "Warn those who are unruly, comfort the fainthearted, uphold the weak, be patient with all" (1 Thess. 5:14). Four conditions dealt with by four verbs—something for every situation. Everything that is broken, every relationship that is strained, every person who is hard to love can be ministered to by God's Word. No person or situation is hopeless because God is the God of hope. Just get into the Book, and you'll soon discover God's counsel for you.

Instruction

The more God's Word dwells in our lives, the more it becomes evident that we have a lot to learn. Willard Stull and his dear wife, Grace, gave most of their lives in service to the Lord as missionaries in

Brazil. Willard has studied God's Word throughout his life. Now advanced in years, Willard often reminds people, "If there's one thing I have learned, it is that I am still learning."

Difficult people can bring out the best in you, or they can bring out the worst. If you bear grudges, stay angry, or seek to get even, you're not allowing God's Word to instruct you. God says, "And be kind to one another, tender-hearted, forgiving each other, just as God in Christ also has forgiven you" (Eph. 4:32 NASB). This has been the household verse in the Peck home for decades. Believe me, with a total of twenty-five biological, adopted, and foster children, our family (including the kids) has had lots of opportunity to put this verse into practice.

Praise

"Teaching and admonishing one another in psalms and hymns and spiritual songs, singing with grace in your hearts to the Lord" (Col. 3:16). When facing hard-to-love people, many Christians have found comfort and hope in singing the great hymns of the faith.

Do you have a hymnal in your home? Perhaps it is in the piano bench, tucked away for safekeeping. With TVs, CDs, DVDs, and VCRs to entertain us, we don't sing those old hymns as we once did, and I fear we are robbing ourselves of a great heritage. Open a hymnal. Find hymns of assurance and hope. Usually there is a topical index. Read the text of hymns that exalt the person of God or describe the hope and help we have in Him. Sing the hymns over and over. Also sing some spiritual songs of praise. Some of the newer praise choruses also lift up God and speak of our hope in Him. If you have a hymnal that sets the psalms to verses and music, such as the *Scottish Psalter*, sing some of the psalms. If not, read them. Besides the psalms of David, there are psalms of Asaph, the sons of Korah, and others. You'll find them right in the middle of the book of Psalms. Allow that difficult person or situation you are facing to become an altar of worship and praise. God has already given you the divine resources. Use them.

Does it sound impossible? Try it and you will be amazed. The psalm, hymn, or song whispered to the Lord can transform a dungeon into a worship center. Read Acts 16:25 and see the results of lifting your heart to the Lord in song.

The Name

"Whatever you do in word or deed, do all in the name of the Lord Jesus, giving thanks to God the Father through Him" (Col. 3:17). How do we deal with difficult people? Take a peek at the shelves in your local Christian bookstore. Books abound with suggested remedies for every situation imaginable. There also are books on how to encourage, how to confront, how to restore. Books provide step-by-step instruction on how to handle rude bosses, unfaithful spouses, unruly children, nosy neighbors, and aggressive telemarketers. Many of these books are quite helpful.

In fact, you are reading one of them now, a book meant to encourage through a better understanding of hope in God. Ultimately, however, hope is not something we can experience by reading books. It's not something we gain by learning. It's something that, as Christians, we already have. Innate within you, the believer, is the hope to handle difficult people. And within God's Word right now is the insight you need to love hard-to-love people. Paul told the Colossian congregation, "Do all in the name of the Lord Jesus, giving thanks." Deal with the hard-to-love person in your life in the name of the Lord Jesus. Reprove, rebuke, and correct as necessary. Love always. Treat the person in a spirit of true thankfulness, and you may be surprised how successful you are.

What does it mean to do all *in the name of the Lord Jesus?* Think of your own name. If I mentioned your name, how would people respond? Would a look of approval come over their faces? Would their reaction indicate that you have a positive influence on them and others? Your whole being is identified when someone mentions your name. Your name instantly summarizes what is known of your character, testimony, and reputation. In the command to do all in the name of Christ, Paul expected the Colossian Christians to stop and consider Christ's character, testimony, and reputation. You and I are to live worthy of Christ's name. Doing all in the name of the Lord Jesus is a grand, one-sentence, bottom-line philosophy of life, especially in the presence of difficult people.

Use God's Tools

Become adept with the tools of hope described above. Don't be like the old lumberjack. His friend became concerned about the old man because he continued to cut trees with a handsaw. The friend bought him a brand new gas-powered chain saw. After a few days the lumberjack returned it to the store and claimed it was terrible at sawing timber. The clerk was astonished and offered to check the problem. When the clerk pulled the chord, the old lumberjack asked, "What's that noise?"

There is hope for you. You hold the power tools to love hard-to-love people. Use them by pulling the cord, trusting the Lord, and seeking His direction. The hope is right there in your hands. Just read the instructions and get started.

By the way, Peter often calls long-distance to tell us he loves us. In fact, he called just the other day to update us about what's going on in his life. He dropped out of school, but God is so good. Peter says that he views himself in a new way. He sees where he made wrong choices and says that God has been convicting him. He told us that, especially at night when he goes to bed, he remembers things Karen said to him while he was living in our home. He reads our letters and thinks about the Scriptures we shared. We praise God that our Peter is beginning to show a sensitivity to spiritual things.

Peter claims he hasn't stolen anything in a long time. In his recent phone call he said, "I know I'm going to have to show you that I really mean it when I say I am different." In a tender moment, Peter said that we are his "real" parents, that his biological family may have brought him into the world, but the Pecks are the ones who loved him. We pray that our hard-to-love son has become different, but our love for him will not vary even if he hasn't changed. Love for a difficult person is God's gift to those who love.

God is so kind to heal broken relationships. He makes broken people whole. And He gives hope where there is nowhere else to turn. Don't give up. There is hope for your hard-to-love person, too. Every time I hear Peter's voice on the other end of the line, I know there is hope.

Chapter Notes

1. Barbara Johnson, *Stick a Geranium in Your Hat and Be Happy* (Dallas: Word, 1990), 59.
2. Oswald Chambers, *My Utmost for His Highest*, ed. James Reimann (Grand Rapids: Discovery House, 1992), November 1.
3. Joseph Stein, *Fiddler on the Roof* (Mirisch Productions, Inc., 1971).

Finding Hope by Breaking Anger's Cycle

Ron Hawkins

IN HIS AUTOBIOGRAPHY, Billy Martin tells a great story about anger. Martin had gone hunting with slugger Mickey Mantle on a Texas ranch owned by a friend of Mantle's. When they arrived at the front gate, Mickey told Martin to stay in the car while he checked in with the owner.

The rancher greeted Mantle at the door and told him it was okay to hunt on his property but asked a favor of him. The rancher had an old mule that was half-blind and needed to be destroyed, but he didn't have the heart to do it himself. He asked Mickey Mantle if he would shoot the mule for him and Mantle agreed.

Arriving back at the car, Mantle pretended to be angry and told Billy Martin, "That old so-and-so won't let us hunt. I'm so mad I'm going to his barn and shoot his mule." Mantle strode into the barn and promptly destroyed the old, blind mule. But much to his surprise, Mantle heard two more shots ring out behind him. Whirling around he saw

Billy Martin with his rifle smoking. "What are you doing?" Mantle inquired. Martin yelled back in anger, "I got two of his cows!"[1]

Anger is a volatile emotion and often hard to control. So is it an emotion you would expect of God? Ask the man on the street if God ever gets angry and you'll probably hear, "What? Are you kidding? He's God. He's love. What's He got to be angry about?" But the Bible paints an entirely different picture.

It was not a good day for Israel. God was speaking through His prophet Isaiah: "They have rejected the law of the LORD Almighty and spurned the word of the Holy One of Israel . . . the LORD's anger burns against his people; his hand is raised and he strikes them down. The mountains shake, and the dead bodies are like refuse in the streets. Yet for all this, his anger is not turned away, his hand is still upraised" (Isa. 5:24–25 NIV).

Anger: An Appropriate Emotion

The Lord had planted His people Israel as a vineyard. "For the vineyard of the LORD of hosts is the house of Israel, and the men of Judah are His pleasant plant. He looked for justice, but behold, oppression; for righteousness, but behold, a cry for help" (Isa. 5:7). God's planting was for a specific purpose and when that purpose was ignored, God was understandably angry. God's anger teaches us that anger in and of itself is not, as many suppose, sinful. God is incapable of sin, and if He gets angry, then there is no inherent evil in anger.

A Godly Response

Anger can and should at times be an appropriate response in the work of God and in the behavior of His workers. Leon Morris, in his commentary on the gospel of John, reminds us that it is "one of the crowning wickednesses of this age that we have starved and chilled our faculty of indignation."[2] When we witness the abuse of children, callous indifference to fetal life, and a host of other dehumanizing practices prevalent in contemporary America, we are far from God's heart if we do not feel sadness and anger.

Jesus was motivated by an anger that "ate him up" when He drove the moneychangers out of the house of God. He was angry because the outer court of the temple was filled with "merchandising." This marketplace was the only place to which the Gentiles were admitted when they wanted to pray or meditate. Making money had become more important than the witness of Israel to the unbelieving Gentiles. Jesus' anger was appropriate and required, in view of the great evil that was occurring in the Father's house. In their interaction with men, both the Father and the Son exhibit anger that is not sinful. Paul admonishes the Ephesian Christians to "be angry, and do not sin" (Eph. 4:26). Whatever else may be said about anger, we must understand that anger is not, *per se,* a sinful emotion. In commenting on Ephesians 4:26, Kenneth Wuest writes,

> When guided by reason, anger is a right affection, so the Scripture permits it, and not only permits, but on fit occasions, demands it. . . . The words "be ye angry" are a present imperative in the Greek text commanding of continuous action. This *orgē,* this abiding, settled attitude of righteous indignation against sin and sinful things is commanded, together with the appropriate actions when conditions make them necessary. [3]

No emotion, in fact, is sinful. Our emotions exist because we are created in the image of God. Our emotions are part of God's design to enrich our lives and relationships with Him and with others. Our emotions find their origin in the person of God Himself, and the Bible never teaches us to extinguish these feelings. Rather, we are to control them through the power of the indwelling Holy Spirit. When anger flows within biblical guidelines, it is a powerful ally in the progress of God's work. The good news is that our anger can be controlled and used for the glory of God. There is hope at the end of anger. If you are struggling with anger, God has a plan in His Word and the power in His Spirit to give you victory over the sinful effects of anger in your life and relationships.

Sinful Responses

When anger flows beyond the presence and control of God's Spirit and biblical guidelines, it becomes a force for great destruction. This movement outside divinely sanctioned boundaries is addressed by James: "The anger of man does not achieve the righteousness of God" (James 1:20 NASB).

Susan's situation is a case in point. Susan's neat appearance in no way matched the chaos in her life. Her marriage was in deep trouble. However, she seemed strangely unmoved by her husband's hurtful behavior. When I asked if she felt any anger toward her husband, she quickly replied, "I don't get angry!" She truly believed that, and she went on at some length about how God's grace kept her from feeling any anger toward her husband's repeated adultery. When she stopped, I asked her if she thought God was angered by her husband's sin and his abandonment of his children and wife. She acknowledged that He probably was. We then discussed the possibility of a connection between her host of physical problems and her inability to be openly angry with her husband's repetitive sinful behaviors. She was puzzled by the question and was not sure that any connection existed, but she acknowledged that there might be. Years of experience, plus reams of research, convince me that there is a dynamic connection between the body and the mind.

Internalizing negative emotions can be appealing, especially to Christians, and may seem quite godly. After all, it allows for peace, since no one is being confronted for sinful behavior. However, the desire to avoid confrontation is often founded in a fear of conflict. Our failure to challenge a person's sinful behavior may suggest that we hold the view that love makes shallow demands on our relationships. We are commanded to speak the truth in love with a view to building others up, not tearing them down (Eph. 4:15, 29). We must confront, for the good of the other person and the good of the body of Christ, even though confronting another may be difficult for us.

A High Price

Dealing honestly with our hurt and refusing to "stuff" it also brings lasting benefits to us. The cost of internalizing the anger that flows from hurt is often very high. It may express itself in

- physical symptoms ranging from a mild headache to ulcers, high blood pressure, or heart attacks;

- psychological reactions such as anxiety, fear, or feelings of tension and depression;
- unconscious or conscious attempts to harm oneself (seen, for example, in accident proneness, a tendency to make mistakes, or even suicide attempts); and
- thinking characterized by self-pity, thoughts of revenge, or ruminations on the injustices that one is experiencing.[4]

Stuffing one's anger without giving vent to it may also increase one's struggle with bitterness. In the New Testament, bitterness contains the ideas of "seized" and "pressed down."[5] When anger is pressed down into the mind, it often surfaces unexpectedly as rage or depression. Refusing to use anger to accomplish godly purposes is not an option for the person who is seeking maturity in Christ.

Too Much Anger

A different set of challenges exists for people who give free vent to their anger. We all know someone who becomes aggressive when angry.

My friend Bill has a history of uncontrollable anger. He often lashes out at his wife and children. His anger is volcanic and hurtful. This kind of behavior is the wrath (Gr., *thymos*) that the Scripture speaks of. This is, writes D. Martyn Lloyd-Jones, "anger roused and nursed and nourished until it becomes a settled condition; it means hatred, bitterness of spirit, vindictiveness. It means that you are determined to get your own back, to seek vengeance and absolutely determined to get it. It is a settled condition of anger, it has become part and parcel of you, and it is a condition which is permanent."[6] Everyone agrees that Bill's anger is sinful, even Bill. Most believe that he needs to be confronted and brought to a point of repentance. He freely acknowledges his sin but believes he is unable to conquer the overpowering force of anger. He sees himself as a little like Billy Martin in the rancher's barn—so caught up in anger that he can't help himself.

Although anger is a powerful emotion, the disciple of Jesus Christ has an even greater power in his or her life. When we become God's children, we are invaded by the Holy Spirit. The invasion of God's Spirit results in our being "born again" (John 3:3). We become the temples in which the Holy Spirit dwells. This is wonderful news and provides the believer with the only real source of concrete hope. The Spirit of God empowers Bill and all of us for victory over anger and the sinful expression of any other emotion. Bill must consciously yield himself to the power of the Holy Spirit and commit himself to obey all that the Bible teaches. Bill's life has been transformed since he committed himself to obeying God's Word and relying upon the Holy Spirit to empower the control of his anger. Hope for victory abounds for all who follow Bill's example.

Volcanic anger wounds people, destroys relationships, and is condemned by God. While internalized anger may appear to be a more civil way to deal with problems, it is not, in fact, Gods' way. God's Word teaches us there is a way to respond to hurt, deal appropriately with anger, and evidence love for God and the offender. It is our responsibility to understand God's teaching on anger management and to apply it in our relationships. To accomplish this, it is important to recognize the elements that make up the negative anger cycle.

Anger: The Negative Cycle

To understand the improper use of anger, it will be helpful to study the following diagram. It outlines the components that make up the cycle of negative anger.

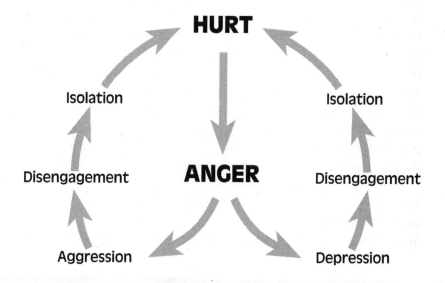

We *cannot* live our lives without *hurtful* experiences. Sometimes we act as though we don't want to believe that. We all long for a place where we can avoid hurt. But the reality of the post-Edenic world is that the number of things that are wrong are so great they cannot be added up (Eccl. 1:13). H. C. Leupold summarized the whole of Solomon's wisdom in Ecclesiastes, that "by engaging in a comprehensive quest for wisdom, you soon begin to realize that you are achieving nothing, you are straightening out none of the many things that have been crooked, and in fact, many things are lacking and ought to be supplied, but they are so many that a man cannot even count 'that which is lacking.'"[7]

Paul shares the same view of life "under the sun." He says, "For we know that the whole creation groans and labors with birth pangs together until now. Not only that, but we also who have the firstfruits of the Spirit, even we ourselves groan within ourselves, eagerly waiting for the adoption, the redemption of our body" (Rom. 8:22-23).

Choose Your Poison

There is no place to hide from the mark of sin on planet earth. Every person, every job, every church, every family presents innumerable problems. We can become depressed with this reality, retreat into isolation, and eat ourselves alive—or we can engage people, trust God's sovereignty, and embrace the pain of life in community. Understand that none of these options is pain free. In some sense, we "choose our poison," but in embracing people, we place ourselves in a position to experience the reward of intimacy, engagement in mission, and the joy of knowing we are fulfilling our God-given commission (Matt. 28:18-20; John 13:13-17).

Archibald Hart observes, "In its early stages, anger is simply a signal that we have been hurt or our rights infringed—physically or psychologically. The feeling of anger is the pain of our psychological makeup. It tells us that we have been violated, and at this point, there is nothing wrong with anger."[8] But deciding where I go with my anger and what I do with it is the defining moment for me. Whether I am carried by my anger into sin or into godly expression is a decision that I must own. Two bad choices are possible. First, I may ignore the anger and push it down. Second, I may translate my anger into aggressive behaviors directed toward the people around me. Neither choice is right. Neither allows hope to grow in the winter of our anger.

Unlearning Anger

The decision of what I will do with my anger is conditioned to a significant extent by patterns that I learned in my family environment as well as by what fits my particular personality style. Some of us grew up in families where anger was openly expressed in volcanic outbursts. We imitate that behavior and/or were traumatized by it. Some people who grew up in families where anger was never expressed imitate that model. This pattern of imitation doesn't mean that we are not responsible for how we deal with our anger. However, it is helpful to realize that, to a significant extent, what we do with our anger is learned. This is good news. What is learned can be unlearned. There is hope for the angry. We can master new and healthier ways of dealing with anger if we commit ourselves to breaking old learned patterns and replacing them with new patterns.

Paul makes it clear that this dehabituation (breaking with old sinful learned habits) and rehabituation (replacement of old habits with new, learned, godly behavior patterns) is the normal process by which believers advance in godly maturity. The "put off" and "put on" passages refer to unlearning and relearning behaviors (Eph. 4:22-27; Col. 3:8-17). The history of the church is filled with believers who have overcome old, sinful behaviors learned through imitation and fueled by sin.

At least as significant as environment is one's inherited personality style. Some people are equipped genetically to fight back against perceived injustice, while others find it suits their nature to submit. Some are overwhelmed by the "shoulds" and "oughts" leveled at them by their parents. These people are by nature more compliant and tend to feel an overdeveloped sense of shame. This shame is often connected to smoldering anger that is unrecognized.

The Challenge

What individuals have experienced in their families, plus their own personality styles, set the tone for natural and preferred methods of dealing with hurt and the anger that flows from it. Often, we are unaware of our own style and its impact on us and those with whom we seek to build relationships. Becoming aware of the style and owning responsibility for its evaluation and management is one of the major challenges faced by Christians who have a desire to move to maturity in Christ. But it is not a challenge without hope. In fact, if there were no hope that, by God's Holy Spirit, we could rise to the challenge, we would never try. Hope gives us the courage to press on.

My own experience is a case in point. I had a terrible temper when I became a Christian. I grew up in upstate New York and my father had modeled explosive behavior all through my childhood. I simply imitated his behavior. That's what children do. I watched him and learned from him. When I became a Christian at seventeen, I was confronted by some brothers in the Lord concerning my angry outbursts.

"Ron. You've got to get control of that anger," they cautioned me.

I agreed because they showed me that God's Word condemned my sinful use of anger. I repented of my sin of anger, immersed myself in God's Word, trusted the Holy Spirit for the power to overcome my anger, made myself accountable to my brothers, and sought forgiveness from God and others when I gave vent to my sinful anger.

I could have said to my friends, "Listen, guys, you don't understand. I can't control my anger. My father lost his temper. I lose mine. Probably my kids will lose theirs. It's a heredity thing." That would have been the easy way out, but I shudder to think what would have happened had I blamed my anger on my family or my genes. I had the power of God's Spirit to transform my genetic predisposition, and a new family (the church) in which I could be reparented for Christlike maturity. Today—thanks to God, faithful brothers, the empowering work of the Word and Holy Spirit in my life—I am virtually free from the evil work of anger in my life. Does that mean I never get angry? Of course not. But I am not controlled by anger. It's an emotion under the control of the Spirit of God.

For those who seem to be driven by an angry spirit, there is hope. It's my hope, and my hope is tangible, concrete, real. It is yours to have as well.

Taking Control

The purpose of anger is to prepare us to fight. Anger brings with it the desire to hurt the person who is the cause of our hurt. This desire is accompanied by significant increases in levels of adrenaline, which can be damaging, particularly to the cardiovascular and digestive systems. The damage that anger can do to us and to others inspires advice from Arch Hart:

> I believe very strongly that, while we must heed our feelings of anger just as readily as we heed a pain in the knee or tooth, we must learn to dispose of our anger as rapidly as possible. Paul's advice is absolutely accurate from an adrenaline-management standpoint: "Let not the sun go down upon your wrath" (Eph. 4:26). Modern stress psychology would say a loud "amen" to this because bringing anger under control helps restore our adrenaline to its lower levels again.[9]

Some would say amen to Hart's advice. They would tell us that is why they "unload" their anger on others: "If you think it, you might as well say it." There are some serious problems, though, with giving ourselves unqualified permission to move from hurt to anger to aggression. First, this commitment to unbridled aggression is condemned in the Bible. Paul advises all to deal with anger in a way that builds up the offender and uses no cutting words (Eph. 4:29-32).

Persons who display aggression when hurt and angry have little concern for the impact their behavior has on others. When people are wounded by anger, they disengage. No one enjoys being around someone who vents their anger. We smile when we read, "Better to dwell in a corner of a housetop, than in a house shared with a contentious woman" (Prov. 21:9). However, when anger fuels aggressive verbal or physical behaviors, people are wounded; they retreat and abandon the abuser.

Living in Isolation

The person who is less aggressive slides into depression because of the hurtful words or behavior of others. These timid souls find themselves retreating in fear from the people around them. Their lack of aggression appears to be commendable and in compliance with Paul's teaching in Ephesians 4. However, that appearance is deceptive. True, they cause no stress for the offender. But they do not speak to the offender with a loving, truth-based message that brings joy to our God, confronts the offense, demands the building up of the offender, and fosters growth in the relationship. Only when we follow this pattern can we begin to fulfill our responsibility to the sinning brother or sister.

Patterns of either aggression or depression cut people off from meaningful and constructive connection. People choose to disconnect from hurtful aggressors and depressed persons disengage from everyone. Thus, these patterns cause people to live alone in their anger and lead to feelings of hopelessness and helplessness. The result in both cases is disengagement leading to isolation.

John was deeply hurt by his dad, who berated him daily. Nothing John did was good enough. He excelled at sports and didn't do badly at school, but he never heard "Well done!" from his dad. It was always, "Think of what you could do if you just gave it everything you had!" John longed for words of encouragement from his dad. One day John finally vented: "Get off my back! Can't you ever say anything good to me?"

John left his collegiate athletic career behind and his father too. He moved to a new city. What he did not leave behind was his anger. The initial outburst at his dad blossomed into full-blown outbursts of volcanic anger at the slightest missteps from his wife and children.

When John came to me for counseling, he knew that his outbursts were out of proportion to the events precipitating them. He felt saddened by his responses, yet he reported feeling hopeless that he would ever gain control of his anger. He felt isolated and cut off from everyone. I shared the gospel with John, and he opened his life to Christ. He was thrilled with his forgiveness and felt a new power to forgive others, even his dad. His life was radically transformed as he obeyed

God's Word and became empowered by the Holy Spirit to walk in his new nature. Where once despair had reigned, John now met every day filled with hopefulness.

Satan loves an isolated person. We are designed by God to live within community. "Though one may be overpowered by another, two can withstand him. And a threefold cord is not quickly broken" (Eccl. 4:12). Strength is in togetherness and in the maintenance of relationships on both the vertical and horizontal levels. Satan may have come to Eve when she was alone, and certainly he attacked when Jesus was very alone in the wilderness. Elijah slid into a suicidal depression, partly because he believed he was all alone in his concern for God's truth. Satan's method is to break us away from relationships and the strengths gained in community and then destroy us. Our inability to deal appropriately with hurt sets us up for Satan, and may result in our being rendered totally ineffective for the work of God.

Is there any hope to break the downward spiral that leads to victory for Satan and the loss of joy and effectiveness for us? The good news is that the Word of God speaks powerfully to this concern. There is hope in God's Word for all who wish to break the negative cycle of anger and use the emotion of anger to promote growth in self and others. There is hope for you.

Breaking the Negative Anger Cycle

Every week as a pastoral-counselor, I see people who are in difficult situations. Their situations are often complicated by not knowing how to deal with their own anger or the anger of another. God gives instruction in His Word that fills us with hope as we seek to constructively manage anger. When we follow His direction, we are empowered to control our anger, and we are free to use anger to accomplish godly purposes in our lives and relationships.

The Believing-Feeling Connection

If we are to break the negative anger cycle, to be effective managers of our own growth and deal effectively with our emotions, we must identify and own our feelings. Feelings are often the first indication that something is happening in our inner world. We usually call that place our mind, or brain, or heart. In that place, our beliefs reign. People generally think that circumstances determine their feelings. In reality it is what we *believe* about the event that determines our feelings. It works according to the formula a + b = c. Filling in that formula, "activating event plus belief equals emotional consequences."[10]

When I don't get a promotion (a) and feel bad about it (c), my feelings derive from such beliefs (b) as "God didn't do right by me" or "I never get the good stuff." These beliefs cause me to feel angry, get depressed, or lose hope. The growing influence of these negative feelings can only be stopped when I am willing to examine the errors that are in my thought life. When the feeling of anger is growing, it is because I am rehearsing in my mind hurtful and error-based beliefs about events, people, and perceived hurts.

It can be helpful to play back for ourselves a tape of the conversation that occurred in our brain while we moved from hurt to anger to aggression or depression. The tape reveals patterns in these internal conversations. Some writers call these patterns "self-talk." Sometimes our "self-talk" is based in truth and other times it is filled with error. When it is filled with error, we might call it "stinking thinking." It is imperative that we dispute this error as early in the process as we can. When we experience hurt, we know that anger will be its companion. The truth or lies we tell ourselves about the hurtful event will set us up for the constructive or destructive use of anger. The better we become at interrupting the rehearsal of error, repenting of it, and replacing it with truth, the sooner the negative anger cycle will lose its power. Hope is recovered and solidified where biblical truth is rehearsed. It sounds amazingly simple, so simple that I dare to hope that I can do it, and in doing it find my hope expanding.

The Muttering Prophet

Elijah is a powerful biblical example of the tragic consequences of "self-talk" that was rooted in "stinking thinking" (1 Kings 18–19). Elijah had been used of God in a wonderful way. He had demonstrated the superiority of the God of Israel over the prophets of Baal. Soon after his great victory, however, he became deeply depressed, harbored suicidal thoughts, and was bereft of all hope.

How did such a radical transformation occur in the life of the prophet? Who can know what terror struck the heart of Elijah when Jezebel determined to kill him? Examine, though, Elijah's self-talk: "I alone am left; and they seek to take my life" (1 Kings 19:10). "It is enough! Now, LORD, take my life, for I am no better than my fathers!" (v. 4). Elijah was angry, depressed, suicidal, and rehearsing self-talk that was rooted in error. As a result, he abandoned any hope of being restored and asked the Lord to take his life. When hope is missing, stinking thinking is ready to move into the vacuum.

At some point, when Elijah's strength was failing due to physical exhaustion, he became introspective. He rehearsed in his mind his worthlessness in view of his failure and the collapse of his inner world. His mind lost hold on God's loving grace and he became unmercifully hard on himself: "I am no better than my fathers." Elijah was a loner, and he may well have thought that he was made of better stuff than were other men in Israel. He was totally unprepared to deal with his own sin and failures. There was little room for grace in his life. He totally lost touch with the truth of God's sovereignty. Has this ever been true of you?

The Help of Hope

Contrast Elijah with Joseph, son of Jacob. Joseph had known many reversals in his life. His brothers had inflicted great pain on him, but he held no anger or malice toward them. He entertained no thought of revenge. He rehearsed in his mind hour after hour this great truth: "You meant evil against me; but God meant it for good, in order to bring it about as it is this day, to save many people alive" (Gen. 50:20). Joseph retained hope.

In his dark moment, Elijah needed to lay hold of hope in God's sovereignty. The situation called for Elijah's self-talk to center on the great truth of God's utter control over all events in the lives of his children. When Elijah lost hold of that truth, fear pulled him down from the stronghold of hope into the abyss of a suicidal depression.

The Lord ministered to Elijah, however, by telling him to sleep, feeding him, and exposing his error-based thinking. He instructed

His prophet, "Yet I have reserved seven thousand in Israel, all whose knees have not bowed to Baal, and every mouth that has not kissed Him" (1 Kings 19:18).

Ask the Right Questions

After identifying and owning our feelings, the crucial second step in breaking the negative anger cycle is identifying errors in our thinking, rooting them out, repenting of those errors, and replacing them with truth. At the moment we recognize that we have been hurt we feel anger making its way into our emotions, and must ask ourselves, *What do I believe about what has just occurred? And what is my responsibility to God, myself, and the offending person?*

We who are in Christ have a tremendous resource, God's revealed Word, when it comes to answering the questions. Scripture prescribes truth and outlines our responsibilities. Against this absolute standard of truth we may test the validity of feelings that stem from the self-talk arising from specific events and persons. The Bible is truth "and is profitable for doctrine, for reproof, for correction, for instruction in righteousness, that the man of God may be complete, thoroughly equipped for every good work" (2 Tim. 3:16–17).

How utterly wonderful to be set free from stinking thinking through replacing error-based beliefs with beliefs anchored in the truth of God's Word! From this truth comes hope. We can be free from the awful effects of anger and live hope-filled lives if we gain a correct perspective on the source of our anger and it's object. It is wonderful to witness the positive use of emotion that comes to those who, with the help of God's Word, are willing to rehearse true self-talk moment after moment, day after day. Hope is ours, regardless of our situation, when we rehearse in our minds God's truth and let that truth define what we have experienced in the past, are experiencing in the present, and might experience in the future. We are then able to respond to others with emotions that are under the discipline of truth. Appropriate and disciplined responses are of great importance as we practice the management of anger and the decision to exercise forgiveness.

Forgive

Our commitment to rehearsing truth in our minds must be accompanied by a commitment to practice behaviors controlled by biblical truth. The command in Philippians 4:8 to focus on truth is followed with, "The things which you learned and received and heard and saw in me, these *do*, and the God of peace will be with you" (Phil. 4:9, emphasis added). Anger brings with it some initial desire to seek revenge. Truth demands that we imitate God in our relationships with others (Eph. 5:1). Imitating God demands that we "be kind to one another, tenderhearted, forgiving one another, even as God in Christ forgave you" (4:32).

Imitating God's love and forgiveness does not mean, however, that we give people permission to practice hurtful behaviors. Many fear applying biblical forgiveness in relationships because they believe that such forgiveness gives the offender permission to continue his/her abusive behaviors. Many examples of forgiveness given in Scripture illustrate that such a notion is unbiblical. Biblical forgiveness that results in the full restoration of a relationship involves the application of God's love, appropriate boundary setting, and the presence of repentance. Read what the apostle Paul had to say in 2 Corinthians 7:2–3.

Kathy and Ken

Kathy was greatly helped when she understood Paul's approach to resolving his issues with the Corinthians. Her husband had a history of adultery and physical abuse. Each time he was caught he would beg her forgiveness and tell her how sorry he was. She felt that it was her responsibility to take him back because she had a high view of the marital covenant.

Kathy came to understand that truly loving her husband meant that, while she expressed her desire to maintain their marital covenant, she must also demand that he repent of his sin and validate that repentance by evidencing over an extended period the fruit of repentance specified in 2 Corinthians 7:10–11.

Church leadership came alongside Kathy. They challenged her husband to recognize the superficiality of his sorrow over sin. He was taught that only through godly sorrow could he hope to change, cease his pattern of sinful behavior, and hope to see the restoration of his marriage. The Holy Spirit empowered Ken for godly sorrow, and the repentance that followed validated itself through the daily production of its fruit. Kathy was then able to forgive him. Over time she was empowered by the Holy Spirit to trust and embrace Ken in a new way that led to the restoration of their marriage.

Such restoration was only possible because Kathy and church leaders expressed love for her sinning husband and courageously set appropriate boundaries that refused to let the sinner continue his covenant breaking and hurtful behavior. Love has many sides and one of those sides is insisting upon compliance with divine standards. Kathy's approach is sometimes called "tough love."

Two-Dimensional Forgiveness

We must understand that forgiveness is two-dimensional. The first dimension is immediate and unconditional, forgiveness granted without the offender even requesting it. This is God-based forgiveness, which we do in obedience to God's demand. It is not something we have to think through or discuss with others. God said if you do not forgive men their trespasses against you, I will not forgive you your trespasses against me (Matt. 6:12–15; 18:21, 35). We cannot survive without His forgiveness and we thus freely forgive all who sin against us. We need to do so immediately when we feel anger over another's offense. The faster we implement forgiveness, the quicker we will be empowered to handle the situation with God's power, and the stronger will be the hope for a repaired relationship. This is forgiveness in the first dimension.

The second dimension of forgiveness actually takes more courage and skill than the first. After completing the first phase of forgiveness, and when the time is right, we must show our love for the offender by sharing our pain and the role the other person played in creating that pain. The person must be called to repentance (Luke 17:1–4; 2 Cor. 7:1–12). We choose our words carefully (sometimes with the help of another) and prayerfully confront the offender with the hope that sin will be recognized and repented of. If that occurs, then it is possible to rebuild trust, to reconcile, and to restore the broken dimensions of our relationships. We may need help with some dimensions of the restoration.

Tom and Sally

When Tom and Sally renewed their vows in a public service at our church we were thrilled for them. A few years ago Tom was totally under the power of drugs. When Sally had all she could take, she divorced him and set out with two young children to rebuild her broken world. Then Tom met Jesus Christ and a hopeless addict became a new person in Christ. Tom gives all the glory to God and to His power working in his life. Sally heard him confess his sin to her, saw the fruit of genuine repentance, found her love and trust for Tom growing, and was empowered by God and her choices to love Tom again. The church offered counsel, support, and encouragement every step of the way, and God was glorified and the saints stirred as a man and a marriage were transformed. Others look on and know that where brokenness once dominated, wholeness has taken root, and they are filled with hope.

The genuine repentance of the one who offends creates an environment of safety in which the necessary things can be learned to assure the restoration and continued growth of the relationship. Genuine repentance is validated by the elements listed in 2 Corinthians 7:10-11. Check them out. The absence of these elements indicates that the professed repentance is not genuine. Without these elements, restoration of a broken relationship is impossible.

Conclusion

Is there hope for you if you tend to be angry? There certainly is. All emotions are gifts from God to enrich our experience of life, relationships with others, and our worship. Anger must be embraced as one of these special gifts, with a wonderful potential for enrichment. Guided by the Scriptures and empowered by the Holy Spirit, we can practice a stewardship of our anger that is honoring to God, good for us, and an ally in our quest to build relationships that edify and promote Christlike maturity. These wholesome objectives are within our grasp when we diligently follow biblical teaching and break the negative anger cycle. Filled with hopefulness for ourselves and others, we are then free to practice a biblical stewardship over our emotions, our thoughts, and our responses to those who hurt us.

If you're living a life filled with anger today, grab on to the hope found in God's Word. Anger is not wrong, but your response to what has angered you may be wrong. The love of God, the forgiveness of God, and the grace of God all make it possible to enjoy the hope of God in overcoming anger and breaking its negative cycle. Everything you need, God has provided. It's not necessary to be eaten up by anger. By following the biblical patterns, you can discover the hope that God provides to help overcome hurtful anger. Even when it comes to defeating destructive anger, hope is a noun. It's something you have, not something you do. Latch on to it and be free.

Chapter Notes

1. Billy Martin and Peter Golenbock, *Number One* (New York: Delacorte, 1980), 117.
2. Leon Morris, "The Gospel According to John," in *The New International Commentary on the New Testament* (Grand Rapids: Eerdmans, 1971), 195.
3. Kenneth S. Wuest, *Wuest's Word Studies in the Greek New Testament* (Grand Rapids: Eerdmans, 1978), 113–14.
4. Gary Collins, *Christian Counseling* (Dallas: Word, 1988), 126.
5. James Strong, *Strong's Exhaustive Concordance of the Bible* (McLean, Va.: MacDonald, 1894).
6. D. Martyn Lloyd-Jones, *Darkness and Light: An Exposition of Ephesians 4:17–5:17* (Grand Rapids: Baker, 1980), 232.
7. H. C. Leupold, *Exposition of Ecclesiastes* (Grand Rapids: Baker, 1969), 54.
8. Archibald Hart, *The Hidden Link Between Adrenaline and Stress* (Dallas: Word, 1986), 143.
9. Ibid., 144.
10. Credit should be given to Albert Ellis, the founder of Rational/Emotive Therapy, for this formula and the observation drawn from it.

Breaking the Grip of Fear

Gil Parker

MAROLYN AND DIANNE ARGUED over which one would ride in the front seat. Dad and Mom decided Dianne would ride up front between them, since she had asked first.

When my wife, Marolyn, was thirteen years old, she and her family traveled to the Thousand Islands in upstate New York. They drove north to Alexandria Bay, and when they came to the crest of a small hill a car was headed south in their lane. There was no chance to avoid a head-on collision. Marolyn's father's last words were, "Oh no!" In an instant, the crash snuffed out the lives of her father, her mother, and her sister, all in the front seat. Marolyn and her three younger brothers, Roger, Dennis, and Gary, ages ten, seven, and twenty months, were injured, but God spared their lives. Four children, barely able to understand what had happened, were left orphans.

That was many years ago. But the emotional consequences of a deadly accident do not disappear easily. One of those emotional consequences is fear. Marolyn was terrified of riding in a car for several years. Although this fear gradually subsided, another fear persisted—that of visiting the Thousand Islands, the family's destination that day.

Marolyn's parents were thirty-four when they were killed. Each time we shared this story with our children and spoke of their grandparents who are in heaven, we did not realize that we were generating a secondary consequence of fear. Our daughter, Dyann, breathed a sigh of relief when we turned thirty-five. We never knew that she constantly lived with the fear that she, too, would lose her parents at an early age.

The Reality of Fear

Much in life makes us afraid. We call these fears "phobias." I have a fear of heights—*acrophobia*—which makes it a challenge for me to climb a ladder when working on my house. People afraid of water have *hydrophobia*. Those afraid of spiders are bothered with *arachniphobia*. Others are troubled by enclosed or confined areas and suffer from *claustrophobia*. There is even a phobia known as *arachibutyrophobia*, which is the fear of peanut butter sticking to the roof of your mouth.[1] We can safely say that everyone has, at one time or another, been subject to fears that have upset their normal life patterns.

Healthy Fear

Normal fear is a God-given emotion that alerts us to danger. Usually fear is present when our personal security or well-being is threatened. This is healthy fear, which may kindle a life-saving response or at least cause us to reevaluate our plans. God may even use these fears to stimulate spiritual growth or to affect other positive changes.

Some time ago a retired Marine, Harold, lay in a hospital bed. The doctor diagnosed his condition and determined that surgery was necessary. Harold wasn't a Christian, but his father-in-law, John, had been a faithful witness to him. Since at that time I was John's pastor, Harold asked to see me. No sooner had I entered the room when Harold called me closer to him and expressed his fear. "I've never been under the knife," he said, "and if something should happen, I don't know what's on the other side. I'm afraid." Harold's was a healthy fear—not knowing what the future held. It was my privilege to tell Harold that Jesus Christ died for his sins to provide a bright future for him in heaven. All Harold had to do was trust what Jesus did for him at the cross of Calvary, and Harold would be saved. Harold trusted Christ as his Savior that day and faced his surgery with peace. He recovered nicely.

Healthy fear alerts us to our vulnerability in dangerous situations. It may say "proceed with caution" or "fasten your seat belt." It forces us to seek out a doctor or a pastor and to follow their counsel. It causes us to warn our children when we see them in dangerous or compromising situations, such as being with the wrong friends. We all experience healthy fear, and we are all better off because of it.

Unhealthy Fear

Some people, however, are plagued by exaggerated fears that produce terror, severe anxieties, or panic. I know a man who suffered asthma attacks as a normal part of his life. Usually he handled them without difficulty. However, on one occasion he had one at an inopportune time, which caused him to panic. The situation triggered a panic attack, and this hindered the proper use of his breathing device. Not only was he afraid, but those nearby were equally frightened because of his inability to breath.

Phobias affect us much like this. Unlike healthy fear, which can protect a person from danger, phobias can actually cause harm. After the accident my wife, Marolyn, for example, was very tense riding in a car. Involuntarily she would be looking out for other cars, grasping and clutching at anything. This made it extremely uncomfortable for her to travel.

When our normal fears become exaggerated, they make a deeper impact on us. They can bring about a temporary paralysis or affect us in some physical way.

Universal Fear

Although salvation brings great changes to our lives, it does not banish fear. We Christians are as subject to fears as anybody else; we just have a better way of dealing with them. For us, hope can help us handle our fear.

Scripture demonstrates that many of God's servants were beset by fear. And these people are our heroes. God reminded Abraham after his rescue of Lot, "Do not be afraid, Abram. I am your shield, your exceedingly great reward" (Gen. 15:1). Possibly Abraham feared retaliation from the kings he had defeated, but God promised protection. Zacharias, the father of John the Baptist, was visited by an angel of the Lord, who said, "Do not be afraid" (Luke 1:13). Just seeing the presence of an angel frightened the old priest. This was a new and unusual experience. Paul wrote to the Corinthians, "Indeed, when we came to Macedonia, our bodies had no rest, but we were troubled on every side. Outside were conflicts, inside were fears" (2 Cor. 7:5). Rather than be ashamed of his fears, the apostle readily admitted them. Paul's life and ministry were being threatened on a regular basis, and the natural consequence of a threat is fear. Don't ever be ashamed because you are fearful. Fear is a reality in the Christian life.

While serious fear may require the intervention of a physician, everyday fears are best handled by hope. Fears that disrupt a normal lifestyle exhaust our strength, cloud our judgments, rob us of hope, and deplete us of joy in our walk with God. And since such fears can even cause us to doubt our relationship with Christ, we must always deal with fear.

The Causes of Fear

Christians often speculate about what causes fear. Many assume that fear arises from a lack of spiritual maturity. They say, "If Bill was really right with God, all his fears would be gone." That statement sounds spiritual, but experience doesn't bear it out. Others associate the presence of fear with character flaws. "I think Jan's problem is that she lacks the courage to trust God. That's why she is afraid." In some cases such an observation might be insightful, but more frequently it is a flawed assumption. We certainly can't explain away all fears so easily. Spiritual and courageous men like David experienced fear (Ps. 56).

Often fear is the result of past experiences that have conditioned a response to the unknown, in which we anticipate possible harm. Whatever the cause of fear, we all will have feelings of terror or dread. The Bible has much to say about fear and its effects.

Nature

Have you ever been caught in a fierce thunderstorm? Lightning flashed all around. Thunder cracked in your ear. Indeed, nature can cause us to be fearful. When Jonah refused the Lord's assignment in Nineveh and fled to Tarshish, the Lord sent a storm. The Bible says, "Then the mariners were afraid" (Jonah 1:5). These were experienced sailors, but so fierce was this divinely flung fury that even old salts were shaky in the knees. And when Jonah confessed his disobedience to the Lord "the men were exceedingly afraid" (v. 10). These men weren't particularly religious men; they were sailors. Yet they were stricken with terror when they learned that God was pursuing Jonah. Hurricanes, tornadoes, and earthquakes often pose severe threats to life. The power of God in nature is a wonder to behold. Anyone who doesn't respect that power is a fool.

Fear of nature isn't merely confined to those backward souls of antiquity either. The book of Revelation peers into the future and records that the inhabitants of earth will be afraid during the upheavals of nature that will take place during the Tribulation (Rev. 11:13).

War

We've heard of acts of incredible bravery during times of war, but bravery doesn't mean there is no fear. Those who have faced losing their lives in battle will tell you that war causes heart-pounding fear. Even Navy Seals or Army Rangers are subject to wartime fear. When the Philistine giant Goliath taunted Saul and Israel's army, fear gripped this elite Jewish force. First Samuel 17:24 reads, "And all the men of Israel, when they saw the man [Goliath], fled from him and were dreadfully afraid." Fear that the Philistine champion would defeat its armies caused Israel to wither under the prospect of fighting Goliath. I don't blame them. Goliath was nearly ten feet tall, almost four feet taller than I am. That's intimidating. Later King Saul was terrified at the size of the Philistine army. Fear gripped his heart, causing him to lose his perspective on life and God (1 Sam. 28).

In the 1960s, when America was deeply engaged in the Vietnam War, my wife's brother, Roger, was deployed there in the Army. He was in constant danger. Thousands of lives were lost in that conflict, and the family naturally feared for Roger's life. But we are people of faith, and we prayed earnestly for his safety and his return to the family. We fear because we are human. But as Christians we have hope because we pray to the One who is able to protect our loved ones wherever they are.

Loss

Sometimes fear is caused by the anticipation of personal harm. My daughter, Dyann, lived with fear of losing her parents. Nagging questions plagued her. Who would raise her brothers and her if we were taken in an accident? What would become of them if they had no parents? The fear of loss often causes people to live with a dread that they cannot logically explain. Bill Boulet speaks of the fear of loss in chapter 11 of this book. The fear of loss may not be as tangible as the fear associated with war, but it is real fear nonetheless.

When the men of Gerar asked Isaac about his wife, Rebekah, he said, "She is my sister." Why would he say such a thing? He was afraid to say, "She is my wife . . . lest the men of the place kill me for Rebekah, because she is beautiful to behold" (Gen. 26:7). The fear of losing his life weighed more heavily on Isaac's mind than the fear of losing his wife. He doubted God's ability to protect him.

As in Isaac's case, fear often causes us to do unreasonable things. Remember all the crazy things people did as they anticipated the failure of computers when the calendar turned to the year 2000. Because of the "Y2K" crisis, they were afraid they would lose their homes, their bank accounts, their food supplies, and their lives. Some misguided and fearful people drew all their money out of the bank, moved to the mountains or the desert, and stockpiled enough dried food to last a year or more. This was a classic case of overreacting fear.

Foolishness

At other times fear is caused by foolish behavior and decisions. Adam and Eve enjoyed all the goodness God could provide in their idyllic home, the Garden of Eden. After they rebelled against God and succumbed to Satan's temptation, our first parents were frightened and tried to hide themselves from the One who created them. Genesis 3:10

records Adam's words: "I heard Your voice in the garden, and I was afraid because I was naked; and I hid myself." Adam's foolish act of sin produced feelings of fear as he stood in the presence of the Lord.

The Bible is filled with records of foolish behavior that resulted in fear. Haman's plot to annihilate the Jews was exposed to King Ahasuerus. The Bible says, "Haman was terrified before the king and queen" (Esther 7:6). Haman knew that the power of life and death was in the hands of the king. He feared because he knew that his foolish decisions would result in his death.

Fear related to foolishness lives on. A teenage girl foolishly lives fast and loose with the boys and then fears that she may be pregnant. A young guy steals a six-pack from the local convenience store. As he leaves the store he notices the security camera. He rightly fears he will be caught. Foolish choices lead to fear. One of the ways to reduce our fears is to reduce our foolishness.

Guilt

Fear is also triggered by feelings of guilt. Jacob is a classic biblical example. Upon his return to Canaan and his impending reunion with his brother, Esau, the Bible says that Jacob "was greatly afraid and distressed" (Gen. 32:7). Twenty years earlier Jacob had deceived Esau, and Esau had threatened to kill him (27:41). Jacob now expected that Esau would exact revenge as soon as they met. That didn't happen, but Jacob's guilt, which produced fear, almost caused him to blow the best homecoming he could ever have.

The sons of Jacob were afraid as a consequence of guilt. They had sold their brother into slavery, and after they knew that he had a powerful position in Egypt, the brothers assumed that Joseph would seek revenge at the earliest opportunity. Riddled with guilt, after their father died they fell before him and begged his forgiveness. But Joseph had long before forgiven them, so now he could encourage them not to be afraid. "You meant evil against me; but God meant it for good" (Gen. 50:20).

The Hand of God

God's activity in specific circumstances caused fear among both Israel and her enemies. God delivered Moses and the children of Israel from Pharaoh's grasp through a miracle at the Red Sea. The Bible says, "Thus Israel saw the great work which the LORD had done in Egypt; so the people feared the LORD, and believed the LORD and His servant Moses" (Exod. 14:31). God used this activity to move His people toward a reverent respect for Him. On the other side of the Red Sea the frightened hoards of Israel sang, "Our God is an awesome God." Sometimes just watching God work on our behalf evokes an awe that is akin to fear.

God's activity also can spread terror—a different kind of fear—among His enemies. Years after God had destroyed the Egyptians at the Red Sea, the Israelites approached the Jordan River and the Canaanites were certain they were about to cross into Canaan. The Canaanite Rahab told the spies that Moses had sent into the land, "As soon as we heard these things, our hearts melted; neither did there remain any more courage in anyone because of you, for the LORD your God, He is God in heaven above and on earth beneath" (Josh. 2:11). The Canaanites acknowledged the power of God, power that commanded respect and fear.

Sometimes the cause of our fear is real; other times it is imagined. Whether or not the cause is real, the fear is real and can have debilitating effects. Marolyn's accident had a tremendous effect on her for decades after she lost her father, mother, and sister.

The Effects of Fear

Fear may be accompanied by various physical symptoms, such as palpitations of the heart, difficulty in breathing, sweating, and various aches and pains. When Belshazzar witnessed the handwriting on the wall, the prophet recorded, "Then the king's countenance changed, and his thoughts troubled him, so that the joints of his hips were loosened and his knees knocked against each other" (Dan. 5:6). Belshazzar was so terrified he could not stand.[2] Fear incapacitated him.

Fear, too, reduces our quality of life. People dominated by fear may have difficulty concentrating or may run from situations where there is even the slightest potential of a threat. My neighbor Bob was a gardener. I often observed him at work, moving dirt with a rake the way he wanted it and where he wanted it. But over the years he worked slower, took longer breaks, and rested more often by leaning on his rake. He explained that he had a severe pain on the right side of his abdomen. "You should go to the doctor," I said.

"No," he said, "I'm afraid I have cancer."

I had that conversation with him a number of times, as did others in his family. One day he had to visit the doctor and was diagnosed with cancer. Within weeks, Bob was dead. His fear prevented an early detection of this dreaded disease and perhaps ended his life prematurely.

Emotional Effects

Fear makes a direct impact on our emotional state. Fear can make a person fainthearted, to lose strength of will and resolve, to give up. On the eve of Israel's conquest of Canaan, Moses exhorted the nation, "Do not let your heart faint, do not be afraid, and do not tremble or be terrified because of them" (Deut. 20:3). Good soldiers must engage the enemy and not retreat in the face of battle. But when those highly trained in combat become afraid, if that fear is not controlled by faith, it could lead to terror, panic, and defeat.

In Gideon's day, God reduced the size of Israel's army because they were fainthearted: "'Whoever is fearful and afraid, let him turn and depart at once from Mount Gilead.' And twenty-two thousand of the people returned, and ten thousand remained" (Judg. 7:3). Two-thirds of the army were excused from the battle because they were afraid. But faintheartedness can be overcome by courage and courage grows out of hope. The secret to overcoming fear is to have faith. Faith comes when there is something concrete to believe in. That's why it's important to remember that hope is a noun, it's concrete. Hope gives rise to courage and courage gives chase to fear.

Mental Effects

Fear also affects our mental processes, undermining our ability to think rationally and distorting our perception of facts. Both Abraham (Gen. 20) and Isaac (26:1–11) resorted to lying because they thought their lives were in jeopardy. When his "heart trembled" because of his fear of the Philistines, Saul consulted a medium, which was a forbidden source of counsel for the people of God (1 Sam. 28:5–8; cf. Lev. 19:31). Fear had pushed him over the edge. But the words of the deceased Samuel, whom Saul sought, made him "dreadfully afraid" (1 Sam. 28:20). Samuel informed him that Israel would lose to the Philistines in the coming battle, and he would die. Rational thought in time of crisis requires trust and confidence in God. Fear is the natural consort of irrationality.

Benjy's story is an example of fear coupled with irrationality. Benjy was a young man who seemed to have the world by the tail. He was a high school senior at the week of his graduation. His mind was fixed on Friday, the day "it would all be over." He and some friends attended a pregraduation party and had a few drinks. On the way home, Benjy, as usual, refused to use his seat belt. He had an irrational fear of being trapped in a burning car. But on this night he lost control of his car, skidded off the road, and hit a tree. Benjy was thrown from the automobile, and his neck was broken from the impact. His irrational fear of being trapped in his car caused him to act foolishly.

Behavioral Effects

Fear influences behavior patterns in other ways. Herod waited to kill John the Baptist because he "feared the multitude" (Matt. 14:5). The religious leaders held off attacking Jesus for the same reason (21:46). Even Peter, out of fear of the reaction of the Judaizers from Jerusalem, stopped eating with the non-Jewish believers (Gal. 2:12). Fear can make us subject to the opinions of others. We do crazy things when afraid. Which brings me back to Marolyn and how she broke the grip of her fears.

The Antidote to Fear

As a result of Marolyn's accident, for years we avoided travel to the Thousand Islands in Watertown, New York. We often talked about visiting there, but she was not sure what emotions would be stirred by returning to the site of the family tragedy. Once we did drive through the beautiful region, but we entered from Canada.

Then thirty-five years after the accident, God arranged for me to preach in a church in Watertown, New York. As we drove by the hospital where many years earlier the family had been taken, my wife again recounted the events that made her and her brothers orphans.

"Gil, I don't know if I can even look." I encouraged her to do so. She gave the hospital a sideways glance and then looked away.

"It's just too painful. I have so many fears, so much anxiety," she said.

"It's okay, Honey. God will help you overcome your fears."

Marolyn said, "You're right. Fear is best resolved by facing it and turning it over to God. I think I can do that."

Right there, as we passed the hospital that held so many painful memories, Marolyn did what sounds so easy but is so difficult—she handed her fears to God, asking Him to receive them and to give her faith and hope. God performed a miracle in my wife's life. Fear that had gripped her for thirty-five years was suddenly gone. It was as if a cloud had been lifted from her life, a cloud that followed her around since age thirteen. God gave her peace. God gave her faith. But most of all, God gave her hope.

Fearing God

What is the antidote to fear? If you live in fear today, how can it be removed as completely as one erases a word by hitting the delete key on a computer keyboard? What does the Bible say?

While fear may conjure up feelings of terror or fright, that is not the only meaning of fear in the Bible. Fear is also used to describe great reverence or respect for God. When we Christians consider our position in Christ, our hearts should respond with wonder, awe, and reverence—holy fear. Solomon said, "The fear of the LORD is the beginning of knowledge" (Prov. 1:7). We who fear the Lord recognize the reality of His being, that He exists as the only true God. We gladly submit to Him. This knowledge becomes the basis of hope and helps control our human propensity to fear. Only God can offer real hope in the face of our fears. Fearing God is the antidote to fear itself.

When we fear God, we concentrate solely on Him and abandon allegiance to other deities, real or imagined. Loyalty to God will become the foundation of life. At every critical juncture, we will desire to be conformed to the will and ways of God. And we will express our reverence and respect for God by pleasing the Lord in our walk, by loving Him in our worship, and by serving Him with our whole being. The apostle Peter reminds us that God-fearing faith motivates holy living (1 Peter 1:17–19). For one who truly fears the Lord, all of life revolves around Him, breaking the grip of fear that binds those who conduct their lives without God.

Knowing God

A sense of awe and reverence toward God is the initial step to overcoming fear. But knowing God intimately provides the daily confidence and hope needed to break the grasp of fear. Peter wrote, "But grow in the grace and knowledge of our Lord and Savior Jesus Christ" (2 Peter 3:18). *Grace* is God's favor toward us and *knowledge* pertains to information that helps us understand Christ and His provision for us. Reliable information is one of the believer's greatest resources for understanding and conquering fear, and there is no more accurate information about God than that found in His Word. In this grammatical context, the present imperative verb *grow* means "be continually growing" or "be continually deepening" in your relationship with Christ.[3] Put what you know about Christ to work in your Christian life. Spiritual growth fortifies the believer against the assaults of fear.

There are things we know about God that help break fear and provide hope.

The Providence of God

First, the *providence of God* means that God exercises foresight over all the details of life. Nothing is left to chance. God is sovereign and nothing comes into your life that He hasn't permitted. While growing up orphans Marolyn and her brothers found it hard to understand that God permitted their family tragedy. But the more they grew in God's grace and in their knowledge of His loving care, the more they came to appreciate the absolute wonder of God's providence. It wasn't an easy lesson to learn, and it was a long time in coming. But it was learned in the school of God's grace, over time, and with great patience.

The Power of Jesus

Second, the *power of Jesus* is wonderfully illustrated in the Bible. One night Jesus sent His disciples across the Sea of Galilee to Bethsaida (Mark 6:45–52). The disciples were "straining at rowing" because of a storm (v. 48). Jesus saw them while He was praying and came to them walking on the water. He cared deeply about them and their safety.

There's a lesson here for all of us. In your battle with fear, recognize that Jesus will rescue you. In fact, when you're up to your eyeballs in life's thorny problems, only Jesus' power can give you hope. Your eyes, like Peter's in this story, may be gazing on the depth of life's swells or the size of the waves, but Jesus will never take His eyes off you. Jesus has power over every fearful situation that you face. Losing your job, facing marital troubles, worrying about what your kids are doing when you're not around—any problem you face in life is outmatched by the power of Jesus. If you cannot find hope to overcome your fears in Him, you have nowhere to turn.

The Promises of God

Third, the believer must depend on the *promises of God*. Isaiah recorded, "Fear not, for I am with you; be not dismayed, for I am your God. I will strengthen you, yes, I will help you, I will uphold you with My righteous right hand" (Isa. 41:10). God's Word is simple and straightforward. God says, "Stop being fearful. I am here." Floyd Barackman counsels, "Get a grip—a grip on the promises of God. His paternal presence assures us of His blessing in our behalf."[4]

Marolyn was born into a home where she had been taught to love and trust God. When God took her parents, she had great confidence that He would continue to take good care of her brothers and her. She was not anxious, for she knew His promises, promises in Scripture that she had memorized as a child. She trusted His care for she had seen Him care for her family in the past. The circumstances were different, but the same gracious, loving God was in control.

The Protection of God

Fourth, when faced with the most severe crises of your life, you must rely on the *protection of God*. "He who dwells in the secret place of the Most High shall abide under the shadow of the Almighty. I will say of the LORD, 'He is my refuge and my fortress; my God, in Him I will trust'" (Ps. 91:1-2). God stresses that He is our strong protection who guarantees our safety. Hope is only as strong as what we place our hope in. Twice in Psalm 42 the psalmist says, "Hope in God" (vv. 5, 11).

Not only does God provide a hiding place for us in the time of trouble, He also assigns angels (Ps. 91:11) to protect us from unnecessary harm. Tenderly they bear us up in their hands. When we are facing our darkest dilemma, God's powerful angels put their arms around us and carry us to the secret place of safety. God's angels are God's messengers. Marolyn and I still do not have answers as to why God sent His angels to carry Roger, Dennis, Gary, and her to safety, but not her parents and sister. God knows, however, and one day He will reveal that to us. Meanwhile, we have the assurance that nothing will happen to us outside of God's providential care. The protection of God is a total package. Knowing all that God has provided to help us ride out the storms of life cements our hope, and that hope breaks the grip of fear like a jackhammer. It was by this concrete hope that God enabled my wife to overcome her fear of riding in an automobile.

Trusting God

Fearing God means to reverence and respect Him. Knowing God means to expand our knowledge of Him and His ways and then apply what we know to difficult situations. Trusting God affirms our commitment to Him when we face life's fears. Based on our reverence for God and our knowledge of His ways, we are prompted to trust Him when we are afraid.

Our ability to trust God grows out of our knowledge and understanding of Him. Indeed He is the object of our faith and trust. To say that we "believe" suggests certainty and conviction with regard to God. Believing is to recognize that He is totally reliable and absolutely trustworthy. Trusting God means we hang on to Him. Here's how it's done.

On a commuter flight from Portland, Maine, to Boston, Henry Dempsey, the pilot, heard an unusual noise near the rear of the small aircraft. He turned the controls over to his copilot and went back to check it out. As he reached the tail section, the plane hit an air pocket, and Dempsey was tossed against the rear door. He quickly discovered the source of the mysterious noise. The rear door had not been properly latched prior to takeoff, and it flew open. He was instantly sucked out of the jet. The copilot, seeing the red warning light that indicated an open door, radioed the nearest airport, requesting permission to make an emergency landing. He reported that the pilot had fallen out of the plane, and requested a helicopter search of that area of the ocean.

After the plane landed, they found Henry Dempsey holding on to the outdoor ladder of the aircraft. Somehow he had caught the ladder, held on upside down for ten minutes as the plane flew 200 miles per hour at an altitude of four thousand feet. And then, at landing, he somehow managed to keep his head from hitting the runway, a mere twelve inches away. It took airport personnel several minutes to pry Dempsey's fingers from the ladder.[5]

What can we learn from this amazing story? Simply this. When you are in deep trouble, when fear presses you hard against life's circumstances, when you are fighting untenable odds, when you find yourself in life's most hopeless situation, hang on to God. Only God can spawn hope from certain disaster.

Our hope is in God who is completely trustworthy and has always demonstrated faithfulness to His children. Ours is a confident expectation that God will deliver us and act on our behalf.

Loving God

Fear of God leads us to bow our knees in reverence and awe to the great God we serve. He is all we need. Knowing God involves a growing relationship with Him, allowing His promises to help us with the dread of fear. Trusting God expresses that we will commit to Him all the fears that trouble us. Loving God prompts us to obey Him in the face of fear. This, too, helps to break the grip of fear.

Our love for God is a response to His love for us (1 John 4:19), which was displayed at the cross. His love dispels the fear of future punishment. We should fear the Lord because we love the Lord, not because we fear punishment from Him. The apostle John said, "There is no fear in love; but perfect love casts out fear, because fear involves torment. But he who fears has not been made perfect in love" (v. 18). As believers growing in our love for God, we are released from the inner torment of fear as we anticipate the future day of judgment. John F. Walvoord and Roy B. Zuck observe regarding this text, "The matured experience of God's love (reached in the act of loving one another) is incompatible with fear and expels fear from the heart."[6]

Love and obedience are linked in the Bible. Jesus said, "If you love Me, keep My commandments" (John 14:15). In the same chapter, a further promise is made: "He who loves Me will be loved by My Father, and I will love him and manifest Myself to him" (v. 21). Upon this basis, the Lord promises peace: "Let not your heart be troubled, neither let it be afraid" (v. 27). When we demonstrate our love for God through obedience to Him, God manifests more love toward us, which results in peace being unleashed in the midst of our fear. It's that peace in the midst of fear that brings us hope, and hope is the ultimate by-product of obedient love.

Some Practical Conclusions

God does not want us to be victims of fear. When we encounter a fearful situation, we must become even more dependent on Him. Dependence on God is enhanced by our personal knowledge of Him, appropriation of what we know about God and His Word, and application of that knowledge to our particular situation. The process of becoming dependent on God as first aid to our fears is like becoming familiar with the Red Cross manual and applying what we learn in an emergency. Success in breaking the grip of fear depends on our spiritual condition and our degree of obedience to Him, and that largely depends on how familiar we are with His Word.

As Marolyn and I reflect on the tragedy that entered her life and the hope that resulted from it, we have come to some conclusions about fear that I pray will be helpful to you.

First, when you are afraid, admit your fears. Recognize them because they can have an impact upon you physically and upon the way you live your life. Great men of God, such as David and Paul, freely admitted their fears (Ps. 56:3; 2 Cor. 7:5). Be on the lookout for symptoms of fear in your own life. Marolyn had to be honest in evaluating her fears. You must too. In fact, you may need to seek godly counsel to help you come to grips with the cause of your fears. Don't hesitate to ask for the help of your pastor or a mature Christian friend.

Second, when you are afraid, take courage. Courage is a blend of optimism and bold action in the face of danger. Jesus encouraged His disciples during the storm on the Sea of Galilee by saying, "Be of good cheer! It is I; do not be afraid" (Matt. 14:27). As the Lord said "Come!" to Peter, the storm still raged, but Peter responded with courage and walked on the water. That's what Marolyn had to do as well. She had to respond to her situation with confidence in God. She talked to God about her fear, she rehearsed it in His ears, and then she released it to Him. You can do the same. Face up to your fears and enlist the help of God in breaking their grip. Replace the negative attitude of fear with positive action and courage.

Third, when you are afraid, recognize that God provides you with the necessary power to face your fears and conquer them. Consider Paul's words to Timothy: "For God has not given us a spirit of fear, but of power and of love and of a sound mind" (2 Tim. 1:7). As a young pastor Timothy was facing many difficult situations, and he feared he wasn't equal to them. Fear was present but so was hope in God's enabling power to give him victory. In your moment of fear, admit that your confidence is in the Lord. Acknowledge your dependence on Him. David said, "Whenever I am afraid, I will trust in You" (Ps. 56:3). If you are prone to fears, try memorizing Scripture texts of hope and courage, for example Psalm 23; 27:1–3; or 2 Timothy 1:7. Then be ready to quote these as an expression of your confidence in the Lord.

Fourth, when you are afraid, God says to practice love (2 Tim. 1:7). This requires active involvement in the lives of other people by sharing your fears and soliciting their encouragement. Let others know how they can help you and allow them to minister to you. Let them encourage you about your position in Christ. When Marolyn and her brothers were left orphans, they sought the help of others in their church. They went to live with their grandparents, who raised them.

They knew that being afraid was not a sign of weakness; it was a sign of wisdom. Don't try to conquer your fears by yourself when God has provided hope through so many avenues, including your friends and family.

Fifth, when you are afraid, bring some good, old-fashioned self-discipline to your thinking. "A sound mind" (2 Tim. 1:7) views life from a realistic perspective. From this perspective we best practice theology. Marolyn reminded herself that God is in control—He knows all about her fears—and then she lived as one who trusted God. She believed it, and then she had the discipline to practice it. David said, "What can flesh do to me?" (Ps. 56:4). Paul asserts, God is on our side (Rom. 8:31). What have I to fear? To further enhance your sound mind, spend more time with godly friends who will help change your perspectives on life. Seek the right company—friends who will understand, encourage, and pray for you. Conversely, remove yourself from fearful places, experiences, and people.

Captive to Fear

Don't let your fears destroy you. They almost destroyed Marolyn until she practiced the discipline necessary to turn them fully over to God and rely fully on Him. She had lived a captive to the constant fear of her family's tragic accident. But God delivered her from this self-imposed captivity.

If you live alone, do not fear. Trust God. If you are facing insurmountable odds at work, do not fear. Have hope. Get a group of friends to pray with you and for you, and turn your fears over to God. Spend time in the Word developing a sound mind with which to combat the fears that Satan is using to badger you. When you are tempted to fear, repeat the commitment of the prophet Isaiah: "Behold, God is my salvation, I will trust and not be afraid" (Isa. 12:2). Nothing destroys fear like faith, and when fear is put to flight by faith, nothing can hold back the hope.

Someone has said, "A man can live forty days without food, three days without water, about eight minutes without air, but only one second without hope." Hope is what you need and hope in God is what you have to overcome your fears. Fear can either hold you hostage or make you more dependent on God. It's your choice. Make that choice carefully, and as you do, remember the words of hymn writer Elisha A. Hoffman (1839–1929):

> What have I to dread, what have I to fear?
> Leaning on the Everlasting Arms.

Chapter Notes

1. Paul D. Meier, Frank B. Minirth, and Frank B. Wichern, *Introduction to Psychology and Counseling, Christian Perspectives and Applications* (Grand Rapids: Baker, 1982), 187.
2. John F. Walvoord and Roy B. Zuck, *The Bible Knowledge Commentary Old Testament* (Wheaton, Ill.: Victor, 1988), 1345.
3. John F. Walvoord and Roy B. Zuck, *The Bible Knowledge Commentary New Testament* (Wheaton, Ill.: Victor Books, 1988), 878.
4. Floyd Barackman, *Practical Christian Theology* (Grand Rapids: Kregel, 1998), 52.
5. Craig Brian Larson, ed., *Illustrations for Preaching and Teaching* (Grand Rapids: Baker, 1993), 114.
6. *Bible Knowledge Commentary New Testament*, 900.

Loving Your Kids
Through Tough Times

George Miller III

IT'S EASY TO LOVE YOUR CHILDREN during the good times. But parenting is about struggles and pain, as well as triumphs and pleasures. Sometimes it's about taking unexpected blows and bouncing back—and nobody can deliver a punch like your kids. You take your lumps, you learn your lessons, and you move on.

It isn't easy to love your children when they disappoint you. As parents, we still love them. We have to; that's our job. But sometimes our kids can really test us.

When It's Tough to Love

This chapter is about loving your children through difficult times. It's about finding the hope to go on when your life comes crashing down. Your kids can drag you through the darkest days, placing a spirit of winter in your heart, but you can all come through to the spring, arm in arm, still very much in love.

It doesn't matter whether our children are young or old. We never stop being a parent, and parents must never stop loving. We never know when that love is going to be strained the most, and needed the most. For most of us it's during our kid's teen years. Things get a little crazy then. But even after your children are grown and married, they can still cause you heartaches.

Do you remember the day you first looked into your child's face? Do you remember holding that tiny baby for the first time? The child you cuddled showed every indication of becoming the smartest, best-looking, and most-talented kid you had ever seen—a real chip off the old block. The whole world lay ahead, and you would do anything to help your child through life. At that tender moment, you never dreamed that this tiny bundle ever could make a choice with negative consequences. "Not my kid; she's perfect." But babies grow up, and they do what they want. Sometimes what they want is not what is best.

Doing the Wrong Thing

There is no greater influence on the life of a child than Mom and Dad. Oh, sure, their peers exert a lot of pressure on them, especially while they are teens, but as a loving parent you teach your children traditional Christian values, you send them to good schools, you attend a caring, Bible-preaching church, and you give them everything they need to succeed—all because you love them and you want them to love you. Because your kids have been blessed with so many advantages, surely they would never make decisions that fail to reflect your values. You've done all the right things and you have great confidence in their abilities. But as someone once said, "Confidence is what you have before you understand the situation."

Parents soon learn that their little darling is a sinner just as they are. Regardless of how young or how old, fallen people are going to make bad decisions. You can count on it. Sometimes they even get off track and make a mess of their lives. That's when, like the prodigal son, they need to be loved and made to feel welcome in the family.

But how do you love them through the tough times? Is there hope for a bewildered parent and a careless child? I know there is. Hope is what you have. Hope is a noun. And hope helped my family get through our darkest winter.

Bewildered Parents

During the past twenty-five years, I have been a marriage and family counselor, with a doctorate from Syracuse University. I have counseled many parents and families as they worked through difficulties resulting from wrong choices. In some families I've helped teens who had lived in rebellion for years. In other families the children were next-to-ideal, but they had simply made a wrong choice. It may have been just one wrong choice with far-reaching, even life-changing ramifications. When our kids make bad decisions the consequences are emotional, physical, and often very visible.

I have kept a box of tissues handy on my desk for the tears of parents as they described problems with their children. I have had in my office parents in pain who were medical doctors, lawyers, pastors, missionaries, and lay leaders. All poured out their hearts to me. Some have been rich and others poor; some were well-educated, others not so well-educated. They have come from all stations, all ethnic backgrounds, all religious denominations. They all had one thing in common—their children had made wrong choices and the parents were in despair. They weren't there to ask me how to punish their children for hurting them. To the contrary, they wanted to know how to survive and how to love that child through the tough times.

It was tough growing up in the twentieth century. It may be even harder in the twenty-first. It's no secret that life is much more challenging for our kids than for many of us when we were growing up. The temptations and enticements to make wrong decisions are everywhere, even when growing up in a moral home. You can't turn on the TV, rent a video, or click on the Internet without seeing something offensive. Society no longer shares the basic values of the Bible, and the institutions that at one time provided some sense of stability are increasingly undermined. Life is different now, and it's hard.

Looking for Answers

I counseled Linda and Tom when their teenage daughter was

pregnant. I sat with Bill and Sue and worked through their response to their son; he was the father. John and Lori's son was in trouble with the law and headed for prison because of a wrong choice. I have wept with and tried to provide direction for parents whose children were addicted to drugs or alcohol. One couple's adult child left his mate for someone else. Rita and Jerry's adult son was fired from a job because of his embarrassing behavior.

All of these are real people, loving and caring parents committed to giving their children every advantage in godly living. But all of them are hurting people, people looking for hope in the midst of despair. If you have been fortunate enough not to have experienced heartaches like these, likely someone you care about has.

It Will Never Happen to Me

Let's face it. Most parents have some teeny tiny fear that they might experience difficulty with one of their children. My wife, Elaine, and I also shared this fear, but we thought the chances were remote. I was a loving father, a minister of the gospel and, at the time, vice president of a Bible college. Elaine was a wonderful wife and a loving, dedicated, model mother. Besides, as a family counselor, I had helped so many other families through difficulties with children. Surely, I thought, God would protect us from serious trouble in our family. I was wrong.

I was in my office one afternoon when a terrible feeling came over me. Something was wrong. I just sensed that it was Jessica, my daughter. I never had a feeling like this before.

Jessica is our youngest. With her two older teenage brothers, Jason and Nathan, I could do "guy" things like shoot hoops and wrestle. But Jessica was my dainty flower—the apple of my eye. And she was a great kid—a good student, faithful at church, and well-respected at her high school. She was planning to become a medical doctor. She had it all together. She was the complete package, and yet that day I just knew something was wrong.

I called Elaine at home to make sure Jessica was there, then I immediately left my office. When I arrived home I called our daughter into our room. Elaine came with her. I asked, "What's wrong, Jess?"

"Nothing," she said, surprised at my question.

But I couldn't shake that weird feeling. With fatherly tenderness again I probed, "Jess, I know something is wrong, and I want you to tell us." I'll never forget the look that came over her face. With hesitation in her voice and fear in her eyes, she said, "Daddy, I think I'm pregnant."

Our World Fell to Pieces

Elaine and I just looked at each other, stunned. Maybe we heard her wrong. Surely our little angel didn't say what we thought she had said. Jessica had been our pride and joy, never in any kind of serious trouble. She was a model fifteen-year-old, and she was pregnant. How could this be? She wasn't even dating. This can't be happening. Not to us.

I admit that our first thoughts were about where we went wrong. What had we done as parents that would lead to such a common but improper decision? What more could we have done to teach her right from wrong? What could we have done to protect her more? Guilt swept over us, and we were inundated with doubt, shame, guilt, and despair.

After talking more with Jessica to find out what had happened and how she was responding to it all, my mind was immediately awash with questions. Should I resign my ministry at the college? Whom should I talk to? What will people think? What will they say? What are we going to do now? Humbled, we wanted to simultaneously run, hide, and cry. We couldn't run and we couldn't hide, but there were oceans of tears. Our nice, neat little world had fallen to pieces. There seemed to be no hope that we could go on.

Thank God for Friends

But there was hope. There is always hope. God had not forsaken us, and we had close friends. Ken and Pam gave us James Dobson's book *When God Doesn't Make Sense*[1] with a note that said, "We have been asking the Lord to show us small ways that we can help and support you." Job could have used friends like this. And there were many others. A note from a relative read, "Not a day goes by when you are not on my mind and in my prayers. Keep your head up and God will get you through this one." Elaine received a card from a friend who said, "Please know that if there is anything a friend can do—this friend would be most happy to." I received phone calls from friends who were well-known leaders. They encouraged me by telling of the difficulties they had faced with their children, situations that I was unaware of, in which God had worked in the family. We couldn't believe the love and support we received. We couldn't have made it without the prayers and hugs and gentle comments from friends. God already had a network around us to support us, and we didn't even know it.

There was no easy solution to our problem, but through it I have learned hope is best found by following God's Word. There is a light at the end of the tunnel, and it's not always an oncoming train. Perhaps some hope-filled advice that has been engendered through my years of counseling and from my own experiences will help you love your kids through the tough times.

Our family went through five stages in dealing with Jessica's pregnancy. Some of the stages are "family" stages—experienced by the whole family. Some of them are "personal" stages—experienced by individuals within the family. All of them are important in loving your kids through tough times.

The Reaction Stage

He who answers a matter before he hears it, it is folly and shame to him. (Prov. 18:13)

When we heard the news of our daughter's pregnancy we were stunned. Our first thoughts were to deny—"This can't be true." But as difficult as it was to accept, it was, nonetheless, true.

Everyone Will Be Watching

A pastor met with Elaine and me the day that we discovered we were facing the greatest challenge of our lives. He wanted to show his compassion and support for us. But one thing he said sticks in my mind to this day: "George, you can be certain that everyone will be watching to see how you deal with this situation." How would I react? What would I do? Would the counsel that I had so often given to others really work for me? It was an awkward situation, but God was so good. He gave us hope.

When loving our children through tough times, we must first come to grips with our own state of mind and our initial reactions to the situation. Ross Campbell and Gary Chapman write, "Someone has said that when children are little, they step all over your feet, and when they are older, they step all over your heart. The rigors of raising children can be extremely draining, physically, emotionally, and financially. Parenting can be hazardous to your health."[2] My heart had a boot print the size of Texas on it. How would I handle my reactions?

If you have encountered some problems with your kids, spend time evaluating yourself and your disappointment. Feelings of fear, anger, embarrassment, depression, and guilt can motivate us to say and do things we later regret. As a counselor, I have heard the hurtful words of parents in reaction to their hurt. Their frustration and anger toward their child frequently spill out in name-calling and unreasonable rage, and this can destroy the child, regardless of age. Hurtful reactions complicate the issue and make it more difficult to move toward restoration and ultimate recovery.

Swallow Your Pride

So what's a parent to do? Swallow your pride. Talk about an untasty meal, but I learned to eat it. And realize you need the help and support of others. Scripture clearly teaches that when we are going through tough times, we need the companionship of those who care about us and understand our struggle (Eccl. 5:9–11). The help of a godly pastor or counselor is important. Spending time in prayer and reflecting on what is going on inside of you as a parent is necessary to gain a proper perspective on the problem and to make correct responses. Let your pastor or trained Christian counselor help you deal with you before you ask for help in dealing with your kids. That will pave the way to understanding and compassion.

Some parents may also wish to join a parent's support group. David

Jeremiah, who has himself experienced a wayward child, writes, "If we had not been willing to swallow our pride and join a parent's support group, we would have struggled on as if we were the only hurting family on the planet. Instead, the mutual sharing in the group enabled us to put our own problems in perspective."[3] Others can help you in loving your kids through tough times, but only if you ask them and only if you let them. Swallow your pride and ask.

Handle Your Guilt

The most devastating feeling that results from a family situation like ours is guilt. Now, to be sure, some guilt is valid—like when we have fallen short of God's requirements. Elaine and I had to evaluate ourselves and the mistakes we may have made as parents. When we evaluate ourselves and discover our own failures, we have to confess them to God (1 John 1:9) and make things right with those we have hurt (Acts 24:16). Then we need to accept God's forgiveness.

No one is perfect and every parent fails in some way, but we need not wallow in self-blame when we have tried to be the kind of parents that God wants us to be. We parents have a tendency to assume too much responsibility for everything our children do as teens and as adults. We must remember that our kids have wills, and when they exercise those wills in ways contrary to our wills, we are not to blame. *Focus on the Family*'s James Dobson believes that the tendency of parents to blame themselves for their children's failures results from the teaching of classical psychologists who believe in determinism— that all behavior is *caused* behavior. Determinism takes away all responsibility for voluntary decisions.[4] But God has given all of us the freedom to make choices. Sometimes even the best kids make a wrong decision that brings about devastating results. Each person, including our children, is responsible for his or her own choices.

It is difficult not to accept all the blame if we believe what David Jeremiah refers to as the myth that "Good Parents Don't Have Problems with Their Kids."[5] Those of us in positions of spiritual leadership feel even more to blame. The embarrassment of and critical comments from family and friends only add to our feelings of guilt and self-blame. The younger the child, the more intense the guilt feelings. We feel that we are supposed to be in total control. But our children are not robots or mindless, passionless androids. They are sinful people Christ died to save, and sinful people sometimes make poor choices. Sometimes we can't prevent the choices, and we need not beat up on ourselves when the unthinkable happens. Believe it or not, the unthinkable happens all the time.

Get a Grip

The day I explained my situation to the man who was then president of Practical Bible College, Dr. Dale Linebaugh, I intended to resign my position as Vice President for Student Affairs. I was so riddled with guilt that I didn't know what else to do. He was gracious and loving, and he said, "There was a perfect parent who had two children, and they lived in a perfect environment free of sin. The children were loved by a parent who made no mistakes. All their needs were met. The two children ignored the warning of their Father and made wrong, sinful choices. The parent was our heavenly Father. His children were Adam and Eve." His point was clear, and I appreciated his wisdom.

The choices, then, are these: First, when your children make poor decisions, you can go to pieces, bury your head in the sand, resign all your responsibilities, and drop out of the Christian community. Second, you can recognize the basic truth that all people are fallen and sin. When they do, they need your strength, not your self-pity. They need your guidance, not your guilt.

Parents must honestly process their negative feelings if they are to love their kids through tough times. We cannot offer hope if we see none. We must get beyond reacting out of guilt, anger, fear, or embarrassment. Those feelings are normal, but we need to turn our reactions into responses that will both honor God and help our children. Compassion and love cannot flow from us when we are controlled by negative emotions. Negative emotions produce negative responses.

We should always ask, *What does God want?* and *What is best for the recovery of my child?* This is the proper way to react to life's setbacks, big and small. This is the way hope reacts.

The Remission Stage

If we confess our sins, He is faithful and just to forgive us our
sins and to cleanse us from all unrighteousness. (1 John 1:9)

No one is exempt from emotional hurt. It is part of life to be deceived,
cheated, lied to, told off, offended, or worse. We are going to experience
misunderstanding, hurt, pain, suffering, and broken relationships. So,
when someone in your family, especially your child, hurts you deeply,
don't allow anger and bitterness to fester. Many parents and children go
through life carrying stored-up grudges, resentment, bitterness, and broken hearts that prevent them from being psychologically and spiritually
healthy. What Christian parents decide about forgiveness will determine
whether they will be *bitter* or *better* Christians and parents.

We usually relate the idea of *remission* to cancer or another dread
disease. Often when someone has completed treatments for cancer,
they receive the happy news that their cancer is abating. Their body is
returning to its precancer condition. Remission is good news. When
we who are hurt decide to release that hurt to God and to allow our
relationship to return to its pre-hurt condition, that's *remission* too,
and it, too, is good news. Remission in this second sense means the
release of the guilty party from the penalty that accompanies their
guilt. Our daughter was guilty of sin. The hurt that accompanied that
sin—to our pride, to our reputation, to our relationship with her—
could not be relieved just because she confessed her sin to God and
received His forgiveness. It could only be relieved when we also forgave her and released her from the guilt we felt.

Making Things Right

What a great object lesson Jesus gave in the parable of the Prodigal
Son (Luke 15:21–24). When the wayward boy realized what a fool he
had been and returned home, he was reunited with his father. Immediately the sinful son began to make his confession before God and
his earthly father. But even before he could finish, the compassion of
the father got the best of him. He snapped for his servants to begin a
great celebration because he loved his son, and he could see that his
repentance was genuine.

Sin must always be confronted, but confronted lovingly. When re-pentance is real and a genuine confession is made, forgiveness must follow. This leads to the remission stage, and we have no choice but to enter it when our kids see the mistakes they have made and genu-inely repent of them. Just as repentance cannot be forced—it must come about honestly as the Spirit of God reveals to our kids the wrong that has been done—so must forgiveness also be honest and timely. When our kids genuinely repent of their sins, we must genu-inely forgive their sin. If we don't, they will be cleared by God and we will be condemned by Him.

True Forgiveness

Parents who love their children through the tough times will re-spond biblically to their kid's wrong choices and will assure them of God's forgiveness when they confess their sin. We must be equally quick with our own forgiveness. There's no difficulty about God for-giving our foolish children, but there is often a problem with parents forgiving children. "They hurt me so deeply. You can't know what this has done to me. I don't know if I can forgive them." These sentiments are common among disappointed parents. Common or not, they are selfish.

Notice that such comments relate, not to the sin of the child, but to the pain of the parent. Everything is about *me*. *I* was hurt. They have done it to *me*. I don't know if *I* can forgive them. When parents take this attitude toward their wayward kids, they clearly have not entered the remission stage, and without passing through this impor-tant stage they can never progress to the others.

Parental Confession

Parents are also required to confess their sins, not only to God, but to their families. If after you review and evaluate your performance as a parent you can identify things that contributed to your child's fail-ure, you must confess them and ask for forgiveness from your kids. This was not easy for us to do with Jessica, but it was necessary and cathartic to our relationship. A clear conscience is essential if we are to enjoy emotional and spiritual health and be the parents God wants us to be. Too often our children do not see us doing what we are encouraging them to do. Repentance and remission on both sides leads to restoration.

Our motivation for forgiving Jessica was the forgiveness that God had granted to us (Eph. 4:32). God forgives us for the sake of our Savior, Jesus Christ. God does not forgive us because we deserve it, just as we do not forgive others because they deserve it. We forgive because God commanded us to do so (Matt. 18:21-22). God has already given to us a model of how relationships are reconstructed and restored through forgiveness. Now we must follow it.

Our Greatest Christmas Gift

One of the greatest days in our lives as parents came on Christmas, four months after Jessica told us she was pregnant. Elaine and I could not have asked for a better present from her. Throughout our ordeal, Jessica had repeatedly told us that she was sorry for the wrong choices she had made, but on Christmas day she gave us a large, beautiful card that wished us a merry Christmas. Inside was a long note that thanked us for all that we had done for her. That was nice, but even better was her honest, sincere, written apology. She wanted to make sure that we had forgiven her. You should have been there. The most delightful emotion I know is forgiveness. It is so freeing, so cleansing, so sweet. It made our Christmas. Our family was passing through a long, cold personal winter. And yet we were discovering together that hope grows in winter.

Forgiveness brings to you a great sense of freedom from the bondage of all your negative feelings. Forgiveness allows you to overcome the hurts instead of dwelling on them. It opens the door for you and your child to be truly close, to deepen an intimate relationship.

Please don't fail to forgive your kids for their bad choices. Remission is the only road to restoration and rejoicing. If you have been forgiven by your heavenly Father, don't you think you can forgive your children?

The Restoration Stage

Brethren, if a man is overtaken in any trespass, you who are spiritual restore such a one in a spirit of gentleness, considering yourself lest you also be tempted. Bear one another's burdens, and so fulfill the law of Christ. (Gal. 6:1-2)

If we are to experience the hope of loving our children through tough times, we must focus on their restoration. We in evangelical circles often concentrate on what went wrong and almost ignore what we must do to bring about recovery. Often I am amazed at how many Christians possess the gift of criticism, but apparently do not possess any desire for restoration. The apostle Paul couldn't be clearer in Galatians 6. We are to provide hope for the fallen. And to do so, we must help in the healing of those who hurt. We are to be concerned with restoring our kids when they make bad choices, not cutting them off from the life of the family.

Right Motivation

Restoration is always to be our motivation as we deal with difficult family issues. Too often our motives are selfish; we just want out of an embarrassing situation. But that's self-love, not true love. True love has the other person's well-being in mind. Rich Buhler noted, "The motive for expressing your disapproval is vitally important. Sometimes when we express disapproval to another person it is not our intention to try and solve anything. Our goal is to vent our anger and frustration or to make the other person feel guilty. Before confronting another person, we need to think about what we hope to accomplish."[6] That's especially true when dealing with our kids' wrong choices.

Paul placed the responsibility of looking out for members of the family of God on those who are spiritual, those who are walking and living in the Spirit. This presupposes the more mature are to help restore the less mature. Parents fit into this category. We are not perfect but, if as believers we are mature in our faith, we bear a special responsibility to those who are less mature in faith, and that includes our children. If our children fall into sin but repent of that sin and confess it to us and we fail to forgive them and take the steps to restore them, which of us is more immature?

Making Useful Again

The word *overtaken* in Galatians 6:1 refers to a person who is caught, someone who has been suddenly seized by a temptation before they could escape.[7] They were caught off guard. The "trespass" is any sin or any deviation from the truth. The central point of the verse is that those who are spiritual should, in gentleness or meekness, restore the one who has succumbed to unspiritual behavior. The Greek word that the apostle chose for "restore" means "to set broken bones or mend fishing nets."[8] In both cases, the word speaks of making something useful once again. It was our main goal as Jessica's parents to help her to regain her former usefulness to God and others. We did not commit her to the woodshed of sin; we restored her to useful service for the Lord she loves.

Considering my own experience, I would paraphrase the verse in this way: "Parents, if your child is caught in a situation that is counter to the truth of God's Word, it is your responsibility as spiritually mature leaders to do whatever is necessary to restore your child to a useful spiritual life. Deal gently with your child, realizing you are not immune from making sinful choices yourself, because sometimes even the strong become weak."

The Word of God is so practical, especially when you really need it. And when Jessica told us she was pregnant, we really needed some practical advice. My wife and I continually asked ourselves some important questions:

- What can we do to correct the problem?
- What is needed to restore Jessica to her rightful position?
- What can we do to help her to succeed?

When we found the answers to these questions, we found God's way of giving hope to us in a hopeless situation. We found that hope is a noun, it is something we have, not something we do. Focusing on blame and our daughter's failure would not help Jessica or us survive and move forward. Only the answers in God's Word could do that and that's where we found our hope.

The Rebuilding Stage

Bear one another's burdens, and so fulfill the law of Christ. (Gal. 6:2)

Suddenly we were faced with two choices. We could allow our fifteen-year-old daughter to bear the consequences of her sin alone, even though we said we had forgiven her, or we could help her bear that burden. The loving thing to do was shoulder some of the burden ourselves. It was the right choice.

Sharing the Load

Loving your kids through tough times means assisting them in carrying the burdens resulting from their wrong choices. Understanding two terms in Galatians 6:2 is critical. The first word is *burden,* which refers to a weight that is pressing or demanding on the person's re-sources.[9] The weight is beyond the capacity of a person to carry by himself or herself.

The second term, *bear,* means to carry or support.[10] Putting those terms together, I can see clearly that Christ expects me as a compassionate dad to come alongside my daughter, who is hurting, and help her by sharing the load. In this case, it wasn't a load of my own making, but it was a load for me to share. The consequences of wrong choices are often great and continuing. We parents dare not shut our kids out of our lives after they make bad decisions. We must share their heavy burdens, so they will not be crushed under the load of their foolishness. Allowing that to happen would be destruction, not restoration and rebuilding.

Paul told us that, by bearing the burdens of others, we fulfill the "law of Christ." This "law" likely refers to the words of Galatians 5:14: "For all the law is fulfilled in one word, even in this: 'You shall love your neighbor as yourself.'"

Unconditional Love

I came to fully appreciate through our family crisis that parents need to be loving and supportive as their children go through the tough times. We need to say with honesty, "I love you, no matter what." When I said that to my lovely daughter, I wasn't showing approval or acceptance of what she did wrong. I was showing approval of who she is—my lovely daughter. We should not withhold or place conditions on our love. Parental love, like God's love, must be unconditional, unselfish, and unending. Only a clear demonstration of that type of love will help our children rebuild their lives. It's what helped the Prodigal Son rebuild his life (Luke 15:20).

Loving our children must not be just emotional love; it must be action love—love with feet. We need to demonstrate our love in practical ways. First Corinthians 13:4 states that "love . . . is kind," meaning that love is serviceable.[11] True love is doing good things to help or assist others. In our case, Elaine and I were demonstrating love to Jessica, even though she made a wrong choice. We supported her by giving her hope and shouldering some of her burden. Elaine would go with Jess for her prenatal visits and was her labor coach. We also faced financial concerns and a need for new living arrangements. We spent a great deal of time with her; we made a commitment to invest time and energy in our relationship. I remember wanting to be by her side in every situation that might be difficult, and we wanted to hold the baby so that people would see our acceptance of our grandson. We always believed that how we demonstrated our love would set the tone for how others would demonstrate their love to Jessica.

The goal in restoring your child is to enable him or her to rebuild his or her own life and one day stand strong alone. I believe this is what Paul meant in Galatians 6:5 when he said, "For each one shall bear his own load." We help bear one another's burdens, with the goal of helping them until they are strong enough or mature enough to bear the load themselves. We support our children in tough times to give them the time to gain the strength and spiritual resources to stand alone. If they do not experience our loving support, the burden of their sin can overwhelm them and rob them of hope. But hope is a noun. It's what we give our kids when they have nothing else.

A Support Strategy

In many family situations, this loving support needs a strategic plan to assure growth and success. Parents and child should decide together the steps for successfully handling their problems. Together they should clarify the difficulties, generate solutions, and design a plan for action. What will be required for the child to rebuild his or her life and see full recovery?

In our situation, we needed to arrange counseling for Jess and to help her finish high school and college. If she was to succeed, she needed an education that would allow her to independently take care of herself and her son. Finances and day care were big concerns. God opened the right doors and provided for everything, but it still took planning. We also thought it was important that the stresses of being a teen single mom did not bring about emotional or spiritual burnout for Jess. We planned time for her to be alone, to do homework, and many nights Elaine or I would stay up with the baby because Jess had an early class.

There are many ways we parents can demonstrate supportive love. We can make sure that there is open communication about things other than the tough times that are before us. We can be good listeners and be tactful when communicating with our kids about their bad choices. We can make sure our talk with them and about them builds up our sons or daughters instead of tearing them down (Eph. 4:29). Positive, reinforcing love will include spending fun times together and expressing love with hugs and kisses.

One of the ways we demonstrated our love for Jessica was through words of affirmation. We spoke words that showed Jess that we see the good in her, not just her unwise decision. There came a time when Jessica needed to hear from me, "I'm proud of you and the way you are dealing with your life." The expression on her face said it all. Look for all the good things in your child's life and mention them often.

Rebuilding Trust

A final important ingredient in the rebuilding stage is trust. Rebuilding trust in Jessica was not difficult for Elaine and me. Our daughter has acted in an incredibly responsible manner, and we are always seeing things to comment on positively. She has moved ahead with her life and has made us very proud. I realize this may not be true in every family, but parents need to search their kids' lives for things to praise and be positive about. If you're committed to it, you'll find them.

For many parents, however, trust won't be restored overnight. Don't kid yourself. It will take time. You have been shocked, saddened, and hurt. But trust must be rebuilt, and you likely will need a plan for rebuilding trust between your child and yourself.

Jessica informed us of her schedule and who she was with. She would go out of her way to make sure we had phone numbers to contact her, and she would often call just to check in. We committed to openness about discussing frustrations. We sincerely committed to investing time and energy in the relationship, to honesty, to accountability, to avoidance of temptation, and to walking with God. Trust can grow and be reestablished, but it takes time and effort—your time and your effort.

The Rejoicing Stage

Rejoice in the Lord always. Again I will say, rejoice! (Phil. 4:4)

Rejoicing was not on our minds when Elaine and I sat down with Jessica and heard she was pregnant. But it is today. Rejoicing is not always easy when we are in the midst of disappointment and difficulty. As Christians, however, we can experience joy because of our relationship with Jesus Christ. As Christian parents, we can face the tough times with our kids and still rejoice because we know Christ is our hope and that God is able to use even our most difficult situations to help us grow. That's tangible hope.

Parents are not always successful in recovering and restoring their kids. There are no magic formulas that assure a desired outcome. Our children must still make the choice to do what is right and to follow God. We cannot do that for them. We can deal with ourselves, making sure that we are filled with the Spirit of God and with His compassionate love, but we cannot repent of sin for our kids.

Part of our hope is that God will allow us to be instrumental in restoring our children to useful lives for His glory. We can also be supportive of one another. Only parents who have faced pain themselves can understand what other hurting parents are going through. God has given me greater understanding and compassion for moms and dads who are going through adversity because of the wrong choices made by their kids.

God's "Nevers"

If your child has done some pretty foolish things, and is estranged from you right now, here are some "nevers" to keep in mind. God never allows us to stop loving our kids, regardless of how much shame and pain they have caused. Paul told us that "love never fails" (1 Cor. 13:8). He also characterized love as bearing all things and enduring all things (v. 7). God never allows us to stop loving our children even when their choices cause tension and embarrassment. Our children must sense from us the kind of compassionate and empowering love that God showers on us.

Also, God never allows us to give up on our kids. We must hang in there with them. My heart goes out to parents who are doing everything in the correct way, but whose son or daughter has not yet responded positively. Don't give up hope. Hope is what you have. God can still perform miracles in changing their lives.

And God never allows us to quit praying for our kids. Prayer may be the best weapon you have against Satan, and that old snake doesn't want you to use it, especially on behalf of your children who have made wrong choices. So the right thing to do, the Devil-disappointing thing, is to continue to pray for them. God hears your cries. Hold on to your faith, regardless of how long it takes.

When God performs a miracle in bringing someone back to Him, it is always because of love. One of my favorite hymns is "The King of Love My Shepherd Is" by Henry W. Baker (1821–1877). The third stanza grips my heart:

> Perverse and foolish, oft I strayed,
> But yet in love He sought me,
> And on His shoulder gently laid,
> And home, rejoicing brought me.

There are times when our rejoicing is due in part to the proper responses of our children. In the parable of Luke 15, the father of the Prodigal was looking for his son. He held onto his hope that the boy would return, and sure enough he did. When the compassionate father saw the son returning, he embraced the young man, kissed him profusely, and lavished honors and gifts upon him. That father doesn't sound like many people whose sons or daughters have made wrong decisions. In Jesus' story there was true rejoicing and that's the way it ought to be. The entire parable gives us a great sense of hope.

Hope Restored

My daughter responded to the leading of her heavenly Father and earthly parents. Jessica graduated from high school and went on to college. After working as a radiology technician for a year, she went back to college and graduated, with honors, from the New Jersey University of Medicine and Dentistry, specializing in ultrasound technology. She was one of nine students accepted and wants to work in obstetrics and gynecology.

What makes my heart rejoice more, Jessica is faithful in her devotions and church attendance. We are proud of what a great mother she has become to her son. We thank God for the way in which He has helped Jess handle the difficult circumstances that came from her wrong choice. God helped her get back on track, as she yielded her life to Him.

Have I Told You About My Grandson?

Oh, by the way. Have I told you about my grandson? I have pictures. You should see him. His name is Keenan, and he has captured all of our hearts. He is God's gift to us, and we treasure him.

Our two sons, Jason and Nathan, love Keenan as a nephew as much as Elaine and I love him as a grandson. Nathan was once assigned to write a college paper on the worst thing and the best thing that ever happened to his family. He chose to write about Jessica's pregnancy, saying it was both the worst and the best thing that we've experienced. Keenan is now five years old. His uncles are always wrestling with him, they take him fishing and to ball games. He is a busy little guy who wants to be doing something exciting every minute of every day. He has many people in his life who love him dearly. One day while I was baby-sitting I asked him why he was such a good boy. He replied, "Because I have so many people who love me, Grampa." And he's right.

Out of life's toughest time, God blessed us with a grandson, and we wouldn't trade him for the world. A dear relative once wrote to us and said, "That baby has a special mission—you wait and see." Though we did not approve of our daughter's bad choice, and neither does she, God brought good out of it. He can bring good out of your situation as well.

While going through the most trying times of our lives, Elaine would read this saying every morning: "There is nothing that touches my life that has not already passed through the hands of God." There is hope for the Christian. That hope is in the God of all hope, the One who can bring life from the ashes and joy from distress. Let Him give you the gift of hope today.

Chapter Notes

1. James Dobson, *When God Doesn't Make Sense* (Wheaton, Ill.: Tyndale, 1993).
2. Ross Campbell and Gary Chapman, *Parenting Your Adult Child* (Chicago: Northfield, 1999), 123.
3. David Jeremiah, *Exposing the Myths of Parenthood* (Waco, Tex.: Word, 1988), xii.
4. James Dobson, *Parenting Isn't for Cowards* (Waco, Tex.: Word, 1987), 74.
5. *Exposing the Myths of Parenthood*, 3-21.
6. Rich Buhler, *Love: No Strings Attached* (Nashville: Nelson, 1987), 112.
7. John F. Walvoord and Roy B. Zuck, *The Bible Knowledge Commentary New Testament* (Wheaton, Ill.: Victor, 1983), 609.
8. W. E. Vine, *An Expository Dictionary of New Testament Words* (Old Tappan, N.J.: Revell, 1966), 290.
9. Ibid., 157.
10. Ibid., 100.
11. Ibid., 292.

Overcoming Temptation with Hope

R. Peter Mason

LANNY WAS LIKE A LOT of young men today—sixteen and eager to explore his sexuality. He and some of his buddies used to hang at the convenience store hoping to get a peek at *Playboy* magazine. It wasn't hard; this store didn't keep magazines of this genre behind the counter. They were right out in plain view and every time Lanny and his friends visited they got an eyeful. But they often were busted and asked to leave. There had to be a better way, and there was.

Lanny's friends and he were perfect candidates for computer geekdom. With a few strokes of a keyboard and access to the Internet, the convenience store was a distant second in the convenience department. Images of nude models or sexy "housewives" would stream across the computer monitor in the privacy of Lanny's room. The guys came over regularly to do "homework." They even dabbled in a cyberspace romance. The guys made up a story about Lanny, changed his name, made him ten years older and bingo—they got a bite. They acted out their impossible fantasies through the things they said to their on-line girlfriend. A virtual romance began, but it wasn't real. It was all a joke to Lanny and his buddies.

Temptation in the Information Age

We live in the information age. More than half the homes in America have a computer. A three-year-old boy reveals the ubiquitous presence of technology in his bedtime prayer: "Lead us not into temptation but deliver us from e-mail."

With technology comes opportunity but also isolation. Technology brings increased opportunities for ministry but also many more avenues for temptation. Recently I read in my local newspaper, *The Times Union,* that 70 percent of college students are guilty of cheating. But here's the catch. The old days of using *Cliffs Notes* have now been eclipsed by the easy availability of term papers from Internet sites. Stealing once meant the bold risk of shoplifting. Today, it is as simple as pirating copyrighted software. With little chance of being caught, the temptation to dishonesty is powerful.

Because I work with churches and pastors, I am exposed to the devastating consequences when spiritual leaders succumb to temptation. One senior pastor lingered with the youth pastor's wife for counseling. They began corresponding over e-mail. She was impressed with his understanding and thoughtfulness, as he listened to her needs. He was weary from the demands of a church building program. Then one day after their relationship turned more intense, they passionately embraced and fell into sin.

Temptation, of course, is not limited to cyberspace. The accounts are frequent and disheartening. A pastor has a sexual liaison with the superintendent of his Sunday schools—a woman with whom he spends extensive one-on-one time in ministry. His young wife is busy at home with the responsibilities of caring for two toddlers and an infant. Another pastor's wife feels unappreciated and unloved by her overzealous husband. Eventually he learns that, while he has been devoting his every moment to his ministry, his wife has been seeing a coworker in the evening instead of attending business meetings at her downtown office.

These are true stories, and how frequently similar tragedies come into the open. Ministries are disrupted, marriages are strained or broken, and churches are demoralized. Succumbing to temptation has terrible consequences.

A Starting Point

To triumph over temptation we need God's power. On our own, we will not succeed. The Bible describes the natural human being as spiritually "dead in trespasses and sins" (Eph. 2:1). Left to our own abilities in an unsaved state, we would never achieve victory over temptation. "But God, who is rich in mercy, because of His great love with which He loved us, even when we were dead in trespasses, made us alive together with Christ" (vv. 4–5).

When we experience this new spiritual life by acknowledging our sinfulness and trusting Christ alone for the forgiveness of our sins, He not only saves us, but He provides the energizing source to live in victory. That source is the Holy Spirit.

- He indwells us (John 14:16–17).
- He seals us (Eph. 4:30).
- He prays for us (Rom. 8:26–27).
- He convicts us of sin (1 John 3:20).
- He teaches us (1 John 2:27).
- He guides us (Rom. 8:14).
- He fills us (Eph. 5:18).

In Romans 8 the Holy Spirit and His work in the believer are mentioned no fewer than eighteen times.

In our Christian lives, we must continue to take a serious view of sin. "Sin is lawlessness" (1 John 3:4). It is a failure to live according to God's revealed will and purpose. Sin extends beyond doing wrong things; it is also failing to do things we ought to do. To use the words of one of the general forms of confession that has been part of the liturgy since Puritan times in editions of the Church of England's *Book of Common Prayer*, as well as the directories of worship used in Reformed churches, we sin when "we have left undone those things which we ought to have done" as much as when "we have done those things which we ought not to have done." It was for sins of omission that those "on the left hand" were judged in Christ's description of the Last Judgment (Matt. 25:31-46). It is not for acts of sin that these people stand condemned, not for lying or cheating or murder. They were sent into everlasting fire because they had neglected to give food to the hungry, drink to the thirsty, and clothing to the naked.[1]

We cannot presume upon God's grace by saying, "If I sin, God will forgive me anyhow. He's got this mercy thing going." Truth is, an evidence of the genuineness of God's grace in our lives is that we resist sin, not flirt with it. "The goal of the gospel is godliness," said Dwight Pentecost when he expounded Paul's words in Titus 3:1-8.

The mere presence of temptation does not indicate that we have not experienced God's grace. Thomas Watson, one of the most popular preachers in London during the Puritan era, observed, "Satan does not tempt God's children because they have sin in them, but because they have grace in them. Had they no grace, the devil would not disturb them. . . . Though to be tempted is a trouble, yet to think why you are tempted is a comfort."[2]

God tests His children as He did Abraham and Job to purify and to strengthen them. In sharp contrast, Satan's strategy is to distort the divine image and to mar the beauty of Christ's character from being displayed through the life of a Christian. Satan comes as an "angel of light" but his goal is destruction. God's goal is to gather the grain and to destroy the chaff (Luke 22:31-32). The Destroyer seeks to tear down whereas the Holy One seeks to build up. We will recognize the source of the testing by its purpose.

Temptations from the Deceiver, from the world system around us, and from the sin principle within us, persist in the Christian's experience. Every believer struggles with temptation, and the Tempter is not going to let up. However, God's Word provides hope that we can be victorious. In this chapter practical tools will be presented for overcoming temptation. Temptation is everywhere, but we can have hope in the face of temptation.

Be Prepared

It is a sad commentary on biblical characters that so few "finished well." A common story is that they began in a close walk with God but lost spiritual stamina and ended in defeat. As a middle school student I was eager to join the track team. I was very naïve as to the demands of running a distance race. My first race was the half-mile run. I completed the first lap with ease, far ahead of my competitors, and felt confident of victory. But I didn't anticipate the stamina needed for the second lap. One by one the other runners passed me as my strength was depleted. I crossed the finish line dead last. What a humiliating defeat!

Don't imagine that experience and maturity will keep you from temptation. In fact, in moments of greatest confidence, we are most vulnerable to temptation. King David was at the apex of his reign and had a false sense of security when he sinned with Bathsheba and entered a period of spiritual compromise (2 Sam. 11). Oswald Chambers warns, "You have gone through the big crisis, now be alert over the least things. . . . You have remained true to God under great and intense trials, now beware of the undercurrent."[3]

We must be alert for temptation at the moment of our greatest weakness. However, in a surprise attack, temptation often strikes us at our points of strength and giftedness. If you have the gift of discernment, you may be tempted toward a critical spirit. If your strength is encouraging others, you may capitulate to falsehood and flattery. "Let him who think he stands," the apostle Paul warns, "take heed lest he fall" (1 Cor. 10:12). Chambers observes, "Bible characters tended to fall at their strong points, not at the weak ones."[4]

We must be alert to the varied forms of temptation: "The lust of the flesh, the lust of the eyes, and the pride of life" (1 John 2:16). As John Bunyan's (1628–1688) character, Christian, in *The Pilgrim's Progress* faced numerous distractions and temptations, so too will we. That's why we must be prepared for spiritual attacks. The apostle Paul described his struggle with temptation: "For the good that I will to do, I do not do; but the evil I will not do, that I practice" (Rom. 7:19).

Only Jesus was victorious over every kind of temptation. The writer to the Hebrews declared, "For we do not have a High Priest who cannot sympathize with our weaknesses, but was in all points tempted as we are, yet without sin" (Heb. 4:15). Clearly, our closeness to the Lord does not immunize us from temptation. Yet our closeness to the Lord does give us the resources to overcome temptation. Vance Havner encourages us with the hope that "God does not keep us from temptation, but He can keep us in temptation."[5]

Defeat Is Not Inevitable

The Deceiver will try to convince you that defeat is inevitable. He will whisper, "You have fallen before, you are sure to do it again, so go ahead!" Yes, Christians who claim, "We have no sin," are deceiving themselves (1 John 1:8). Yet God's forgiveness and fortitude enable us to experience consistent victory over sin.

We do not need to succumb to temptation. We face a defeated foe. Our hope and victory are in Christ—in His sure promises, His personal presence, and His resurrection power. The apostle Paul assures believers that because of our union with Christ in His death and resurrection, "we should no longer be slaves of sin. For he who has died has been freed from sin" (Rom. 6:6–7). This means we have been set free from the reign and rule of sin. We are dead to sin's dominion. The bottom line? There is hope. If you are a Christian, you can stand up to sin and say no.

Jerry Bridges shares a helpful illustration regarding the power of temptation.

> In a particular nation two competing factions were fighting for control of the country. Eventually, with the help of an outside army, one faction won the war and assumed control of the nation's government. But the losing side did not stop fighting. They simply changed their tactics to guerrilla warfare and continued to fight. In fact, they were so successful that the country supplying the outside help could not withdraw its troops.[6]

So it is in the life of a Christian. Satan has been defeated and the reign of sin overthrown. But indwelling sin resorts to guerrilla warfare to tempt us. Thus the apostle Paul writes, "For the sinful nature desires what is contrary to the Spirit, and the Spirit what is contrary to the sinful nature. They are in conflict with each other, so that you do not do what you want" (Gal. 5:17 NIV).

A battle plan must be in place "because your adversary the devil walks about like a roaring lion, seeking whom he may devour" (1 Peter 5:8). We are facing spiritual forces. "We do not wrestle against flesh and blood, but against principalities, against powers, against the rulers of the darkness of this age, against spiritual hosts of wickedness in the heavenly places" (Eph. 6:12). We need to be armed for the fight.

Thomas Adams was right when he said that, "Satan, like a fisher, baits his hook according to the appetite of the fish." Satan tempts, but he knows what we like and only our consent permits us to enter into the sin. Our vulnerability to temptation corresponds to the condition of our hearts. When we entertain the tempting thought, we are tilling the heart, making sowing the seed of sin easier.

Make a Decision First

Temptation will come. Decide before it arrives what you are going to do. A teenager should have a firm decision, based on God's Word, about how far to go in expressing affection. The young man or woman should not go on a date with an "open" mind on the subject. Having convictions up front helps to hold the line. Decide where you are going to go on your date and what you are going to do when you are there. To help you to stick to your convictions, invite emotionally and spiritually mature friends to go with you. Make a pact to honor God together.

Experiencing temptation is not sin. How you respond to temptation determines whether or not you have sinned. "But each one is tempted when he is drawn away by his own desires and enticed. Then, when desire has conceived, it gives birth to sin" (James 1:14–15). Note, it is when "desire has conceived" that we enter into sin. Don't allow desire to penetrate your thoughts and conceive the life of sin.

You may blame others for your falling into sin, but ultimately there are no excuses. You must take responsibility. There is no place for the victim mentality when it comes to the believer and sin. Regardless of what the late comedian Flip Wilson said, the Devil did *not* "make you do it." You did it because you wanted to.

But there is hope, real hope—hope that is concrete, because it is a noun. God's Word gives this hope in the face of temptation. "No temptation has overtaken you except such as is common to man; but God is faithful, who will not allow you to be tempted beyond what you are able, but with the temptation will also make the way of escape, that you may be able to bear it" (1 Cor. 10:3). There is always an escape from yielding to temptation. That's God's promise. There is a way out. Here's how.

Call It What It Is

Don't cover sin with euphemisms such as "It is only a white lie" or the ever-popular "I had a sexual indiscretion." Don't justify your indulgence in sin, rationalizing it as a "research project" to help you be wise. Real wisdom comes when we avoid temptation, not when we test it.

Call sin, sin. It's the only way to deal with it. It's God's way. "If we confess our sins, He is faithful and just to forgive us our sins and to cleanse us from all unrighteousness" (1 John 1:9). To *confess* is to say the same thing about sin that God would say—to see sin as He sees it. Charles Spurgeon in *Morning and Evening* admonishes us, "Learn in confession to be honest with God. Do not give fair names to foul sins; call them what you will, they will smell no sweeter."[7]

We must admit that there is a problem before it can be solved. We must acknowledge the disease before the doctor can help us with a cure. Don't beat around the bush when it comes to identifying sin. Call it what is. That's the first step in overcoming sin. Honesty is where the hope begins.

Stop Feeding the Sin

The apostle Paul admonishes the believer, "Let us walk properly, as in the day, not in revelry and drunkenness, not in lewdness and lust, not in strife and envy. But put on the Lord Jesus Christ, and make no provision for the flesh, to fulfill its lusts" (Rom. 13:13–14). *Make no provision* means to starve the sin; don't feed it. Cut off the sinful thoughts just as they begin. Don't invite them into the home of your mind. Don't show them to a comfortable seat in the room of your heart.

In the debate that rages about physician-assisted suicide and euthanasia, there is one arena in which euthanasia is not only appropriate, it is necessary. Euthanasia is appropriate when dealing with temptation. Remove the respirator and the feeding tube—all the life supports. Permit the temptation to die. How are you going to let sin die? Sometimes you have to change your location.

Joseph, when confronted with seduction by Potiphar's wife, employed a very effective strategy for overcoming temptation. He ran (Gen. 39:12). A wise mother avoids the candy aisle in the grocery store when her young children are with her. Timothy's mentor, the apostle Paul, admonished his spiritual protégé, "Flee also youthful lust. . . ." (2 Tim. 2:22). Fleeing temptation doesn't show cowardice; it shows good sense.

The Puritans spoke of "darling sins." These are sins that we pet and allow to live and to thrive. We don't deal with them. We excuse the sin and rationalize it. Charles Spurgeon counsels the Christian, "Beware of light thoughts of sin. It is sadly true, that even a Christian may grow by degrees so callous, that the sin which once startled him does not alarm him in the least. By degrees men get familiar with sin. Do not little strokes fell lofty oaks?"[8]

Dr. Jerry Jenkins, in an interview with James Dobson for the "Focus on the Family" radio broadcast, was talking about his book, *Loving Your Marriage Enough to Protect It.*[9] Dr. Jenkins promised, "If you take care of how things look, you will take care of how things are." He illustrated that principle by saying, "Don't travel alone with a woman who is not your wife. Don't open the door of temptation. Put hedges of protection around your relationship with your wife." Take care of how things look. Take sin seriously.

When in battle we give ground to the Evil One by surrendering to the army of temptations, we find ourselves battling for that ground again and again. Yielded land is subject to disputed ownership. It is better never to yield the territory in the first place.

The Real Price

Temptation's attraction is that it presents the pleasurable part of sin. Like buying a car, the sticker price is only the beginning of the expenses. There are interest payments and insurance premiums and maintenance bills and fuel costs and much more. Similarly, sin is very costly.

Pornography, for example, exploits your time, your money, your good conscience, your contentment, your peace of mind, and even your fellowship with God. Pornography robs you and your spouse of the joy in your relationship. Instead of thinking that sin is gaining you something, you are, in fact, losing so much.

Sin deteriorates healthy relationships, including the one with God. Sin does not bring contentment. It never has enough. Its desire cannot be quenched. Its yearning cannot be satisfied. The greedy billionaire was asked, "How much money is enough?" His answer, "A little more!"

Find Us Faithful

When you and I are faced with temptation, we must review the consequences of submitting to sin. We will hurt our witness for Christ. We will let down our Christian friends. We will damage our relationship with our spouse. Most of all, we will cloud our fellowship with God. That's a significant penalty to pay for a few moments of pleasure.

Whenever I am tempted, in my mind's eye, I visualize the faces of my children, and I recall Jon Mohr's song, popularized by Steve Green, which pleads, "May all who come behind us find us faithful" and at one point speaks about the "fire of our devotion" lighting their way.[10] All of that can be lost in an instant of yielding to temptation.

Deadly Wages

Finally, we must reflect on the ultimate cost of sin. "The wages of sin is death" (Rom. 6:23). The most famous sermon ever preached in America was delivered by Jonathan Edwards on July 8, 1741, in Enfield, Connecticut. In that fiery sermon, "Sinners in the Hands of an Angry God," Edwards began his application by appealing, "O sinner! Consider the fearful danger you are in: it is a great furnace of wrath, a wide and bottomless pit, full of the fire of wrath." As Christians, Christ bore this terrible price for our sin. We should not regard the consequences of sin lightly. We should not participate in something that was so costly for our Savior.

Recognize the false promises of sin, the real price of indulging in it, and the high price already paid for it.

Sin and Genuine Needs

Evil is a twisting of the good. Sin will turn the natural instincts of our physical body into lust. Sin will warp our need for food into gluttony, our need for clothing and shelter into materialism, and our God-given sexual interest into immorality.

My older brother, Paul, gave me this counsel about defeating temptation: "Try to delve into why you feel needy or what void you are trying to fill through that sin. The better you feel about yourself and your relationships, the less the draw of sin. Low self-esteem—due to distance from God or past negative experiences—opens you up to try to fill the need or to dull the pain with a temporary pleasure instead of deep contentment and worth."

Lust, for example, is a phony, shallow substitute for true love. It is self-seeking and short-lived. True love is sacrificial, stable, and satisfying. Lust is impersonal and superficial. Love is deeply personal and has depth. Recognize that sinful patterns emerge out of genuine needs, and fill those needs in God's way and in God's timing. Do this and you will have hope in the midst of temptation.

Positive Alternatives

A two-year-old is told, "Don't do that!" But without a distraction, the child returns to the forbidden behavior. The same is true for older children. When I was a teenager, my wise mother directed me toward positive activities as distractions from wrong actions. Mom would encourage and enable me to be active in school, church youth groups, sports, and service to others. When she was heading out to the nursing home to play hymns for the residents, she would urge me to bring along my trumpet, and she would accompany me. Saying no to the wrong action needs a stronger yes to the right action.

Lisa was determined to avoid eating chocolate cake, so she decided not to focus on the chocolate cake. She said, "I will not eat the chocolate cake. I will not eat the chocolate cake. I *will not* eat the chocolate cake!" You can guess what happened. She ate the chocolate cake. ·

We are pulled toward whatever we focus on. When we concentrate on sin, even undue concentration on avoiding a particular sin, there is a tug toward the temptation.

Rather than simply avoiding the sin, cultivate positive alternatives—community service projects, healthy hobbies, recreational activities, meaningful relationships, and church work. Channel your desires and thought energy into appreciating and enhancing the opportunities you already have. After Paul warned Timothy to flee from temptation, he urged him instead to "pursue righteousness, faith, love, peace with those who call on the Lord out of a pure heart" (2 Tim. 2:22).

Replace temptation with positive thought patterns. "Whatever things are true, whatever things are noble, whatever things are just, whatever things are pure, whatever things are lovely, whatever things are of good report, if there is any virtue and if there is anything praiseworthy—meditate on these things" (Phil. 4:8). Replace the sinful preoccupation with positive patterns of thought and behavior.

Accountability

People once had less privacy and more accountability to others. Now we can isolate ourselves behind the walls of our homes. Researchers say that three out of four Americans don't know the people who live next door to them, and one in seven don't even know the neighbor's name.[11] We live in an increasingly individualistic culture in which relationships do not develop with frequency or depth. An effective tool of the Evil One is to isolate his opponent. Temptation is more seductive when we are alone.

Mobility moves us away from the circle of family and friends who provide the network of support for wise decisions. The mobility of our society makes for widespread rootlessness and disconnected relationships. People are not settled in a place, community, and family for stability and accountability.

Accountability in the Family

I have a road job. My work as regional executive minister of the Conservative Baptist fellowship of churches requires many miles of travel. Travel exposes me to the world of truckers and road-weary salespeople. It can be a world of anonymity. Into that world of lonely hotel rooms comes temptation. Accountability has practical applications. I make sure my wife holds me accountable for my schedule and activities. She knows where I am and with whom, and we frequently phone one another.

At home, place your computer where others can observe your use of it. Numerous software programs are available to help control Internet content. These programs can block access to adult sites, rate sites based on pornography or violence, and establish time controls, for example blocking usage after a particular time at night. It can also supply accountability by logging surfing activities to review what sites have been visited. You would be wise to have someone else enter the software password for you so that you are not tempted to remove boundaries in a time of weakness that you established during a time of strength.

Accountability in Friendship

There is encouragement and support in having mentor relationships to hold us accountable. Richard Tyre helped guide me through a doctoral research project on "mentoring." He defined *mentoring* simply as "a brain to pick, a shoulder to cry on, and a kick in the pants." We need close friends who care enough to give us "a kick in the pants." Solomon reminds us that, "Faithful are the wounds of a friend" (Prov. 27:6).

Jeremy was pastor of a successful, growing church in the East. He had been at the church since he graduated from seminary. He and his wife, Jenny, had a wonderful marriage. Everything seemed to be going their way. But as pressures at church mounted, so did Jeremy's stress. He felt his elders couldn't help him shoulder the load; there were some really difficult people. He wanted to protect Jenny from the problem, so Jeremy tried to carry the load himself. Before long Jeremy began to unburden to Sally, one of the ladies who worked in the Christian Education department. Sally seemed to understand. The rest, as they say, is history.

Jeremy simply disappeared with Sally one day, leaving the announcement that they were not coming back. They weren't really in love; this was a relationship of convenience. There was never any immorality involved; it never went that far. But it went far enough for Jeremy to make a fool of himself and ruin his ministry. What Jeremy really needed was someone with whom to share his burden, and Sally was just "there."

Now Jeremy is back in the church, not as pastor but as a man being restored. He confessed his failings to Jenny, to the elders, and to the church at large. Several senior elders are working with Jeremy to hold him accountable along his road to recovery. This kind of accountability is necessary for restoration, but if it had been in place earlier for Jeremy, perhaps restoration would not have been necessary.

Satan's strategy is to isolate and destroy. We need a Paul to guide us, a Barnabas to come along side us, and a Timothy in whom to invest our lives. Genuine accountability produces authenticity.

Accountability in the Church

Accountability should be a vital motive for our participation in the local church. We all need to be an active part of a Sunday school class, a discipleship group, or a small group ministry. We need people who know us and develop bonds of care, prayer, encouragement, and accountability.

During my pastoral ministry on Long Island, a new member of the congregation shared with me his need for accountability in maintaining sobriety. Together we developed a ministry called Twelve Steps to Christ that encouraged abstinence. The support group met together at least once a week. "As iron sharpens iron, so a man sharpens the countenance of his friend" (Prov. 27:17). Build relationships of accountability.

Temple Watch

"And the LORD God formed man of the dust of the ground, and breathed into his nostrils the breath of life; and man became a living being" (Gen. 2:7). By the creative act of God, we are both physical and spiritual beings. We face the demands of long hours at work, family responsibilities, church ministry expectations, and social commitments. Stress and weariness of the body break down our resistance to temptation and lead to the vulnerability of the soul.

Depriving ourselves of sleep, neglecting exercise and good nutrition, and failing to see the doctor for regular checkups all can lead to physical problems that make us spiritually vulnerable. Get rest. Take a day off. Prioritize time for reflection, exercise, and recreation. If your body is fit and rested, you become more resilient to temptation.

The body is the temple of the Holy Spirit. Caring for the temple shows respect for the One who indwells it (1 Cor. 6:18-20). Strengthen your physical body to take on the spiritual challenges of your day.

A Closer Walk

I can identify with Robert Robinson when he wrote the text for "Come, Thou Fount of Every Blessing." He lamented, "Prone to wander, Lord, I feel it." When all is said and done, there will still be moments when you are alone, where there is no accountability, when because of life's demands you are weary, and temptation is available. How do you stay strong?

Even when you are very careful and you have placed hedges all around, only God can provide complete protection. "O LORD, You have searched me and known me. You know my sitting down and my rising up; You understand my thought afar off. . . . Search me, O God, and know my heart; try me, and know my anxieties; and see if there is any wicked way in me, and lead me in the way everlasting" (Ps. 139:1-2, 23-24). We must guard our hearts, where sin seeks a foothold. We need to protect the inner self.

Purity is essential to closeness with a holy God. "Blessed are the pure in heart, for they shall see God" (Matt. 5:8). Sin grieves our Savior and hinders our fellowship with Him. His sorrow must break our hearts. Thomas Watson in *The Ten Commandments* warns, "He who loves God, hates that which would separate him and God, and that is sin. Sin makes God hide his face; it is like an incendiary, which parts chief friends; therefore, the keenness of a Christian's hatred is set against it. . . . One cannot love health but he must hate poison; so he cannot love God but we must hate sin which would destroy our communion with him."[12]

To protect our hearts for God we need to develop spiritual disciplines because godliness comes through discipline. Thus we are told in 1 Timothy 4:7 to discipline ourselves "for the purpose of godliness" (NASB). Begin by developing a personal devotional life with the Lord. E. M. Bounds wrote, "God's acquaintance is not made hurriedly. He does not bestow his gifts on the casual comer and goer. To be much alone with God is the secret of knowing Him; of influence with Him."[13]

Spend quiet time with the Lord consistently and attentively. Come before the Lord reading and reflecting upon His Word and pursuing Him in prayer. Practice a devotional life that includes reading God's Word, praying, *and* slowing down to spend some time in quiet stillness, reflecting upon what the Lord wants to teach you that day. That time of listening, meditating, and reflecting is important. The psalmist promises, "Blessed is the man who walks not in the counsel of the ungodly, nor stands in the path of sinners, nor sits in the seat of the scornful; but his delight is in the law of the LORD and in His law he meditates day and night" (Ps. 1:1–2).

The Word of God resonating within our souls and renewing our minds (Rom. 12:1–2) is the sword in spiritual battle (Eph. 6:17). The psalmist reflected, "Your word I have hidden in my heart, that I might not sin against You" (Ps. 119:11). When the Lord Jesus was tempted in the wilderness by the Devil, He responded to the Tempter three times, "It is written. . . . It is written. . . . It is written" (Matt. 4:4, 7, 10). His Father's Word was His defense.

We succumb to sin when we fail to embrace a close walk with God. At a recent men's retreat, the speaker quoted German Lutheran pastor Dietrich Bonhoeffer's warning about the tragic moment of sin. Bonhoeffer said that when we are tempted to sin, at that moment, God is quite unreal to us. Satan doesn't fill us with hatred toward God, but with simple forgetfulness of God. How true that is. It's when we are most distant from God that we are closest to being entangled in temptation.

Encouragement and Hope

Remember how great a price Christ paid to deliver you from the penalty of sin. That price was also paid to deliver you and me from sin's power. Consider how great a power is available through the resurrected Lord.

As believers we are dead to sin and its reign over us. But there's more. Not only are we dead to sin, but we are alive to God who strengthens us. That recognition takes away the sense of hopelessness that we once felt because of the persuasive power of sin, and it instills in us a lively sense of hope. After all, we are born again to a living hope (1 Peter 1:3), not just to new life. Martyn Lloyd-Jones explains what it means to be born to a living hope: "I lose my sense of hopelessness because I can say to myself that not only am I no longer under the dominion of sin, but I am under the dominion of another power that nothing can frustrate. However weak I may be, it is the power of God that is working in me."[14]

Threefold Hope

Our hope is threefold. First, our hope is in the Savior's resurrection power, which gives us triumph over temptation daily. In the great resurrection chapter (1 Cor. 15), the apostle Paul makes this observation as a result of Christ's resurrection: "So when this corruptible has put on incorruption, and this mortal has put on immortality, then shall be brought to pass the saying that is written: 'Death is swallowed up in victory.' . . . But thanks be to God, who gives us the victory through our Lord Jesus Christ" (vv. 54, 57). The victory that comes through Christ's resurrection is not just future but present. It is that resurrection power to live a life of victory over sin now that drives Paul's ambition "that I may know Him and the power of His resurrection" (Phil. 3:10).

Second, we have renewed hope in the reality of our salvation when we see God give us victory in our spiritual growth. That reality is never more vivid than when we realize that our Savior, our Intercessor, our Advocate, our Abundant Life is not millions of miles away, attempting to help us from afar. He is Christ in us—the hope of glory (Col. 1:27). This "Christ presence" is accomplished through the indwelling of the Holy Spirit of God in every truly born-again person

(John 14:25-26; Rom. 8:23-27). Again the apostle observes, "And if Christ is in you, the body is dead because of sin, but the Spirit is life because of righteousness. But if the Spirit of Him who raised Jesus from the dead dwells in you, He who raised Christ from the dead will also give life to your mortal bodies through His Spirit who dwells in you" (Rom. 8:10-11).

And third, we are "looking for the blessed hope" when Christ will return to remove every temptation and sin (Titus 2:13-14). But even though we are not yet pure and are still looking for the ultimate blessed hope, the event itself bears on our overcoming temptation now. The apostle John writes, "Beloved, now we are children of God; and it has not yet been revealed what we shall be, but we know that when He is revealed, we shall be like Him, for we shall see Him as He is" (1 John 3:2). The link between hope and purity is a strong one: "And everyone who has this *hope* in Him purifies himself, just as He is *pure*" (v. 3, emphasis added). All who have hope will also strive to triumph over temptation.

Richard Sibbes observes, "There can be no victory where there is no combat. The victory lieth not upon us but upon Christ . . . to conquer for us . . . to conquer in us. Let us not look so much who are our enemies, as who is our Judge and Captain; not what they threaten, but what He promiseth."[15]

It really is possible to triumph over temptation. Defeat is not inevitable. Hope is the enemy of defeat, for as long as there is hope there is light to vanquish the darkest temptations. Don't let go of hope. Do the right things. Cultivate a deeper relationship with God. And hang on to hope. After all, hope is a noun. It's something you have, even when Satan is hounding you.

In *The Pilgrim's Progress*, Hopeful was one of Christian's devoted companions who helped him overcome temptation on the road to the Celestial Kingdom. Similarly, hope is our daily companion who helps us stay on the winning side—to triumph over temptation.

Chapter Notes

1. Kenneth Prior, *The Way of Holiness* (Downers Grove, Ill.: InterVarsity, 1982), 33.

2. I. D. E. Thomas, *The Golden Treasury of Puritan Quotations* (Chicago: Moody, 1975), 295.
3. Oswald Chambers, *My Utmost for His Highest* (Toronto: McClelland and Stewart Ltd., 1935), April 19.
4. Ibid.
5. Dennis J. Hester, *The Vance Havner Quote Book* (Grand Rapids: Baker, 1986), 230.
6. Jerry Bridges, *The Pursuit of Holiness* (Colorado Springs: NavPress, 1981), 60.
7. Charles Spurgeon, *Morning and Evening* (reprint, McClean, Va.: MacDonald, n.d.), 197.
8. Ibid., 142.
9. Jerry Jenkins, *Loving Your Marriage Enough to Protect It* (Chicago: Moody, 1999).
10. Jon Mohr, "Find Us Faithful," © Jonathan Mark Music (administered by Gaither Copyright Management) and Birdwing Music (division of The Sparrow Corporation, Chatsworth, Calif.).
11. According to James Patterson and Peter Kim, 72 percent don't have friendships with their next door neighbors, 45 percent have never spent an evening with them, 27 percent have never been inside their homes, and 15 percent don't even know their names (*The Day America Told the Truth* [New York: Prentice-Hall, 1991], 172).
12. Thomas Watson, *The Ten Commandments* (1890; reprint, Carlisle, Pa.: Banner of Truth Trust, 1986), 8.
13. Donald S. Whitney, *Spiritual Disciplines for the Christian Life* (Colorado Springs: NavPress, 1991), 17.
14. D. Martyn Lloyd-Jones, *Romans: An Exposition of Chapter 6: The New Man* (reprint, Edinburgh: Banner of Truth Trust, 1972), 144.
15. *Golden Treasury of Puritan Quotations*, 294.

Recovering Hope During Serious Illness

Carol Miller

To LEARN THAT YOUR LIFE IS in jeopardy is a life-changing experience. The time and place you hear the news will forever be etched in your mind, as was the case for the generation that heard of John F. Kennedy's assassination on November 22, 1963, or those who heard the news of the explosion that destroyed the space shuttle Challenger with all aboard in 1986. In exactly the same way, the details of the day on which I was told that I had a serious medical problem are forever engraved in my mind.

God created us with the ability to experience a full range of emotions. Of course, people react in very individual ways to shocking or troubling news. But beyond this, God's Word tells us that God created our innermost beings, and He knows the thoughts of our entire lifetime long before we think them (Psalm 139). So while we may not always know how to handle bad news, God knows how we will react and can help us find hope throughout even the most desperate time of need.

As a physician, my specialty of obstetrics and gynecology, I usually deal in happy news, delivering babies and presenting them to their parents. These moments give immeasurable joy to both the parents and to me as a doctor. I participate in an event God ordained to be sacred and beautiful. But there are also times of sorrow in my specialty: fetuses diagnosed with malfunctions and chromosomal abnormalities; miscarriages, stillbirths, and ectopic pregnancies; chronic disappointment with infertility; and the diagnosis of cancer in a woman's body.

I have prayed that God would help me to sympathize and empathize with my patients at moments of crisis, that God's Holy Spirit would endow me with the compassion of Jesus. Only when I realize that the precious blood of Jesus was shed for my life and I seek His forgiveness can I truly be moved with compassion for my patients. Beyond that, something draws me near to those who are hurting and causes me to pray for them as if I were praying for myself: I want to obey every commandment in the Bible. As suggested in the book of James, I want to make a decision of faith and follow it with good works my entire life (James 2:20).

It took me a long time in my spiritual journey, however, to pray, "Lord whatever it takes, bring it into my life so I will walk with You more deeply." Perhaps superstitiously, I didn't pray this because I felt that God would immediately bring calamity into my life. But calamity came anyway—not to the lives of patients for whom I had cared compassionately, but to my life.

When Serious Illness Strikes

Life as I knew it changed forever when I was diagnosed with an early stage of cancer several years ago. Every reaction and emotion I had witnessed in so many patients became a reality to me. My stomach heaved with waves of nausea. Fear and dread filled me to the core. I could barely believe the news, and I was immediately thrown into the arms of Jesus in prayer. For a number of weeks I retreated to my room praying, reading God's Word more than ever, and trying to make sense of a life that was falling apart.

When I was diagnosed with breast cancer, I was in my thirties. My baby was seven months old and my two older children were four and six. I am so thankful to the Lord for an early diagnosis, and the fact that no further treatment other than removing the abnormal growth was recommended. When I heard the initial diagnosis, however, I did not know how far the cancer had spread, and I immediately gave myself a death sentence. As the weeks and months passed, I read as much as I could, not only on medically related topics, but in my Bible. When I realized I was not about to die, the fear did not end. Instead, I felt a new fear creeping in: Would there be a recurrence of the breast cancer?

Many of you reading this are suffering from cancer. Some of you are cancer survivors. Some of you, unfortunately, will be diagnosed with this awful disease in the future. As a physician, a woman, a mother, and a Christian, perhaps I bring a perspective on what it's like to pass through the cold winter of cancer that others do not bring. Through my own sudden illness, I learned what years of medical training could not teach me—how to have hope in the midst of despair. I also learned, as a result of that hope, how not to return to a normal life after the reason for the despair was past, but to adopt a better lifestyle. In the process of recovering from my cancer, it has become evident that a Christian must pass through stages of recovery.

The Initial Shock

As a physician, I have seen all kinds of reactions to illness. If patients are having symptoms and are in pain, they are relieved when a proper diagnosis is finally made. Frequently though, with modern ways of diagnosing problems, patients learn of their illnesses before they have any symptoms whatsoever. For example, we live in an age of frequent mammograms and early detection of breast cancer. Many women learn of the cancer, not because they detect any problem, but because of an x-ray. A woman's world is changed forever with the news, although physically she feels great.

I have walked the road of bad news with my patients many times. When a serious problem with a fetus has been detected on ultrasound or a patient has been diagnosed with uterine cancer, before I enter the consultation room I pray for God's Holy Spirit to give me direction.

Then I pray for a heart of compassion so that I can show the love of Jesus to my patients. Wisdom and compassion are an awesome twosome. Who better to possess this combination than a Christian physician. I asked God to give me both in my profession.

Jesus was a man of sorrows and well acquainted with grief (Isa. 53:3). Knowing this should transform the way we as Christians respond to illnesses. While we roll over in our minds for the thousandth time the grief we are experiencing because of our illnesses, the Lord has a way of bringing us hope just when we need it most. Thank God that, in His gracious compassion, He has given us the dimension of time, for in it the healing of the mind occurs.

Psalm 6:2-3 speaks of experiencing gloom and apprehension with our affliction. David pleaded with God, "Have mercy on me, O LORD, for I am weak; O LORD, heal me, for my bones are troubled. My soul also is greatly troubled; but You, O LORD—how long?" These are the plaintive cries of someone who is suffering both physically and spiritually. But by the end of the psalm, David had recovered hope. He knew the Lord had heard him (v. 9).

Responding to Impending Doom

A young patient of mine, diagnosed with breast cancer, suffered depression because of her fear of dying. She told me that shortly after her diagnosis she visited an art gallery. In her state of mind she thought it a waste to enjoy the pictures because she was probably going to die anyway. Of course this is an incredibly hopeless attitude, but it is all too common. People need hope, both physical and spiritual, and the Bible gives us the best guide to the recovery of hope.

Our Savior is our great High Priest, one who can sympathize with our weaknesses (Heb. 4:15). He has been there. He knows what anguish of soul is like. Just read His story in the Garden of Gethsemane the night before He was crucified (Luke 22). He also knows what the anguish of physical pain is like. Read of the events of the next day (Luke 23). How did Jesus deal with His impending doom? He knew that obedience to His Father meant certain death. He would be taken from His friends and family. Far more difficult, He would bear our sins in His own body in His crucifixion (1 Peter 2:24). Part of Jesus' grief stemmed from His knowledge that He would be separated from all that was familiar on earth.

It is difficult to imagine not being filled with extreme sadness at the thought of dying and being separated from everyone you know and love. Jesus offered up His own life as a sacrifice for us when He knew He could have called ten thousand angels to set Him free. He also permitted His dearest friends and His family to endure the pain and horror of watching Him be nailed to the cross to die a slow death. But while His arrest, trial, and crucifixion came suddenly, they were not a surprise to the sovereign Savior. He was prepared from before the foundation of the world for His traumatic death.

Prepare for Illness

But this is not the case with many of us. When illness occurs, particularly sudden illness, many are totally unprepared for it. We feel we are drowning in distress. Absolute terror sets in. "Why me, Lord?" is the universal question of the sufferer. This seems to be the normal response to every life-threatening situation. We tend to throw up our hands and give up hope immediately. But the loss of hope is one of the greatest deterrents to physical and emotional recovery. There is a way to recover hope during serious illness. A key ingredient of this hope is being properly prepared and equipped before it occurs.

How do we prepare ourselves for any difficulties in life, particularly illness? We do what Jesus did.

Trust in the Sovereignty of God

Often the sovereignty of God is a theological issue, something to be discussed and debated in the halls of learning. But for the sufferer from serious illness, it has to become a personal issue. Is God sovereign or isn't He? Maybe you know all the verses. "The LORD has established His throne in heaven, and His kingdom rules over all" (Ps. 103:19). "The king's heart is in the hand of the LORD, like the rivers of water; He turns it wherever He wishes" (Prov. 21:1). "For I am God, and there is no other; I am God, and there is none like Me . . . saying, 'My counsel shall stand, and I will do all My pleasure'" (Isa. 46:9–10). But is the sovereignty of God more than a theological concept to you? Is it real to you? Have you been able to trust yourself in His hands? And if the answer is yes, are you able to trust your cancer to His hands?

Trusting in God's sovereignty is easy until you have to do it with your life. Being prepared to face serious illness requires complete faith in God's sovereignty in the "little things" of life so you are ready to trust Him with the "big things" too.

Become Familiar with the Character of God

Before serious illness strikes, you can prepare for it's devastation by becoming familiar with God's character. In fact, from my own experience as a physician and as a victim of cancer, I believe it is imperative to be familiar with God's character before serious illness invades your life. You have to be convinced, as was Abraham, that the Judge of all the earth will do right (Gen. 18:25). You must wrestle with the issue of whether or not God has your best interests at heart before the roof caves in because when the roof caves it is no time to be wrestling with the issue of God's character.

Jesus most aptly demonstrated His familiarity with God's character that night in the Garden. In His prayer to the Father, recorded in John 17, He said, "Father, the hour has come. Glorify Your Son, that Your Son also may glorify You" (v. 1). Do these sound like the words of one who questions the Father's character? He also thanked God in the midst of His greatest trial, "for You loved Me before the foundation of the world" (v. 24). Jesus was about to die, but do these sound like the words of someone unfamiliar with God's character? And in His prayer He referred to God as "righteous Father" (v. 25). Does that sound like Jesus had a problem with God's allowing Him to endure crucifixion and the anguish of death? Jesus was familiar the character of God and would not question that character in the cold winter of His night in the Garden.

Be Obedient to the Will of God

Perhaps the most tender and touching words Jesus spoke in His night of anguish in the Garden of Gethsemane are these: "Father, if it is Your will, take this cup away from Me; nevertheless not My will, but Yours, be done" (Luke 22:42). Jesus prepared Himself for death by making the commitment to submit to the will of God the Father, no matter what.

Obedience to God and the precepts of His Word is important preparation for when cancer or some other disease comes. God has given us a different perspective from those who have no faith in Him. As the old song says, "This world is not my home, I'm just a-passin' through." No matter how long they last, our lives are but fleeting shadows or thin vapors. A psalm that has been attributed to Moses proclaims the sad news that "all our days have passed away in Your wrath; we finish our years like a sigh. The days of our lives are seventy years; and if by reason of strength they are eighty years, yet their boast is only labor and sorrow; for it is soon cut off, and we fly away" (Ps. 90:9–10). Life isn't always easy, and it isn't always fair. But it can be filled with hope, if we submit our lives to His divine will. "So teach us to number our days," Moses continued, "that we may gain a heart of wisdom" (v. 12). David echoed these sentiments in Psalm 39:4: "LORD, make me to know my end, and what is the measure of my days, that I may know how frail I am." These Bible passages do not mean that we are to count the number of days remaining until death. We cannot possibly know that, nor would we want to. Rather, we are to live each day as if it were the last, and to apply the knowledge learned thereby to both the hope we have in this life and the sure hope we have in the next. Ultimately, our only hope is in the Lord and in spending eternity with Him.

When I learned that I had cancer, I was devastated. But I had learned how to prepare for bad news by helping others prepare to receive bad news. All I had to do was to heed my own advice to them. You, too, can prepare yourself for illness. It will enable you to receive the news you didn't want to hear with hope.

Replenish Your Storehouse

But preparing to receive bad news is only half the story. Once you have dealt with serious illness, once you have become, in my case, a cancer survivor, you need to replenish your storehouse. Because I am a physician writing about restoring hope during serious illness, I would be remiss if I failed to share something of what I have discovered about diet, exercise, and worry, as they relate to recovering from serious illness. Relying on God's hope and personally recovering hope does not mean that we as believers sit back and do nothing to restore our bodies to health. After the initial shock of my cancer diagnosis had passed, I was depleted in emotional and spiritual strength, and I was physically exhausted. When faced with a serious illness, it is essential to restore your defense system by replenishing your spiritual, emotional, and physical storehouse. Although I am not into the "health and wealth" gospel, I believe that God's Word gives us His recipe for health. It is my contention that the Bible supports current research on the elements of optimal health. A sensible diet, with exercise, and improved morale all help the body avoid the descent into spiritual hopelessness.

Many people believe diet has nothing to do with health and disease, that it is simply bad luck or fate when someone ends up with cancer or heart disease. On the contrary, that the United States ranks above most countries in rates of heart disease and cancer is not attributable to mere chance. It is now widely accepted that dietary habits are inextricably linked to health. Even with this knowledge, many patients opt for surgery and medication rather than make lifestyle changes.

Diet and Illness

Dr. John McDougall, a board-certified internist, has written broadly on diet and lifestyle as the direct cause of most illnesses. His excellent books describe the way we were meant to eat. He, and others, refer to the diet we consume as the Standard American Diet (SAD). We would all readily agree that most fast food is junk, but what we eat at home is often only slightly more nutritious than the fare at our favorite fast-food place.

A quick search of the literature comparing rates of heart disease and cancer in the U.S. with those of other countries will reveal statistics that are staggering. There is an extremely low rate of cancer and heart disease in many countries, particularly in the Orient. In Japan, for example, the rate of breast cancer among women is very low.

When adult Japanese women come to the United States, their rate of breast cancer stays very low as long as they continue their traditional low-fat, mostly vegetarian diet. Second-generation Japanese women have a rate of breast cancer nearly equal to that of other American women, as they consume the typical American diet.

Hippocrates, the father of medicine, said, "Let food be your medicine, and medicine be your food." Many believe that the answer to cancer is not under a microscope but on our dinner plates. I have personally found helpful the book *The Bible Cure* by Reginald Cherry, MD. He points out that diets eaten in certain areas of the world today, such as the Mediterranean countries, closely parallel the diet eaten in ancient times. On average, these people live healthier and longer lives than Americans who eat so many processed foods and fats every day.[2]

Interestingly, Daniel and his friends avoided the king's rich food and were depicted as looking and feeling healthier on their diet of vegetables and water (Dan. 1:12–15). Of course the main reason they avoided these foods was religious and not dietary; nonetheless, avoiding the king's meat enabled them to practice a healthy diet while refusing the luxurious lifestyle of the Babylonian palace.

I am thankful for many aspects of modern medicine. I am thankful I can perform a cesarean section when the life of the mother or baby is in jeopardy. I am thankful for anesthesia and antibiotics. People rely heavily, however, on the medical establishment to cure all that ails them. Doctors act as if it's fate that their patients have chronic, debilitating diseases. But so many serious illnesses are lifestyle induced. Patients are quite familiar with the fact that they should eat more fiber (fruits, vegetables, and whole grains), but most think they're doing well by eating an apple a day. In fact, we fail miserably, consuming about half the fiber as do the populations of other countries. Once we have survived serious illness, it shows a good deal of godly wisdom to make lifestyle and eating adjustments that will enable us to live healthier lives as a testimony to God's goodness and grace to us. We can best replenish our depleted bodies with the right kind of foods. That's a natural ally to restored hope.

A Total Change

Proper diet and exercise together are effective in promoting excellent health. One enhances the other. In illness and in health there are numerous perks to exercising. If one is not eating properly, exercise is of little value. We all know an aerobic workout helps the heart, but it also helps the head. In illness, exercise improves morale and reduces the feeling of being a victim. It is well documented that regular exercise helps depression, as Chick Kiloski will relate to you in the next chapter.

I have totally changed the way I look at life as a result of my illness. Not only do I reflect on my experience from a medical standpoint, but also from a spiritual standpoint. I am now concentrating heavily on my responsibility before God to take care of my body. Following God's directives, in accordance with His Word, gives peace and joy. I cannot express the hope and encouragement gained by actively taking part in improving my health. If the serious illnesses and chronic problems we face are totally devoid of our own intervention, we experience little hope for self-improvement. We can only look to our physicians as the center of command and expect all recommendations to come from that person. Clearly we who live in North America particularly harm ourselves by our lifestyles. We are what we eat. Never is this so important than when we are ill.

Thus, it is important to get educated concerning your illness. Get educated about God's standard for taking care of your body, and ask for His forgiveness, help, and healing if you have failed in this area of Christian stewardship. Only then will you be able to establish a complete course of action. Only then will hope flourish.

God's Command to be Free from Worry

As a young physician entering private practice, my first patient was Sarah, a thirty-five year old woman diagnosed with ovarian cancer. I have seen her many times since, and she has done very well from a physical standpoint. However, I cannot adequately relate the way this patient has suffered. She dreads coming to the office, though not enough to miss her appointments. With each visit she relives, to some extent, the horror and pain she experienced when she first received the bad news. She cannot avoid the anticipation that I will have more bad news for her. Although she tries to look collected, the intense worry permeates her countenance. I genuinely feel for her, but Sarah cannot conquer those fears. She tells me that she has been a worrier from her early years.

I have seen the fearful look a thousand times. A patient visiting my office for follow-up appointments or tests often relives the sorrow and pain experienced at the original diagnosis. I ask each patient about her emotional state. Is she carrying on a normal routine and able to care for her family? As an obstetrician and gynecologist, I deal only with women, so I can put myself in the shoes of my patients, not only as a wife and mother but as one who has also received bad news. As I said earlier, now with God's perspective and perfect hindsight, being diagnosed with cancer has changed my life forever—for the good.

The Death of Hope

We know that many times God brings us to Him when we are broken; often broken bodies lead to broken hearts before God as we realize our frailty and mortality. With every patient I encounter, I wonder if this person cares about God and has room in her life for Jesus. The patient database gives patients a chance to state their religious preference, and sometimes that information serves as a springboard in our conversation. Because I take care of many obstetric patients, frequently I have to relay bad news about a birth defect or a genetic problem. I know as I walk into that examination room that lives will be changed forever by the news I bring. The worry that follows can be long-term. Sometimes a strong character, a capable understanding spouse, and a caring family are the mainstays. For other patients, brokenness and worry so drain the spirit that hope may die.

The Recovery of Hope

No matter what our physical, emotional, or spiritual state, God meets us where we are. What an opportunity the Lord has given all of us to help the hurting, and what an opportunity and responsibility He has given me to tell of His love and forgiveness! I can be a healer and a hope giver at the same time. I thank Him for the privilege of helping others to recover lost hope.

God also touches each person at the point of our differences in personality. Some of us are worrywarts and some of us are laid back, cool cucumbers. To those who don't have the hope that comes from a dynamic relationship with a loving God, I try to impress upon them that He will help them in the winter seasons of their life and He can even ensure that hope grows in winter. Even those who know the Lord are frequently beset with worry, particularly in the face of life-threatening illness. Many believers may not realize, however, that worry is a sin. I am the resident expert on worry. It is the sin that I have had to bring repeatedly before the Lord to ask His forgiveness. Worry depletes our zeal for life, making us immobile. The fear of impending doom caused by anxiety is far worse than any physical pain the illness can inflict. It steals our joy and anything we do that robs us of joy is a sin.

When the initial shock of learning of an illness is over, the months or years of waiting set in. If someone's disease is a type of cancer and it goes into remission, patients worry about recurrence. They may develop extreme concern over other things that are wrong with their bodies, such as a high cholesterol count or worsening osteoporosis.

I frequently share with patients the story of my own illness and how God has helped me. When God commanded us not to worry, He also gave His Holy Spirit to empower us not to worry, even in the face of impending physical setbacks. God has laid it on my heart to share printed material with my patients, like James Dobson's *When God Doesn't Make Sense*.[3] My audience is always receptive, and I know God has used the printed word to His glory.

Hope and Prayer

Giving to God all our anxieties and fears about our illness is an ongoing process. Paul wrote, "Be anxious for nothing, but in everything by prayer and supplication, with thanksgiving, let your requests be made known to God" (Phil. 4:6). That is excellent advice. Anxiety, fear, and that nagging sense of impending doom, you see, make us spiritually and physically vulnerable and can easily rob us of hope. Paul is saying, don't worry, pray. Pray with thanksgiving. Pray that God will take away your fear and anxiety. But you say, "What if they come back?" I believe the apostle would say, "Then go back to God in prayer."

The apostle Peter believed the same, telling us that the secret to win out over worry is, "casting all your care upon Him, for He cares for you" (1 Peter 5:7). The word *casting* suggests continuing action. It is natural that new cares will arise, or old ones will return. We are to refuse to carry these fears, cares, and anxieties upon our own hearts.

What are we to do? Cast them upon God. We do the casting. He does the caring.

If you are a cancer survivor like I am, I have a question for you. "Have you, indeed, cast all of your cares upon Him? Have you even cast your cancer cares on Him or are you holding them in, letting them eat you alive inside, causing each day of life to be joyless and hopeless? And, do you really believe that He cares for you, really cares?" I had to learn to answer those questions in the affirmative, and so must you. That's when we discover that hope is a noun, something we possess, not something we do. And hope grows, not only in winter, but in the spring of serious illness as well.

Free from Fear

To feel free from the fear of death is a crucial test in our walk with God. When Paul was aboard the ship on his way to Rome to appeal to Caesar, he encountered a terrible two-week long storm that ultimately ended in shipwreck on the island of Malta. Paul was not afraid in the face of death, and he was an encouragement to the other 276 passengers (Acts 27:14–37). In the face of impending disaster, Paul possessed concrete hope because of his faith in God. The night before Peter was to be executed, he was asleep in jail and not fearful of what seemed like certain death (12:6).

Why did these men have such peace, strength, and courage when it seemed they would die within the day? Because they had a hope that "does not disappoint, because the love of God has been poured out in our hearts by the Holy Spirit who was given to us" (Rom. 5:5). As a physician, I never undervalue the power of hope. Often it is stronger than the power of medicine.

Is this true of you? If you are facing a life-threatening illness, are you at such peace with God that if you believed death would occur in a day or two, you would be able to sleep the night through? Do you have that kind of concrete hope in the Lord?

In reality, we must all die unless Jesus returns first. We must let Peter and Paul's example typify our reaction to illness. Only with God's Holy Spirit empowering us can we be free of human worry. By God's grace, and in the power of His Spirit, we can replace worry with hope. I know. I have done it, and so can you.

What God Requires in Illness

When we lean on our own understanding in illness we become self-absorbed. Rather than the joy of the Lord being reflected in our lives, we become angry and bitter because of our physical setbacks. Paul was thinking about others when he was ready to die. Jesus didn't come to be served, but to serve and focus on a dying world that needed and still needs Him.

The glory will be God's through our illness if we claim Psalm 118:17-18: "I shall not die, but live, and declare the works of the LORD. The LORD has chastened me severely, but He has not given me over to death." As long as God gives us life and breath in our sickness, we have work to do for Him. There is no reason not to pray and work toward healing. That's where the hope lies.

Thank God for Serious Illness

The Bible tells us we suffer so that we will be able to comfort others (2 Cor. 1:3-4). While we are leaning on Jesus and His promises, we are commanded to give thanks in all of our situations, even if they are life-threatening (1 Thess. 5:18). We will probably never understand outside of heaven the mystery of giving thanks to God in illness, but He has said to do so.

When He left us to return to heaven, Jesus promised that the Holy Spirit would reside in us and give us hope. The Holy Spirit's power helps us beyond any human understanding. To be free of worry, to lean on Jesus, to reach out to others, to give thanks to God in the face of serious illness is ludicrous in man's wisdom. But the Holy Spirit empowers us to recognize that the results of suffering are gifts from the heart and hand of God.

Ultimately, we are only passing through this world, and our physical and spiritual bodies belong to God our Creator. Nothing can touch my life that doesn't go through God the Father because He owns me. Through my own cancer, and through the hundreds of women I have counseled and treated who have experienced serious illness, I have learned to say with Job, "Though He slay me, yet will I trust Him" (Job 13:15).

Many years have passed now since I was diagnosed with cancer. It has not been an easy road. There are days when I feel down emotionally, physically, and spiritually. I have learned not to overrate my everyday aches and pains, and assume they are a recurrence of cancer. The Lord's kindness and mercy have been overwhelming. He has given me, among many gifts, the gift of life on this earth. I must constantly ask myself, *What am I doing with this gift?*

Through the daily study of God's Word, a meaningful prayer life, by maintaining a healthy lifestyle (diet, exercise, and managing stress), and because of the love and support of my husband, family, and friends, I feel that my spiritual and physical health are far superior to what they were prior to my diagnosis. God has become my refuge and my lighthouse in every storm, and I wait daily for His instruction and guidance to show me the course for my life.

I am a cancer survivor. I have learned that there is hope, even when you are diagnosed with a serious illness. My hope is in the Lord. That's where you'll find hope too.

Chapter Notes

1. John A. McDougall, *The McDougall Plan* (Clinton, N.J.: New Win, 1983),15.
2. Reginald Cherry, *The Bible Cure* (Lake Mary, Fla.: Creation House, 1998), 3.
3. James Dobson, *When God Doesn't Make Sense* (Wheaton, Ill.: Tyndale, 1993).

Hope Over Depression

Charles F. (Chick) Kiloski

DO YOU KNOW WHAT STATESMEN Abraham Lincoln and Winston Churchill, hymn writer William Cowper and preacher Charles Haddon Spurgeon shared in life? Each of these famous and productive people battled with feelings of melancholy, despondency, and even despair. They all suffered from depression.

Depression is one of the most widespread afflictions in our society. Each year it affects more than eleven million in the United States alone. As many as one in four women and one in ten men will experience at least one debilitating episode of depression during their lifetimes. What's worse, depression is considered a factor in the suicides of as many as twenty thousand each year.

Just a few of the prominent sufferers of depression in our day are journalists Mike Wallace and Art Buchwald, and entertainers Dick Cavett and Patty Duke. Maybe you are one of us. I say "us" because I have battled depression, on and off, for more than thirty years and recently came through my most serious bout. Are you shocked to learn that a Christian—and a pastor at that—suffers from depression?

Well, don't be surprised. Depression is a part of the curse that resulted from Adam's sin, and the effects of sin affect us all.

While the causes of the different types of depression vary, in many cases depression is genetic. This is true for me. Other members of my family have been afflicted, and doctors have concurred, that mine is an *endogenous* (i.e., originating within the body) *depression*, the result of a chemical imbalance. But am I bereft of hope? Not in the least.

In these thirty years I have enjoyed long periods of emotional well-being and excellent health. God has blessed me with significant ministry. But for some reason there have also been recurring periods of darkness and despair. Through it all, there has been the brightness of hope. God has been faithful, and His grace has enabled me to carry on as a pastor, loving people and helping some of them through their own episodes of depression. Added to this has been the loving support of my wife, Pat. I don't know what I would have done without Pat, my constant beacon of hope. I have also depended on the understanding and support of my congregation, plus the prayers of my family and many friends.

Questions, No Answers

Like so many others, over the years I have questioned God about my illness. "God, I know that You love me, but why do I find myself in the pit of despair? I'm a pastor. You've called me to minister to other people's needs. How can I do that when I'm afflicted with feelings of desperation and despair myself?"

As you may have guessed, God never answered me. I have to say like Eli of old, "It is the LORD. Let Him do what seems good to Him" (1 Sam. 3:18).

Iain Murray wrote, "Faced with the question why God allows mental illness in His children we are brought back to a fundamental spiritual fact: there are matters about which the Christian has to be prepared not to get light in this world, for it is clear that there are some dispensations about which God is reserving the explanation until eternity. There are mysteries which He calls us now to leave unsolved."[1]

Suffering plays a vital part in the sanctification of God's saints. Our heavenly Father sees our heartaches, grief, trials, and troubles. And when those seasons of darkness come they are not, as we are all prone to think, a meaningless horror but are His way of preparing us to be more intimately in fellowship with Him (Phil. 3:10). Even the darkest winters of depression profit the growth of our souls, because hope grows in winter.

When I have faced those long days and nights of mental agony, the psalmist's prayer has been my prayer: "Be merciful to me, O God, be merciful to me! For my soul trusts in You; and in the shadow of Your wings I will make my refuge, until these calamities have passed by" (Ps. 57:1).

There is hope over depression. I am living proof of that. I share the following details of my life, things that are difficult to talk about, so that you, too, may latch onto that hope. Hope is a noun and it's something we all can possess when we have a dynamic relationship with God. Even during the darkest days of my life, I cling to hope. Sometimes it's all you may have, but it is enough.

The Darkness

William Styron, in his book *Darkness Visible: A Memoir of Madness,* expresses the feelings of many who have battled depression: "To most of those who have experienced it, the horror of depression is so overwhelming as to be quite beyond expression."[2]

One of the best descriptions of depression I have ever seen is from Anna Larina's memoir *This I Cannot Forget,* a moving account of her twenty years in Stalin's gulag during his reign of terror. Larina was the wife of Nikolai Bukharin, whom Lenin had called "the golden boy of the revolution." Bukharin, however, fell out of favor with Stalin and was arrested, tried, and executed.

Interred in the infamous Tomsk Camp with other Russian wives and mothers, Larina tells of her depression and her reaction when she learned of her husband's execution. "Everything around me grew dim and became one huge and spiritless zone of gray. It was scarcely credible that life, human happiness, and mundane joys existed anywhere on earth."[3]

This is the world I live in when depression overtakes me. From this darkness, I look with envy upon those who seem happy and wonder how anyone could smile and laugh in such a "huge, spiritless zone of gray." The lament of Psalm 137:4 becomes my cry: "How shall we sing the LORD's song in a foreign land?" My world, which had been a place in which to live for the Lord and sing His praises, becomes a twilight zone and a strange land in which it is almost impossible for me to lift up my voice in praise and adoration of God.

I have grappled with what I know to be true: God "doeth all things well." I am all too aware of Romans 8:28: "All things work together for good to those who love God." While intellectually I know from Hebrews 13:5 that God will never leave me nor forsake me, experientially that is exactly how I have felt. To pour salt in the wound, I was often overwhelmed with guilt because I felt that my doubts were unbelief and rebellion against God.

Pain Unimaginable

During bouts of depression life becomes pointless. In her book *Prozac Nation,* Elizabeth Wurtzel places her finger on the pulse of every depressed person: "Why do anything—why wash my hair, why read *Moby Dick,* why fall in love . . . why spend time trying to get in the right schools, why dance to the music when all . . . of us are slouching toward the same inevitable conclusion?"[4] For the person suffering from depression, the world often becomes totally hopeless—even for a dedicated Christian who falls prey to this demon of darkness. Looking back from the vantage point of good health, it seems incomprehensible that I had those thoughts or felt that way, but I did.

Styron notes, "Depression is a disorder of mood, so mysteriously painful and elusive in the way it becomes known to the self . . . as to verge close to being beyond description . . . the pain of severe depression is quite unimaginable to those who have not suffered it."[5]

If the pain of depression were readily describable, sufferers would be able to depict for our loved ones some of the dimensions of our torment. Any lack of understanding by the family and friends of a depressed individual is not due to a failure of sympathy but to the inability of healthy people to conceive of a torment so alien to them.

As I look back over these episodes of horror in my life, I stand amazed that I was able to function as a husband, father, and pastor. God's grace is indeed sufficient and is the only explanation for my survival. Even now I find myself cringing as I relive the misery of those days and the feeling that I would never be well again.

Styron speaks for all who have suffered depression when he says, "The sufferer from depression . . . finds himself, like a walking casualty of war, thrust into the most intolerable social and family situations. There he must, despite the anguish devouring his brain, present a face approximating the one that is associated with ordinary events and companionship. He must try to utter small talk, and be responsive to questions, and knowingly nod and frown and, God help him, even smile. But it is a fierce trial attempting to speak a few simple words."[6]

In the mind of a depressed person, everything becomes distorted. The smallest problem looms like Mount Everest, every molehill grows into a mountain and, although during those times I realize that I am thinking irrationally, I cannot see things as they really are. The thought of doing something as simple as writing a check overwhelms me; making a phone call requires an almost superhuman effort. Concentration is virtually impossible.

In my case at least, depression has a companion affliction. During bouts of depression, when I lie in bed at night my mind races nonstop. Many times sleep eludes me and, as a result, I am exhausted the next day. Sleeplessness combined with exhaustion makes for an exquisite torture. The consequence is a sense of hopelessness.

Depression's Companions

Along with the feeling of hopelessness is the pervasive fear that fills every moment. My wife asks, "Chick. What are you afraid of?" My glazed response is, "I don't know, I'm just afraid."

Actress Patty Duke speaks about this fear. In the book about her struggles with depression, *A Brilliant Madness: Living with Manic-Depressive Illness*, she confesses, "I was afraid—I didn't know of what. I cried all the time and I was completely unable to function. I'd stand in my closet for hours on end. I'd go in there to get dressed to go to the supermarket, and my husband would come back hours later, and find me still standing there."[7]

Filled with this terrible fear, I would be at the same time reminded of the exhortations and promises of Scripture regarding fear. I'd say to myself, *Doesn't the Lord say over and over "Fear not?" Doesn't Paul remind us that God has not given us a spirit of fear? C'mon, Chick, get over this.* And yet, knowing all this, I could not shake the terrible fear.

Crying, too, was a part of my experience. I would sob for hours on end. For no reason at all I would burst into tears. Every morning, without fail, I would awaken and begin crying. And then when I had to be with other people, I would try to put on a happy face and pretend that everything was all right. This only increased my feelings of guilt because I felt like a hypocrite.

In addition to the exhaustion, the fear, and the crying was the awful anxiety. I worried constantly about my family, my friends, my finances, my future. Here again, these things increased the terrible guilt that filled my heart. Jesus said, "Do not worry about your life. . . . Do not worry about tomorrow" (Matt. 6:25, 34 NIV). Paul wrote, "Be anxious for nothing (Phil. 4:6). And worst of all, in light of these and many other Scripture passages, I would sometimes imagine that I could not possibly be a child of God. I would ask myself, *How can you be a Christian and be so depressed? You must not be saved, or this wouldn't be happening to you.* Satan is very clever in the way he plays mind games with you.

Where was the peace and joy that Jesus promised? Whatever happened to "Now thanks be to God who always leads us in triumph in Christ" (2 Cor. 2:14)? William Cowper was a man of God who wrote such well-loved hymns as "There Is a Fountain Filled with Blood" and "God Moves in a Mysterious Way." Ravaged by depression, he convinced himself that his was a unique situation and that the promises of Scripture did not apply to him. As a result, he lived his entire life convinced that he was not saved, and more than once he attempted to take his own life. These are the kinds of crazy notions held by those in the grip of this monster.

Despair

It is a bit inaccurate to speak of the despair of depression. Actually, it is a despair beyond despair. John Milton in *Paradise Lost* speaks of

"A dungeon horrible, on all sides round, as one great furnace flamed; yet from those flames no light, but rather darkness visible served only to discover sights of woe, regions of sorrow, doleful shades, where peace and rest can never dwell, hope never comes that comes to all, but torture without end still urges."[8] He, of course, is speaking of the awfulness of being separated from the Lord for eternity, but his words aptly describe the hopelessness of a depressed person. "Most people in the grip of depression at its ghastliest are, for whatever reason, in a state of unrealistic hopelessness, torn by exaggerated ills and fatal threats that bear no resemblance to actuality."[9]

It is, therefore, so important for the families and friends of depressed persons to pray for their sick ones. But more than that, families need constantly to persuade their depressed loved ones of their own worth in God's sight, which is in conflict with their own feelings of worthlessness.

This despairing sense of hopelessness is, I think, the worst part of bouts with depression. In that state I am convinced that those feelings are permanent and that I am destined to spend whatever remains of my life in that awful state.

I'm ashamed to admit that the thought of suicide has often passed through my mind, and I would imagine different scenarios in which my life could be ended. Thank God these fantasies were never acted upon. I did, however, go to bed every night hoping that I would never wake up. I would long for death to come. My constant prayer was, "Lord, if I am really saved, please take me to heaven now." It is a rare person who, during a severe bout of depression, has not considered self-destruction. Some might dispute this, and most Christians who enjoy a life free from this affliction recoil in horror from the thought that a child of God would even think of such a heinous act.

Many depressed individuals inside as well as outside the church have committed suicide. One of the godliest men I ever knew took his own life years ago. At the time, which was before I had experienced depression, I was dumbstruck and asked how a Christian could possibly commit suicide. Now, I can well imagine the despair he must have felt. Some Christians might question the reality of such a person's salvation, but those of us who have walked the dark road and experienced the despair understand how it happens.

In the mind of most people, suicide is either an act of cowardice or, paradoxically, an act of courage. Actually, it is neither. The anguish, torment, and despair in the mind of a depressed person often make suicide a blind act of necessity. It is important that people who have never experienced depression try to grasp the nature of its pain so that they can, at least in some measure, understand why a depressed person would talk about ending his or her life. I reiterate, it is important to continually persuade the sufferer of the value of life. I believe that many suicides could have been averted if the victims had received the support—as I did, thank God—from my spouse, children, family, and friends.

Cowper died at the age of sixty-nine without ever being delivered from his malady. His was not a pleasant departure from this life. After Cowper's death, his close friend John Newton wrote these poignant words:

> The Lord's thoughts and ways are so much above ours, that it becomes us rather to lie in the dust in adoration and silence than to inquire presumptuously into the grounds of his proceedings. It may reconcile us to lighter troubles when we see what the Lord's most favored and honored servants are appointed to endure. But we are sure that God is rich enough, and that eternity is long enough to make abundant amends, for whatever his infinite wisdom may see meet to call them to, for promoting his glory in the end. . . . The last twelve hours of [Cowper's] life he lay still, and took no notice, but so long as he could speak, there was no proof that his derangement was either removed or abated. . . . There was no sigh either of joy or sorrow when near his departure. What a glorious surprise must it be to find himself released from all his chains in a moment, and in the presence of the Lord whom he loved, and whom he served![10]

Despair was Cowper's constant companion and is the companion of all those who are passing through the valley of depression.

One might ask, "Where is the hope in all of this?" David, when depressed, said, "My hope is in You" (Ps. 39:7). The sons of Korah counseled themselves, "Hope in God" (42:11). And again David said to the Lord, "I hope in Your word" (119:114). If there is any hope for the sufferer of depression, that hope will be found in God and His Word. Indeed, the God of hope can turn hopelessness into something good.

The Design

To say that a Christian can suffer the hopelessness of depression and harbor suicidal thoughts is to invite ridicule and anger from many well-meaning believers who have experienced neither. And to say that there is something good about depression or that it is part of God's design for some of His children is to invite ridicule and anger from many who suffer from this malady. Nonetheless, I as a Christian believe that God is sovereign in our lives, and I thus conclude that there is nothing accidental or incidental in anything that occurs in our lives. "And we know that all things work together for good to those who love God, to those who are the called according to His purpose" (Rom. 8:28). This verse is not a crutch; it is a promise of God to His children, and God keeps His promises.

A verse in the Old Testament has come to mean a great deal to me in my seasons of darkness and despair: "Who is among you that feareth the LORD, that obeyeth the voice of his servant, that walketh in darkness, and hath no light? let him trust in the name of the LORD, and stay upon his God" (Isa. 50:10 KJV). Even the most spiritual and gifted of Christians have at times walked in great darkness—times when life could be summed up in one big, ugly question mark. At those times, the only thing we know is that we don't know. We find ourselves hemmed in by trying circumstances that seem meaningless, and when we cry for light, we only increase our darkness.

For the person in the throes of clinical depression, reading the Bible becomes a chore; prayer is almost impossible. When I knelt to pray I would immediately be confronted with my own sinfulness and unworthiness and would break down sobbing. The one thing I always felt I could count on—my faith in God—seemed to evaporate.

In the light of all this, how can I say there is something positive about depression and that it is a part of God's design? Throughout my periods of depression, I had a faint conviction, bolstered by my wife's encouragement, that God was working and that something good was going to come out of the nightmare. Martin Luther once said, "Affliction is the Christian's theologian." Robert Browning Hamilton wrote:

> I walked a mile with pleasure,
> She chatted all the way,
> But left me none the wiser
> For all she had to say.
> I walked a mile with sorrow
> And ne'er a word said she,
> But oh the things I learned from her,
> When sorrow walked with me.[11]

My theologian of affliction has taught me many things about depression and hope. Three important insights follow.

A New Awareness of Sin

Almost all the books on depression mention that those who suffer, Christians and non-Christians, are overcome with guilt and a sense of worthlessness. Many professional therapists would say that these feelings are unhealthy. And while we must guard against morbid introspection, it is nonetheless of spiritual benefit to periodically examine our lives and ask the Lord if there is any wicked way in us (Ps. 139:24). Modern culture may perceive self-examination of this sort as detrimental to self-esteem. But God is more interested in our holiness than our happiness, and His concern is for our characters and not our comfort. The only way to increase in holiness is to clearly understand the awfulness of sin.

While I hope that I will never again have to experience deep depression, I look back at it with gratitude, because in that condition I saw my depravity as I had never seen it before.

In its chapter on Providence, *The Westminster Confession of Faith* contains this paragraph concerning God's dealings with His children:

The most wise, righteous and gracious God, doth oftentimes leave for a season his own children to manifold temptations, and the corruption of their own hearts, to chastise them for their former sins, or to discover unto them the hidden strength of corruption and deceitfulness of their own hearts, that they may be humbled; and to raise them to a more close and constant dependence for their support upon himself, and to make them more watchful against all future occasions of sin, and for sundry other just and holy ends.[12]

Whether it is Satan accusing me or God convicting me, during times of depression I am aware of many things that have never been dealt with properly, things that affected my wife and children and my ministry. Having gone through depression, I know myself better. And this knowledge of myself causes me to better appreciate the Lord Jesus Christ and His grace and mercy.

John Newton's hymn "I Asked the Lord" has taken on new meaning for me:

> I asked the Lord, that I might grow
> In faith, and love, and every grace:
> Might more of His salvation know,
> And seek more earnestly His face.
>
> Twas He who taught me thus to pray;
> And He, I trust has answered prayer:
> But it has been in such a way
> As almost drove me to despair.
>
> I hoped that in some favoured hour,
> At once He'd answer my request,
> And by His love's constraining power,
> Subdue my sins, and give me rest.
>
> Instead of this, He made me feel
> The hidden evils of my heart;

And let the angry powers of hell
Assault my soul in every part.

Yea more, with His own hand
He seemed intent to aggravate my woe;
Crossed all the fair designs I schemed,
Blasted my gourds, and laid me low.

"Lord, why is this?" I trembling cried,
"Wilt Thou pursue Thy worm to death?"
"'Tis in this way," the Lord replied,
"I answer prayer for grace and faith.

"These inward trials I employ
From self and pride to set thee free,
And break thy schemes of earthly joy,
That thou may'st seek thy all in me."

Depression taught me more about my sinful self, about my need to be holy. It increased my gratitude to God for providing the righteous sacrifice of His Son to secure my holiness. But there's more that the theologian of affliction has taught me.

A New Appreciation of Need

Depression brought me to the place where I sought my all in Him. When God refused to remove Paul's thorn in the flesh He said, "My grace is sufficient for you" (2 Cor. 12:9). When doctors, medications, and counselors could not help me, my only hope was the sufficiency of God's grace. He was my only hope. Never before did 1 Timothy 1:1 have such deep meaning for me. It's easy to breeze by the first verses in each of Paul's epistles, because they are just his salutations. In the first verse of 1 Timothy Paul says the Lord Jesus is "our hope." As Charles Wesley put it in his hymn, "Jesus, Lover of My Soul,"

Other refuge have I none;
Hangs my helpless soul on Thee;

> Leave, ah! leave me not alone,
> Still support and comfort me.

Peter Kramer, who wrote the best-seller *Listening to Prozac*,[13] says that what links men and women to God is precisely their guilt, anxiety, and loneliness. During my bouts of depression, my wife would constantly remind me that God had not forsaken me and that He was at work fulfilling His purpose. Even though I felt alone, in my heart I knew that His promises were sure and that He would be with me always.

In depression or in any kind of suffering, the Christian's answer is not an explanation or a theory but a reinforcing presence. Christ stands beside us in the darkness and says, "I will never leave you nor forsake you" (Heb. 13:5). His companionship makes every trial a sacrament.

There is a final benefit that I have gained through my battle with depression.

A New Ability to Help Others

In 2 Corinthians 1:4, Paul says that God "comforts us in all our troubles, so that we can comfort those in any trouble with the comfort we ourselves have received from God" (NIV).

For years I kept my depression a closely guarded secret lest people think I was weak, mentally unbalanced, or unspiritual. Once my secret was revealed, however, I have been amazed at how many people are, or have been, in the same boat. They are eager to talk with someone who has been there. Thus a new dimension has been added to my ministry, and there have been numerous opportunities to counsel with and encourage others who suffer in the same way as I.

During my time of depression I eventually was hospitalized. The Lord used this to bring about my healing. Two weeks after I was released from the hospital I received a call early one morning from an area pastor who had heard about my illness. He was at the point of desperation; he didn't know what to do. His wife was in the depths of a serious depression, unable to do anything except lie in bed. I spoke with her, prayed with her, and encouraged her to seek professional help. The next day I went with her and her husband as she was admitted to the hospital. Today she is depression-free and is functioning in her role as a pastor's wife.

The other morning I was visited by a pastor who has battled depression for most of his adult life. On one occasion he attempted suicide by swallowing sixty-four sleeping pills. I was able to share with him that, although I too had reached the point of total desperation, I clung to hope and found help. As I write these words, I'm in the process of making arrangements for him to see the doctor who was instrumental in my recovery. I am being well used by God in this new ministry, a ministry of caring, a ministry of compassion, a ministry of hope.

How thankful I am for a Sovereign God who "works all things according to the counsel of His will" (Eph. 1:11). How wonderful to know that my times are in His hands (Ps. 31:15) and to know the truth that "the steps of a good man are ordered by the LORD. . . . Though he fall, he shall not be utterly cast down; for the LORD upholds him with His hand" (Ps. 37:23–24)!

Deliverance!

The majority of people who go through depression survive it. Acute depression inflicts few permanent wounds. However, a great number of those who are devastated by depression will be struck again. It has the habit of recurrence.

At the age of thirty-five, when I first experienced this illness, I was grossly overweight, primarily because of the sedentary life of a traveling evangelist. At that time, since medications did not seem to be helping, a doctor suggested an exercise program. In the more than thirty years that I have contended with this illness, I have survived only by the grace of God and by a consistent physical fitness program.

Taking Care of the Temple

Research shows that exercise has an antidepressant effect. No one is certain exactly how exercise elevates mood. Some experts believe that simply moving large muscle groups in regular, rhythmical ways is inconsistent with depression. Others maintain that exercise produces a fundamental alteration in brain chemistry, affecting neurotransmitters and endorphins (naturally occurring morphine-like substances).

Realizing that I must do something if I was going to maintain my sanity and continue in the ministry, I went at the exercise program with a vengeance. I lost more than sixty pounds, began running every day, and in the ensuing years ran twenty-seven marathons and countless shorter races. I have no doubt of the efficacy of aerobic exercise.

In my last bout with depression, however, exercise did not seem to be as beneficial as in previous years. Perhaps getting older had something to do with it. Possibly the attack was simply more severe than those in the past, for it was by far the most serious episode I have faced. Whatever the cause, one morning I awakened my wife and told her, "Pat, I can no longer stand this torment. Something has to be done." That afternoon I was admitted to a local hospital's mental health unit. As a highly visible pastor in my community, I felt humiliated to admit how weak and sick I was. The medical staff gave my tie to my wife and went through my suitcase to make sure that I had no glass containers or sharp objects. They confiscated my razor, trying to forestall any suicide attempts. Looking back, I appreciate how the Lord used that experience to knock out of me whatever vestiges of pride remained.

"Don't worry, Pastor Kiloski. You aren't the first clergyman I have admitted here," one gentleman told me. "I've taken care of pastors, priests, politicians, and doctors. Depression is no respecter of persons; it strikes indiscriminately at all ages, races, creeds, and classes." That was little comfort at the time, but he was right. Depression is no respecter of persons.

The hospital became my sanctuary. As reluctant as I had been to enter it, I was even more reluctant to leave when the time came for my discharge. I cannot say enough about the compassionate care given by the nurses, the doctors, and other staff. They were exemplary in every respect.

The psychiatrist put me on a combination of medications in which I had little, if any, confidence. But on the fifth day I awoke knowing that something had happened. I felt better. The doctor was as surprised, since it usually takes weeks for medications to take effect in the treatment of clinical depression. Shortly thereafter I was released from the hospital and continue to see my doctor on a regular basis.

I believe that all healing is divine healing. In this instance God saw fit to use modern medication to alleviate my symptoms of depression. Since beginning treatment there has been steady improvement, and at this moment I am free from depression.

Facing the Future

Depression is mysterious in its comings and goings. Will it come back? Only the Lord knows, but if it does, I have confidence that I will, by God's grace, be able to endure it. The fear is gone, and I do not live in dread of a recurrence. Instead, I enjoy reflecting on the old hymn "Children of the Heavenly Father," from the pen of Carolina Sandell Berg:

> Neither life nor death shall ever
> From the Lord His children sever;
> Unto them His grace He showeth,
> And their sorrows all He knoweth.
>
> Though He giveth or He taketh,
> God His children ne'er forsaketh;
> His the loving purpose solely
> To preserve them pure and holy.

A country preacher once put a personal spin on the frequent biblical phrase "And it came to pass." He said, "Our troubles and trials didn't come to stay, they came to pass." His hermeneutics are questionable, but his theology is accurate. The troubles of life will pass, if not in this world then in the next. What has sustained me throughout is my hope in Christ. Paul says that "we also rejoice in our sufferings, because we know that suffering produces perseverance; perseverance, character; and character, hope" (Rom. 5:3-4 NIV). The book of Hebrews speaks about the reasons we have "strong consolation, who have fled for refuge to lay hold of the hope set before us. This hope we have as an anchor of the soul, both sure and steadfast, and which enters the Presence behind the veil, where the forerunner has entered for us, even Jesus, having become High Priest forever according to the order of Melchizedek" (Heb. 6:18-20).

Concrete Hope

Do you want to know my hope? Edward Mote expressed it in the words of his hymn, "My hope is built on nothing less than Jesus' blood and righteousness. . . . His oath, His covenant, His blood, support me in the 'whelming flood. . . ." In the midst of my season of despair, a dear friend wrote me a letter, part of which said,

We long to hear that the Lord has melted away the mists of that long depression with the sunbeams of His presence. For some unaccountable purpose, unknown to us and indispensable to you, God has hid His face and withdrawn from you the joy of salvation. His Fatherly love has prompted Him to lead you through the valley of gloom and darkness with its terrors and trials. How long this unhappy journey will endure, none of us knows. What anguish, self-recriminations, despair, and suspicions have already overtaken you and will yet assail you there, only Divine omniscience can disclose.

I can but remind you that in His good time and according to His gracious pleasure He will lead you out again to gladness and victory. From the long and somber tunnel you will emerge to know yourself better and to preach the secret of His presence more persuasively. I have no doubt that now He is teaching you the magnitude of your weaknesses so that when He lifts you up, you can boast in His strength. The power of divine grace is invincible."

Styron expresses similar sentiments:

For those who have dwelt in depression's dark wood, and known its inexplicable agony, their return from the abyss is not unlike the ascent of the poet, trudging upward and upward out of the black depths and at last emerging into what he saw as "the shining world." *E quindi uscimmo a riveder le stelle*. And so we came forth, and once again beheld the stars.[14]

There is hope over depression. That hope is the stuff of survival.

Without it, life holds little meaning. With it, life holds little defeat. Even depression cannot defeat hope. "Now thanks be to God who always leads us in triumph in Christ" (2 Cor. 2:14). Charles Wesley spoke for me in 1746 through his hymn, "Rejoice, the Lord Is King."

> My hope is in the Lord,
> Who gave Himself for me.
> And paid the debt of all my sin at Calvary.

Chapter Notes

1. Iain Murray, "William Cowper and His Affliction," *Banner of Truth Magazine,* September 1971, 31.
2. William Styron, *Darkness Visible: A Memoir of Madness* (New York: Random House, 1990), 83.
3. Anna Larina, *This I Cannot Forget: The Memoirs of Nikolai Bukharin's Widow* (New York: W. W. Norton, 1993), 73.
4. Elizabeth Wurtzel, *Prozac Nation* (Boston: Houghton Mifflin, 1994), 42.
5. *Darkness Visible,* 7.
6. Ibid., 62.
7. Patty Duke, *A Brilliant Madness: Living with Manic-Depressive Illness* (New York: Bantam, 1992), 8.
8. John Milton, "Paradise Lost" in *The Norton Anthology of English Literature* (New York: W. W. Norton, 1974), 1363.
9. *Darkness Visible,* 76.
10. Murray, "William Cowper and His Affliction," 31.
11. Robert Browning Hamilton, "I Walked a Mile with Pleasure," in *Masterpieces of Religious Verse,* (New York: Harper, 1948), 436.
12. *The Westminster Confession of Faith* 5.5.
13. Peter Kramer, *Listening to Prozac* (New York: Viking, 1993).
14. *Darkness Visible,* 84.

Hanging on to Hope When You Lose Everything

Bill Boulet

THE BOSTON RED SOX last won the World Series in 1918. That means Red Sox fans have persevered through a long period of disappointment and loss. It's not easy, but we have learned to cope.

On the other hand, some fiercely competitive people really hate to lose—whether a card game or an athletic contest. None of us likes to lose, but some people treat it like the plague. They just have to win. Some years ago a man was so upset over losing a golf match that he threw his club at the golf cart. The club snapped in half when it struck the cart and the metal shaft part rebounded with such velocity that it stuck in his throat. He pulled the shaft out of his neck and bled to death. Not an effective way to handle loss.

Western society generally puts a high priority on winning, and those who have been enculturated in the United States are among the worst. Losing is a fearful thing in our culture. Americans who are honest might go so far as to say, "We have to win at everything. It's our destiny." That is not a healthy attitude, for in reality human beings face losses every day and sometimes experience monumental losses. These losses that cut the heart out of life are the ones that bring us to face the question "Is there any hope?"

How can we win when we lose? Is it even possible? How should we handle the death of a spouse or a child? The loss of a home or a job? The breakup of a marriage? The loss of dignity that can result from a mistake in judgment? Is there any hope for us when we experience devastating losses?

Of course the seriousness of a loss is relative, and every loss we experience brings genuine feelings of grief and pain, whether the loss of hair, the loss of a game, or the loss of youthful beauty. But these losses usually do not debilitate a person or threaten happiness. In this chapter we consider the losses that affect us far more deeply, losses that cut to the heart and threaten to suck the hope out of life. At one time or another, we all have faced or will face such losses, and we need to be skillful in seeking out the hope that comes from them.

Family

The loss of a husband or wife should feel like more than the loss of a partner. If there was any love and satisfaction in the relationship, the person who endures the death of a spouse, or a divorce, has lost a friend and life companion. Even in most divorces, the former marriage partners have laughed and cried together. After a spouse's death, it is normal for a widowed spouse to acutely feel the loss of the one who knew him or her best, the one who was loved most intimately. This is the loss of the other half of life, the one who had made the survivor complete. Here is the loss of one of God's greatest gifts. Now he or she is gone, and the loneliness seems impenetrable. If you have experienced this kind of loss, the hands which once held your beloved's hands now are cold and empty.

Of course, somewhat different dynamics govern your feelings after a broken or wounded relationship. For some, the loss of a spouse can come when the spouse is, in fact, still physically present. When a husband or wife loses interest in the relationship, it can seem like a sort of death. Husbands become absorbed in their work, or in their softball team, or just in spending time "with the guys." Their wives feel the loss. Wives spend much of their free time shopping or watching their favorite soaps. Their husbands feel the loss. Though somewhat different from the loss due to death, the feelings of rejection and neglect are real nonetheless. The neglected spouse has lost a meaningful relationship. Life goes on, but living and loving together stops.

Infidelity is a particularly painful loss. A typical scenario is that the relationship grows cold with disinterest. Then comes the announcement that she simply doesn't love you anymore. He may deny that there is someone else, but soon the truth comes out. Who was at fault? What should you have done differently? How can you possibly find hope to endure the pain and the loss?

Perhaps the most painful loss is that of a child. Bill and Sheila sat in the doctor's office as he explained that their six-year-old daughter, Brittany, had a rare form of cancer. When Dr. Burke went over the treatment options, the couple realized how serious this was.

"I was stunned," Bill said. "I couldn't believe this was happening to us. Brittany was so young, so full of life." Weeks and months flew by quickly as Brittany's condition worsened. Bill and Sheila tried to keep it all together, and friends from their church helped. But the painful day finally came when little Brittany's battle was over. There are few things more painful than watching your child's coffin being lowered into the ground.

There is another sort of loss that parents experience. You may not have lost a child physically, but maybe you have lost your child to drugs, to godless friends, or to the allure of the world. You may have provided every spiritual benefit. But little by little, your child rejected everything, pulled away, and became unreasonable, unmanageable, unstoppable—all but unlovable. As a pastor, I've comforted far too many parents grieving over a wayward child. Many parents live in continual emotional pain, wondering what could have been done differently.

Such loss is real and painful. But if you cry out to God for hope, you will discover what you never thought possible—God gives hope in the midst of your sorrow.

In Bill and Sheila's case, the pain of Brittany's death was mitigated when another bundle of hope, Barbie, was born. While Bill and Sheila will always feel the pain of losing their lovely, lively six-year-old, God encourages them daily and has given them the opportunity to find hope and joy in a new child.

Careers

The loss of a family member is devastating, but other losses also create feelings of hopelessness. Brad was fifty-six and at the top of his career. He had climbed the corporate ladder much higher than he ever expected. He was upper management, working directly under the CEO. Brad had given twenty-five years of his life to the company. They were good years, too. He loved his work. Retirement was less than a decade away, but he wasn't looking forward to it. Every day in the office was a joy to him.

But profits and growth suddenly went flat. The company wasn't growing and the answer was to restructure, "downsize." The company had to become leaner if it were to be stronger. Brad was deemed expendable. Without warning, he found himself out of work. How could he start over? Who wants to hire a fifty-six-year-old?

Brad had experienced one of life's most devious losses—the loss of his identity. For twenty-five years, when people asked, "What do you do for a living?" Brad had a ready answer. His job defined who he was. He had given his best years to his company, and it had become his life. Now, life seemed to be over. Brad would have to learn how to write a résumé. He would have to file for unemployment and endure the shame of being the "old guy" in line. Brad knew that he would likely have to spend months or even years retooling his skills, and it would be expensive. He might end up frying hamburgers at minimum wage for a while. Brad was depressed and without much hope.

Downsizing has become a common corporate solution to a weak bottom line. The layoff of managers often results in a loss of dignity and self-worth, as well as a life's savings. But just as in the loss of a family member, God gives hope in the loss of a career. Remember that Abraham, Moses, Peter, Paul, and Matthew all went through midlife career changes. Somehow God gives hope in the midst of our most hopeless losses.

Material Possessions

Perhaps not as life shattering, but no less hope shattering, is a significant loss of material things. Some people lost their retirement portfolios on one single black day of stock market downturn in 1988. My parents lost their home to a fire. They most miss the family pictures. It's easy for outsiders who want to be "spiritual" people to say, "Well, that's what happens when you get too attached to material things." The reality is, we all get attached to material things. It's part of our nature. I know people who are attached to their boats, their computers, their fine china, their pets. People are attached to cars, souvenirs, coin collections, and clothes. We get attached to things we value. That's why people often become unduly attached to their financial portfolios, their Individual Retirement Accounts (IRAs), and their savings plans. Having material things is not wrong. Job was the wealthiest man in the ancient Near East (Job 1:1–4), yet he was blameless and upright before God. Abraham was a wealthy sheik, "very rich in livestock, in silver, and in gold" (Gen. 13:2), yet God told him to "walk before Me and be blameless" (17:1). Solomon had vast wealth, yet "God gave Solomon wisdom and exceedingly great understanding, and largeness of heart like the sand on the seashore" (1 Kings 4:29). Joseph, "a rich man from Arimathea," was a disciple of Jesus as well as a prominent member of the Sanhedrin. He provided his own new family tomb as a place for the Lord's body when it was taken down from the cross (Matt. 27:57–60).

Jesus instructed those who would follow Him not to seek the things of the world alone, but to "seek *first* the kingdom of God and His righteousness, and *all these things* shall be added to you" (Matt. 6:33, emphasis added). It is not wrong for Christians to be wealthy. It is wrong to be wealthy yet untouched by the needs of the world and the needs of eternity (1 John 3:17–18).

No one wants to lose everything they have saved for through a lifetime. Nobody anticipates the loss of a home and everything in it. Even if we have a healthy, biblical view of possessions, losing them is painful.

Dreams

One of the more disappointing losses is the loss of a dream. The dream of financial freedom dissolves with bad investments. The dream of being a doctor fades with rejection after rejection from medical schools. The dream of a happy marriage vanishes in divorce. The dream of a particular sort of ministry disappears when circumstances in life make it impossible. When dreams die, so does hope.

In 1987 Dave Dravecky started pitching for the San Francisco giants and life was good. Playing pro baseball was the fulfillment of a lifelong dream, and Dave had a wonderful wife, two terrific kids, and a big salary. In 1988, however, a lump on his pitching arm was diagnosed as cancer. After surgery and a short-lived comeback attempt with the Giants, the cancer returned. Despite more surgeries, ultimately the arm had to be amputated in June of 1991. The loss of an arm meant the loss of a pitching career, but not the loss of hope. As Dave shared, "I believe in miracles, that God can and does heal people, but more importantly than that, I believe in the eternal hope of heaven."[1]

Jack and Paula were made for each other. They met in college. Jack invited Paula to the student center "just for fun." Well, fun turned into affection, affection turned to love, and love led to marriage. Jack and Paula were married shortly after graduation from college.

Both of them held a variety of jobs to pay off college loans. Finally, Jack was called to be pastor of a church, the vocation that he believed to be God's calling. He was thrilled. Jack and Paula dreamed of having several children. Both of them loved children, especially Paula. All the smaller children in church loved her, so that she looked like the Pied Piper in leading children to the sanctuary.

But after three years without a pregnancy, Jack and Paula were worried. They went together to their family doctor and had the usual tests. Physically they could not have children. The dream died, and they were crushed. Paula cried for days. Her maternal instincts were strong, and so was her dream. Their original dream was lost.

In the case of Jack and Paula, a new dream was born. They decided that if God wouldn't bless them with children of their own making, He would bless them with children they could adopt. Dreams sometimes seem to be lost when they really only have to be adjusted. But even readjusted dreams sometimes cause hope to fail.

Can We Lose It All and Survive?

Can we hang on to hope when we lose everything? Plenty of people have. When hope is strong, survival is certain.

One of those who lost everything but hope was the John D. Rockefeller of his day. He was the Warren Buffet of the ancient Near East. The Bill Gates of antiquity. We know him only as Job. The Bible records his tragedy of spectacular personal, material, and family loss. How Job responded to his loss and how he tenaciously maintained hope in the process is not only instructive but inspiring.

To fully appreciate what Job lost, we must first understand his original blessings. This godly man had a large family, enormous wealth in livestock, and a place of honor in the community. Everyone, young and old, knew of Job. He was a legend to the local town's folk. Some people may see Job as an oxymoron—a godly millionaire. Job had it pretty good. He had every reason to see hope as something you have, because Job had it all.

"It is easy for Job to be godly," Satan complained to God, "Why shouldn't he be happy with all that?" In Job 1:6-12, Satan accused God of buying Job's affection. The underlying accusation to God was, "Job doesn't follow You for who You are, only for what You give him. His hope is in his stuff, not in You." Satan assumed that Job was one of the many who follow God only because He has blessed them. They have a nice house with a pool, they take expensive vacations to exotic places, they even show God that they appreciate His goodness by giving a little to the Lord's work. Why not follow a God who gives you all that?

The Endurance of Job

But the story recorded in Job 1:13-19 is of a rich man who lost everything—possessions, business, and, most painful of all, his children. I personally don't know anyone who has suffered a greater personal loss. I can't even imagine watching, as Job did, ten bodies carried into the family tomb. All his children—gone. All his dreams—gone.

All the good times with them—gone. His memories couldn't console him. His wife wouldn't comfort him. All he had left was God, but he soon learned that God is enough when He is all you have.

Chapter 2 of this book related the story of Don and Betty Hall, who suffered the loss of a child. Don Baker and his wife, Martha, also experienced the death of a child, in their case their only child. Like the Halls, this was a devastating loss. Don Baker writes with special awareness of Job's loss:

> Martha and I have stood on a wind-swept hillside, transfixed by the sight of a little white casket in which lay the lifeless form of our only child. Occasionally the sun would break through the clouds and shine like a spotlight on that little wooden box. And then it would drift back into hiding, and the gray gloom of an early spring day would again fall down around us.
>
> Friends were there. Family was there. Beloved Pastor was there. And yet we remember nothing but the awesome feelings of emptiness, as if all life, all joy and all hope, all laughter had been squeezed from our very souls—forever.
>
> The memory of that little white casket silhouetted against the green hillside is just as vivid today, thirty years later, as it was on that May afternoon. The pain has eased and yet occasionally I'll catch sight of a single tear as it rolls down Martha's cheek, and I'll know that something has stirred the memory of a little life that was loaned to us for such a short period of time.
>
> It hurts—deeply—to lose someone we love. To multiply that loss by ten and to be forced to stand beside the caskets of seven sons and three daughters—all you have—is beyond comprehension."[2]

Job lost almost everything that he held dear. If in the course of this most crushing blow Job had lost his hope, who would blame him? Well, at least he had his health, but not for long.

Satan now maintained that the only reason Job was true to God was because God was keeping him healthy. Satan truly believed Job's devotion to God was a spiritual façade. "If Job lost his health," Satan surmised, "Job would crack and walk away from God." Satan just couldn't imagine that anyone would want to follow the Lord simply for who He is and not for what He gives us.

How bad did it get for Job? Well, focus on the description recorded in Job 2:1-8. Just imagine what it must have been like for him:

- He could not sleep, he constantly tossed until dawn.
- He used dirt clods to cover his running sores.
- Maggots crawled into his sores.
- He bit his flesh to relieve the pain.
- He continually itched.
- His eyes were sunken due to loss of sleep.
- He could hardly breathe.
- His skin was turning black.
- He burned with persistent fever.

There could be no relief for his excruciating pain. Even morphine would have done Job little good. He had hit bottom. His life couldn't get any worse. Think of your struggles with arthritis or migraine headaches or gall bladder attacks. When you are experiencing your worst pain and are tempted to lose hope and doubt the goodness of God, Job is a convicting and sympathetic presence. As Baker observes,

> Pain speaks a strange language—it plays funny tricks on us. It makes us think things and say things and even believe things that are not true. When pain begins to bore its way through human flesh and on into human spirit and then just sit there and hurt and hurt and hurt, the mind becomes clouded and the brain begins to think strange thoughts like: God is dead, or He's gone fishing, or He's just plain not interested.[3]

We can only imagine what was going through Job's mind. He was experiencing the most devastating winter of life. He was a super saint, but even super saints are subject to the adverse effects of pain. How can you hold on to hope when you lose everything to the extent Job did? Job showed that he believed that hope is a noun, a concrete, confident expectation that God is in control. We can have hope when we have lost everything else. Job's hope was firm because his eyes were riveted squarely on God. Ours must do the same. Notice Job's focus.

Job Focused on God's Sovereignty

Job's response proves that hope was tangible to him. Keep Job's example in mind. No one is exempt from losing everything. Job was disturbed and distracted by his problems. But he endured through them because the focus of his mind was elsewhere. Job focused on God's sovereign wisdom, His holiness, justice, and purpose.

Focusing on God's sovereignty means that Job didn't swear and shake his fist at God. Lately there has been a spate of books by Christian authors suggesting that it is okay to question God, to lash out at Him, to give Him a piece of your mind. But Job didn't do any of those immature things. He was so convinced that God was in control—even though things were turning out all wrong—that Job worshiped God (Job 1:20–21). How could he worship at that time in his life? Job worshiped because he had a clear head, free from doubt. Job worshiped because he had clean hands, free from dirty dealing. Job worshiped because he had a trusting heart, convinced that God was in control. Job worshiped because he had hope, the cement that holds life together when everything falls apart. Worship is an act of recognition—recognition that God is worthy of our trust even when we don't understand.

We need strong convictions about the sovereignty of God *before* hard times come. We must be convinced of His righteous character before the bottom falls out because afterward is no time to be wrestling with questions about God's character.

One might say, "But Job was a great man, a super believer. I'm just an ordinary person. How can I expect to hang on to hope when I lose everything?" Actually, Job was just a person like you and me, a man who realized that God could be trusted, even when he didn't understand.

Fanny Crosby (1820–1915) was like that. The poet for many great old hymns, such as "Praise Him, Praise Him," "Blessed Assurance," and "To God Be the Glory" was accidentally blinded when she was just six weeks old. She could not see her mother, her friends, or her surroundings. When her father died, Fanny's mother had to leave her with a grandmother and go to work each day. Although she did not receive Christ as Savior until she was thirty, Fanny learned to love the Bible and her grandmother who read it to her. Fanny learned verses and whole chapters by heart. This way, even though she could not see to read, she always had the Bible with her. Was Fanny Crosby bitter about being blind? Apparently not. She wrote this bit of verse when she was eight years old:

> O what a happy soul am I!
>   Although I cannot see,
> I am resolved that in this world
>   Contented I will be;
> How many blessings I enjoy
>   That other people don't
> To weep and sigh because I'm blind,
>   I cannot, and I won't.

It may be that Job was more spiritually mature than some of us, but how does one explain an eight-year-old girl with such maturity? What did Job and Fanny Crosby have that so many seem to lack? They both had a solid hope in a sovereign God.

Job Focused on God's Holiness

One immediately is impressed with Job's initial attitude when his world fell apart: "In all this Job did not sin nor charge God with wrong" (Job 1:22).

The more common attitude is to say, "If God is sovereign, and He allowed these horrible things to happen, God must be the author of evil." But Job not only focused on God's sovereignty; He also believed that God was holy and the disasters that had befallen him could not be mistakes. No matter how bad things got, no matter how deep his hurt, Job knew better than to charge God with wrongdoing because He knew God.

Since God is sovereign, He has the right to do whatever He wants whenever He wants. But since He is holy, whatever He wants is always right. Sovereignty and holiness—it's a dynamic combination. It means that whoever possesses both of these attributes must, of necessity, always do what is right. It may be difficult for us to understand this, but our inability to understand doesn't change the goodness of God in all His actions toward us.

Abraham understood this as he negotiated with God to save Sodom and Gomorrah and the cities of the plain from destruction. Abraham rhetorically inquired if God would slay the righteous with the wicked, then answered his own question with another question: "Shall not the Judge of all the earth do right?" (Gen. 18:25). God would do right—both in punishing the wicked and in protecting the righteous. He does what is right. Because Job understood this, he could have confident hope.

Did Job grieve over his losses? Absolutely. He was human and humans grieve in reaction to loss. Did he like what happened to him? Of course not. Did he understand what was happening? It was all a mystery to him. But despite all of that, he did not impugn God. He trusted in God's holiness.

Job Focused on God's Justice

Historically Job's wife has received a lot of bad press because she encouraged her husband to give up, to curse God and die (2:9). But because we are concentrating on Job, we often fail to recognize how much she too was suffering. She lost her children. She lost her home and belongings. She lost everything, just as did Job. Her husband was desperately ill, so ill that recovery seemed unlikely. Mrs. Job may have thought in her desperation that if Job cursed God, the Almighty would take his life and end his misery. All she could think of, knowing that her husband would not commit suicide, was to goad God into divine euthanasia. This may have been the way Mrs. Job coped with the tragedy. You can be sure that, wherever there is a suffering husband, there is a grieving wife.

But Job wasn't buying it. Life may have been tough, but it was a gift from God. In responding to his wife, Job confirmed his faith that whatever God does is just. "Shall we indeed accept good from God, and shall we not accept adversity?" (Job 2:10). Job focused on the justice of God. While his wife could challenge that focus, she couldn't change it.

Job teaches us that when we can't understand what is happening, we must hold tightly to the conviction that God is just. He will do what is right every time because His righteous character will permit Him to do no less. God is under no obligation to make us comfortable, but He is under obligation to make us conform to His image (Rom. 8:29). Often God is glorified more in times of trial than in times of blessing. He reserves the right to bring the unpleasant into our lives in order to show Himself strong on our behalf.

In spite of his wife's comments, Job kept his focus riveted on the character of God. As Joe Stowell reminds us,

> Job realized that in suffering the issue is not why. The issue is who! That too is the issue for us. We rest in the reality that our God is the true and the living God, worthy of our trust regardless. We affirm that He has the right to be the sovereign God of our life, death, wisdom, and power. Though this may not make the hurt any less painful, it does get us through victoriously in a way that honors Him.[4]

Do you know what this means? It means that you can lose and still win. It means you can sorrow and still have hope. It means you can lose a spouse, lose a dream, lose a job, even lose a child and still trust that God knows what He is doing. It isn't easy, but it is possible. Not only is it possible to trust in God, it is life-changing. Ruth Harns Calkin wrote these penetrating words:

> O God, I trust you. I don't understand, I cannot begin to comprehend the wisdom of your way in my torn and tangled life. But I am steadfastly believing that your plan for me today must be, surely it must be, as kind, as loving, as profitable as

your plan for me in joyful days past. After all, you are the same yesterday, today and forever, so dear God although my feelings cry out differently, I choose at this moment to trust you![5]

To help people who are going through any kind of a loss, remember that what they need most is hope. Since hope is a noun, it can be shared. Often hope is shared by a hug or by a word of encouragement. Sometimes hope is shared simply by your silent presence. Job's three friends began by giving him hope through their presence. After showing Job how much they cared for him by committing seven days and nights of silent mourning, however, they opened their mouths and yanked that hope right out from under him. We would do well to remember that, when grief is the freshest, words should be the fewest.

Job Focused on God's Purpose

Job focused on one additional characteristic of God that carried him through his time of loss. God does not act on a whim. God always acts consistently with His purpose and plan. What purpose could God have in allowing all of Job's sheep and shepherds to be destroyed? What possible purpose could there be for Job's body to be covered with sores? Was there any discernible purpose to these things? No purpose was discernible. From Job's point of view, none of this had any meaning.

An important lesson about hanging on to hope when everything has been lost seems almost paradoxical: Trials and calamities have to be meaningless in order to have meaning. If Job understood what God was doing in his life, Job could have reasoned, "All I have to do is hang in there for a while and this will all be over. I know God will reward me for enduring all this without a complaint." But Job didn't know why these things had happened to him. He was not party to the conversation between Satan and God. Job didn't have a clue. And that's what makes his focus on God's purpose so important.

The question is not whether Job would trust God in the midst of adversity, but whether he would trust God when he had no idea why adversity had come. It's one thing to hang on to hope when you know the purpose or what the end will be. It's quite another to hang on simply because you believe in the righteous character of God. Job looked into the faces of his friends and he didn't see the hope of God. He listened to the words of his wife and he didn't hear the hope of God. He looked at the devastation around him and he didn't feel like hoping in God. But hope was not a feeling in his life. It was something concrete that was part of him—what this book stresses as noun faith. It's not what Job did; it's what Job had. Job had so much hope in God's character that he said with confidence, "Though He slay me, yet will I trust Him" (Job 13:15).

Our Greatest Resource

Here is a rich truth. Our greatest resource in the time of loss is not how we feel but what we know for sure. More specifically, our greatest resource in the time of loss is what we know about God. That's what the apostle Paul meant in Romans 8:28: "And we know that all things work together for good to those who love God, to those who are the called according to His purpose." That's not wishful thinking. That's not a Christian crutch. That's a promise of God rooted in the character of God. It's something you hold on to when you lose everything else.

I have a dear friend with whom I went to college. She learned through a time of great trial that God is a God of purpose. Debbie Searles was hospitalized for an extended period. The hospitalization was particularly difficult because the doctors were not certain what her problem was. She endured months of questions with very few answers. Some people wondered if she was under the discipline of God. But all through her ordeal Debbie hung on with great tenacity to the God of hope. Finally she was released from the hospital and began her rehabilitation. Later, reflecting on her days in the hospital, Debbie wrote the words to a song that was popularized by Christine Wyrtzen. One line in that song says, "Sometimes we need the hard times to bring us to our knees. Otherwise, we do as we please and never heed Him." Debbie knew that sometimes it is not in our strength but in our weakness that we best understand God's care for us. She concluded in her song,

> But He always knows what's best
> And it's when we are distressed
> That we really come to know God as He is.

Hear the hope in those words. It's when we are on our knees that we know God for who He really is—the God of holiness, the God of help, the God of hope.

Knowing God Means Having Hope

James taught this principle about knowing God as He is in James 1:2-3: "My brethren, count it all joy when you fall into various trials, knowing that the testing of your faith produces patience." James reminds us that our chief resource in the time of loss and trial is not how we feel, but what we know. The better you get to know God, the more you'll understand Him to be a God of purpose.

Is it possible to have hope in times of monumental loss? Not only is it possible, it is God's will for your life. He will give that hope to those who focus on Him. The Bible consistently teaches that our God allows losses in life so that we may gain. Ironic, isn't it? Gain comes from loss. The gain may be perspective, maturity, endurance, perhaps even a deeper longing for heaven, but God does not haphazardly allow things in His children's lives. He always allows them for our benefit. That's the lesson Job learned. It's the lesson we need to learn, too.

If you're in the middle of a tremendous loss—the loss of a dream, a spouse, a child, a marriage, or a profession—if you hang on to hope, you will gain. Will you still hurt? Yes. Will you still wonder why God is allowing this in your life? Likely. But your questions will not exhibit a lack of faith, nor will they inhibit your strong hope. God will see you through.

In times of loss, we can not only survive the loss, but we can actually grow through it. The key to growth is to focus on God—that He is sovereign, holy, just, and a God of purpose. That focus will bring you hope and with this hope, even your unexplainable losses will be gains. And the losses you can appreciate will be greater gains. The tragedy, but we don't appreciate that truth unless it is forced upon us. No, those kinds of bad things certainly wouldn't happen to me. I had always enjoyed good health and this AIDS thing—it belonged to other people, not to me.

With diploma in hand, I set out in 1984 on my life as a pastor, Patti and the kids faithfully trailing along. There were some minor setbacks, but life was good.

I loved the work of a pastor. The people I've shepherded and the churches I've pastored have been a delight. God's blessings were abundant. There were always people coming to know the Savior, and there was consistent growth in the lives of those in my congregations.

Both our kids went to my alma mater for their college and ministry education following high school. Holly married a young pastor named Tim Tangen. Tyler became a youth pastor and married a pastor's daughter, Kim. Then came the granddaughters. What more could a guy want? The blessing of God, a godly family, praise of people, and good health; life was better than okay—life was great.

Everything Changed

By 1996 I was well established in my third church, Grace Bible Church in Holidaysburg, Pennsylvania. This time I was senior pastor in a much larger church with multiple staff members. The challenges were stretching me, but I enjoyed the warmth of our church family and my ministry among them.

In February I started losing weight—slowly, but with ease. For a man who was five feet nine inches tall and weighed 231 pounds, it was a dream come true. By Easter I had lost twenty pounds. This phenomenon was totally out of character for my body, but it was a nice change. "Pastor, you really look great. How are you doing that?" I didn't really know. There were no magic diets, no strenuous exercise program. I was just slimming down nicely. Summer came, and I had a few minor health problems, but nothing serious. I was not alarmed.

However, autumn proved to be another story. I wasn't well and I knew it. My doctor ran tests, and just before Thanksgiving, I was diagnosed as having parasites in my body. The effect of parasites was horrible. The diarrhea was almost continuous. My body was weakened;

difference between trouble that makes us a loser and trouble that makes us a winner is hope. When your roof caves in, hope makes all the difference in the world. Let it make a difference for you.

Chapter Notes

1. Dave and Jan Dravecky, *When You Can't Come Back* (Grand Rapids: Zondervan, 1992), 122.
2. Don Baker, *Pain's Hidden Purpose* (Portland, Ore.: Multnomah, 1984), 23.
3. Ibid., 34.
4. Joseph M. Stowell, *Through the Fire* (Wheaton, Ill.: Victor, 1985), 131.
5. Ruth Harns Calkin, *Lord, I Keep Running Back to You* (Wheaton, Ill.: Tyndale, 1979), 11.

Finding Hope in Cultural Diversity

Dino Pedrone

THE SIGN ON THE BACK OF THE eighteen-wheeler read, "A Place Called Hope." The truck was plastered with other signs and bumper stickers, but none caught my eye or pierced so deeply into my spirit. If there is a place called hope, where is it? How do we get there? Can people in the city find this place? Can anybody have hope, or is it reserved exclusively for the rich and the beautiful? If one lives in North America, is it reserved for descendants of European immigrants?

Is There Any Hope for the City?

I know of no places more bereft of hope than the giant cities of our planet. Still, urban life has become the preferred lifestyle at the dawn of the twenty-first century. The flight to the suburbs has reversed, and the flight today is back into the great urban centers of the world. Rich farmland is being chewed up by developers, who are rapidly expanding the edges of our great cities.

Urban Growth

Population growth is staggering. But while population growth has been phenomenal, city growth has been even more spectacular. In 1800, only about seven hundred and fifty cities in the world were larger than five thousand in population and only fifteen cities had a population above one hundred thousand. Just two hundred years ago you could count the number of cities with populations of six figures on your fingers and toes.

Today, megacities are springing up everywhere. At the turn of the last century only eleven cities claimed more than a million residents. In 1950, the world had seventy-one such cities, and in 1975 there were 181 cities of a million-plus residents. That's a remarkable growth of 155 percent in only twenty-five years. At the beginning of the new millennium, cities with more than 1 million residents dot the globe: Russia has 27 million; Europe 34 million; Eastern Asia 42 million; Southern Asia 46 million; Latin America 48 million; Oceania 56 million; North America 59 million. While the world population swelled by 271 percent during the twentieth century, the urban population surged a whopping 2,736 percent. As a case study, the United States urban population dramatically increased in the 1980s to a new high. In 1990 there were 187.1 million people in the cities and 61.7 million rural residents.[1]

Urban Problems

With the swell of city life has come a corresponding deepening of urban problems, some though not all associated with poverty. People in great cities are isolated as they walk among the masses. Looking for meaning in their lives, they are susceptible to the allure of New Age religions, Eastern mysticism, and even satanism and the occult. However, none of these belief systems really provides the satisfaction that these teeming millions want. Eventually most of these seekers realize that and are left without hope. Many identify with cults and quasi-religious movements but are left dissatisfied, disillusioned, and defeated. Their religious experience has produced only despair.

Urban Flight

For over four decades the church has been "solving" the problems of the cities by moving to the suburbs. Sprawling megachurches spring up on out-of-town acreage with ponds, parks, fountains, and enough asphalt that one could use them to land the space shuttle. Perhaps it seemed unpromising to remain in the city to do God's work, but ministries need to be where the people are, and the people are definitely in the cities. In addition, we have biblical and historical precedent for urban ministry. It may be helpful to reflect on the beginning of Christianity and how unpromising the cities then looked to those who had the message of hope.

Making a Difference in the City

When Christ died, His disciples' vision of a Christian kingdom on this earth died with Him. With their leader gone, the idea seemed futile. With Him died hope for the future. However, three days later Jesus Christ arose from the grave. The resurrection of Jesus meant the resurrection of hope for the fledgling church.

Jesus Christ lived at a time when the *pax Romana* had brought administrative strength and economic prosperity to the empire that ruled the world. The Romans were master builders of roads and cities. They erected great public buildings, including baths and stadiums, wherever they went. The excellent Roman road system took the early Christian message of hope to a largely urban church that reached to the ends of the empire. The apostle Paul and others planted churches in city after city. Under the power of the Holy Spirit, their passion drove these early church planters to accomplish things that astounded even their most cynical critics. Difficulty or distance could not deter them. Ridicule and hatred would not slow those who knew that Christ had risen from the dead. He had been seen alive by hundreds of credible witnesses. He had returned to the Father and now His disciples had a job to do.

The Son of God set the stage for building His kingdom. The early church pioneered many forms of evangelism that reached their generation. Today, if we are to see a rebirth of hope where the people are, we must exemplify that pioneering spirit in the great cities of the world.

Pioneering in the City

Pioneering for the gospel has a rich tradition. William Carey (1761–1834) was discouraged by church elders who badly misunderstood God's Word and plan. They refused his request for help to go to India with the comment "When God chooses to win the heathen, He will do it without your help or ours." Perplexed by this attitude, Carey wrote his analysis of missions, called "An Enquiry into the Obligations of Christians to Use Means for the Conversion of the Heathens." His vision was the prelude for an evangelical awakening in Great Britain.

About fifteen years later, in the midst of revivals that were sweeping colleges in the young United States, five college students were aroused by Carey's book. Taking refuge in a haystack during a rain storm, they prayed for God's direction. This unobtrusive haystack prayer meeting resulted in the American Board of Commissioners of Foreign Missions and a mass student missions movement. In the midst of industrialization in Europe and North America, much of the missions emphasis was to begin works among urban dwellers.[2]

Ralph Winter has identified four stages in missionary activity that are applicable to church growth in our cities:

1. *Pioneer.* With few or no believers in the target area, missionaries must lead and do the work themselves.
2. *Parent.* The young church has a growing child's relationship to the mission. The "parent" must teach and nurture but avoid paternalism.
3. *Partner.* The parent-child relationship matures to an adult-adult relationship. Both groups usually find this changing dynamic difficult, but partnership is essential if the church is to mature.
4. *Participant.* A fully mature church assumes leadership. As long as the mission remains it should use its gifts to strengthen the church to meet the objectives of Matthew 28:19–20. Meanwhile, the mission should have become involved in stage one work elsewhere.[3]

As the mission progresses through these stages, there will be hope for all whom the church touches. When this progression is interrupted, hope is interrupted.

South Florida is a playground for much of the United States and Canada. It is also one of the most unchurched areas of the country. According to a 1999 Cable News Network (CNN) report, only the Pacific Northwest has a smaller church attendance. But within this unchurched area, God has planted the New Testament Baptist Church of South Florida, which I serve as senior pastor.

Today our church has two locations, one in northwest Miami and a second approximately twelve miles to the north in an unincorporated area near Fort Lauderdale. And we are not alone. Other churches are springing up in South Florida because there are still so many who need a place called hope. The challenge is to minister to the needs of this great multicultural population with confidence and trust. How do we bring hope to such cultural diversity?

The Myth of Equality

What flashes through your mind when you hear words like illegal immigrant, the Ku Klux Klan, African-American, Cuban, multicultural, Jewish, Latino, red, yellow, black, white, multiracial? More than likely, your response to these words depends on the geographical location of your childhood, the spiritual instruction you received while growing up, and the relationships you fostered throughout your lifetime. In fact, a good part of our belief structure may be more mythical than factual.

Urban evangelist Tony Evans says, "Myths are traditions passed down over time in story form as a means of explaining or justifying events that are lacking in either scientific evidence or historical basis."[4] Myths exist within the church. Consider the belief of many Christians: "All believers are equal under the blood of Jesus Christ, and we in the church treat one another accordingly." Many Christians truly believe that the Church freely incorporates, without reservation, everyone who is a believer. Unfortunately, more often than not, this is a myth. Look around you on Sunday morning. How monocultural is the congregation? Is it because there are no peoples of color in your community? Is it because evangelicalism does not mix with a multicultural congregation? When we see how uncomfortable we are with those who are not just like us, it becomes evident that practical equality in Christ is still a myth.

Two of the highest hurdles to providing hope in the midst of cultural diversity are the hurdles of racism and the condition of the human heart. Racism exists because of the hardness of our sinful hearts and it manifests itself in three ways.

The Three Faces of Racism

The first face of racism is painted by our attitudes, actions, and words. When jokes, threats, or disparaging comments are made about a person of another race, our words reveal a face of ugliness. It is a revelation of who we are down deep. Racial slurs, unkind comments, or verbal threats reveal more about a person than most of us care to have known, even within the church.

In antiquity, there were two kinds of atheism—practical and theoretical atheism. Theoretical atheism was true atheism which denied the existence of God or any gods. It was referred to by the Greek word *asebeia*. Practical atheism, on the other hand, was simply a practical refusal to pay any attention to God or the gods. Here the Greek word was *atheos*. When Socrates walked through a cemetery, he was accused of *atheos*, a practical disregard for what is sacred. I believe this same distinction can be made with racism. When we truly hate another person of another race, that is theoretical racism. It is real. It is deep-seeded hatred. It holds attitudes and beliefs that belittle another person merely because of his or her race.

The second face of racism shows itself in the violence that plagues urban centers. Sometimes this violence is gang related; sometimes it is racially motivated. In the United States, the National Youth Gang Center, in collaboration with the U.S. Department of Justice, says that gang activity is steadily growing in cities. In 1989 only 15 percent of high school students claimed that street gangs operated within their schools. By 1993 that number had risen to 35 percent and it has continued to climb in the years since 1993. Gang activity varies with race, ethnicity, and cultural heritage. For example, in the last survey of high school students, 51 percent of Hispanic students claimed membership in a gang, 42 percent of African-Americans, and 31 percent of Caucasians. Most organized gangs identify with four major groups: the Crips, the Bloods, Folk Nation, and People Nation. The

Crips and the Bloods are Los Angeles-based, while Folk Nation and People Nation are Chicago-based. All four have a growing national identification with groups of young people.

A third face of racism, and perhaps most telling, is the blank face. This is the face that knows something wrong is happening but doesn't want to get involved. It is akin to practical atheism. It's the attitude of a person who just doesn't care, or at least care enough to do something. It is the face of the white moderate who is apathetic about the whole matter, a practical racist.[5] This face may appear to be anonymous, but it is the one we see most often when we look closely into the mirror, for it has tended to be the face of the church during the twentieth century. We have allowed latent racism to keep us from helping an ethnic congregation down the street. We have not spoken up when others, with hatred in their hearts, have spoken out. We are afraid as evangelicals to speak out, because that might mean we are embracing a liberal social gospel. But that is a faulty dichotomy. Jesus certainly did not preach what is now called a "social gospel." He just embraced people—of every kind, every gender, every social strata, every race.

Modern Racism

Though prejudice is as old as fallen humankind, the peculiar sort of racism that plagues North America and parts of Europe today arose in the sixteenth-century European conquests.[6] Spanish soldiers saw the Indians they encountered in the New World as subhuman savages and therefore they were free to enslave or slaughter them. Conquistadors were more than explorers; in many cases they were butchers. As European immigration spread west, the Native Americans who had befriended the early Christians settlers were viewed paternalistically by many who followed them and eventually as threats to the conquest of the West. The result was an increasingly brutal systematic conquering, and at times annihilation, of Native American peoples.

While slavery is an ancient, pervasive fact in world society, the cruelty of slavery as practiced in the United States is a peculiarly despicable chapter in American and Caribbean history. It is more so because many of those who owned and degraded slaves considered themselves Christians. American church history is a mixed record, but in general the church did little to stop, or even supported, the institution. Slavery came to an end only after the most costly war in terms of lives lost ever fought on the continent (1861-65). U.S. President Abraham Lincoln's Emancipation Proclamation ended the practice of theoretical racism, but it did little to end the practice of practical racism.

Despite the specter of potential prejudice, Cuban refugees still flee via rafts to this nation. They are routinely turned back by the U. S. Coast Guard, and their plight is little understood or recognized outside of South Florida. In a Midwestern state where I was preaching, a Christian asked, "What do you do with all of the Cubans down there?" The very question reveals prejudice. "All the Cubans" are people for whom, just like the rest of us, Christ died. The problems of illegal immigration, infectious diseases, and a variety of other social/ethnic questions are debated in the halls of Congress and the corner barbershop. Far less is said within the walls of the church. Where is the hope for these people? When will the church become a place called hope for them?

Every Tribe and Tongue

All human beings are created in God's image and the body of Christ will include Jews and Gentiles of every stripe and color. Those who sang a new song in Revelation 5 were redeemed "out of every tribe and tongue and people and nation" (v. 9). The apostle Paul informs us that Christ's church is "built on the foundation of the apostles and prophets, Jesus Christ Himself being the chief cornerstone, in whom the whole building, being fitted together, grows into a holy temple in the Lord; in whom you also are being built together for a dwelling place of God in the Spirit" (Eph. 2:20-22). The Scriptures teach that the building is harmoniously constructed together in Him, and it is to rise to be a temple that is holy unto the Lord.

How is it possible for Christians to believe in salvation by grace through faith in Christ, to accept the truth that all believers are welcomed into God's family, and yet to attend churches that close their doors to the diverse peoples around them? In my view of Christendom today, the equality of believers under the blood is still a practical myth, and both theoretical and practical racial prejudice continues to hamper our ability to offer hope to all of God's creation.

Scriptural Principles

Can churches in the twenty-first century really become culturally diverse? Not every church serves a culturally diverse community, of course, but we may find our local communities are more culturally diverse than we think. We must get out into our communities and take the love of Christ to everyone we meet, and not just program our churches so that the "right" people are attracted to us. American churches in our post-Christian, postmodern climate must come to grips with our lack of cultural diversity.

If we are to provide concrete hope to those in our communities who are ethnically, culturally, socially, or politically different, two scriptural principles must be understood. The first is that in God's eyes there is only one race—the human race. All of us have descended from a common ancestry, our first parents, Adam and Eve. While differences in language and cultures have come from sin at the Tower of Babel and the resulting dispersion of people throughout the earth, linguistic and cultural differences are not themselves sin. It was the humanistic flexing of muscle at Babel that God condemned. The resulting cultures and languages simply reflect the variety of individuals within the human race. We are still of the same fallen, human race, regardless of culture, color, or language distinctions.

The second scriptural principal is that, through the redemptive work of Christ, the barrier between our relationship with God as well as with each other should be removed. Political persuasion, cultural heritage, financial ability, or skin pigmentation should never exclude anyone from a local assembly of believers. We may hold theological distinctives, but we are not permitted to hold cultural or racial ones. The Bible forbids it. "For as many of you as were baptized into Christ have put on Christ. There is neither Jew nor Greek, there is neither slave nor free, there is neither male nor female; for you are all one in Christ Jesus" (Gal. 3:27–28). It isn't just coincidence that Paul addressed the three categories of race, social status, and gender in this statement. In our world, these are the things that divide us; in Christ, they are to be the things that unite us.

Isn't it time those of us who have concrete hope in Christ provide hope for those around us, those within the very shadow of our church buildings? To accomplish this, we must begin with ourselves and those close to us. We must pray much about our priorities and prejudices and then specifically plan to reach out to a culturally diverse community. It will take all the creativity that God has given us to develop ministry ideas and activities with the ultimate goal of nourishing hope within all the community. It can be done; I've seen it happen. From the experience of New Testament Baptist Church, several methods have been developed to help you make a difference and bring hope to the urban world.

Reaching Diversity Through Diversity

Most active ministries have developed a mission and vision statement. As church trends analyst and social researcher George Barna writes, "Vision transcends time. True visionaries have much in common regardless of when they live. As people of God seek to lead their churches, grasping God's vision for their ministry requires an investment in the vision. Those whom God chooses as leaders can be effective regardless of their lack of worldly qualifications."[7]

Many of today's megachurches focus on a certain target group. Although this may be an effective tactic, it is incredibly shortsighted. It's a great way to build a big church and get lots of media attention, but the result inevitably will be a homogeneous church, a church of look-alike clones. But the church's mission in the twenty-first century must be broad in its appeal if we are to bring hope to the hopeless. Remember that the Great Commission is inclusive—racially, nationally, and economically.

Jewish Population

Rather than adopting a strategy profiling one cultural group, we at New Testament Baptist have determined to reach out to many cultural groups. An example of this "strategy of diversity" is an active ministry to the Jewish population of South Florida. According to

International Baptist Jewish Missions in Chattanooga, Tennessee, there are fifty cities in America with a Jewish population of twenty thousand or more. Miami-Dade County has 535,000, unincorporated Broward County has 63,000, and Fort Lauderdale has 174,000, making a total of 772,000 Jewish friends. According to the 1998 *American Jewish Year Book,* South Florida ranks sixth behind cities like Tel Aviv and New York in total Jewish population. That's quite a mission field. Should we overlook it just because it's Jewish?

We have several missionaries and numerous church personnel who direct "Jewish Roots" classes. Century Village, a well-known retirement community, has ten thousand condo-owners of Jewish heritage. One Jewish couple living at Century Village was led to Christ, and now there are several Bible studies in that village. "To the Jew first" is still a principle of evangelism, because hope is still a need in Jewish hearts.

Hispanic Population

South Florida has an ever-growing Hispanic community. According to the 1990 U.S. census, Hispanics make up 49.2 percent of the population of Miami-Dade County. Our church has a vibrant Spanish ministry in response to the growing need for hope in the Hispanic community. We provide Bible classes in Spanish for those for whom this is their native tongue. One teacher, Jorge Granda, related, "Because of the influx of Hispanics to South Florida, churches in Miami have the awesome responsibility of becoming like the church of Philippi in Asia Minor—an evangelistic church with an open door policy to lost souls of diverse Hispanic backgrounds." Since Cuban and other Hispanic people make up our backyard, they also constitute our mission field. That's the way it always has been in the church.

Gypsy Population

Walter Stevens is a Gypsy. Walter and his family have relocated to South Florida and are building a dynamic ministry to the Gypsies of our community. With the closing of numerous work parlors for the Gypsies in other parts of the country, many migrated to South Florida. One young lady named Carla made a profession of faith in Christ as a teenager. When she was saved, she gave up her fortune telling business. Her husband, although a Christian, became concerned about their financial prospects and pressured her to stay in the fortune telling business. Fortune telling usually earns a six-figure annual income. One Easter night, however, Carla made a decision to leave the business. Gregor, her husband, also agreed and both are now growing in Christ. A new day of hope is dawning for their family. Walter Stevens's ministry to the Gypsies of South Florida is bringing hope to a people who have been without hope for generations.

These are living examples of how a church can minister to pockets of people with the goal of winning them to the Lord and mainstreaming them into the synergy of the church. Our church has grown tremendously because of an outreach that meets people where they are and gives them genuine, concrete hope.

The Vision for the City

Charles Kettering once said, "My interest is in the future because I'm going to spend the rest of my life there." Vision is at the heart of a place called hope. If a ministry has a mission but no vision, it likely will flounder because its perspective is too broad. "Where there is no vision, the people perish" (Prov. 29:18 KJV). The vision provides the ideal image of the church, and when the vision is clearly in focus, it provides the impetus to carry out the mission.

So often churches are circumstantial and self-focused. There is no energy to commit to a vision and focus on a dream beyond the present. Vision is not a program but the result of a process that begins in infancy and is progressively understood. Vision-making involves questions; questions require explanation; and explanation leads to focused understanding. Vision is not a solution to problems, but it helps visualize a new day beyond those problems. Trepidation must give way to vision. And for this to happen, we must recognize that God is the true source of vision.

Having a vision makes the difference. In *Turning Vision into Action*, John Richardson states, "When it comes to the future, there are three kinds of people: those who let it happen, those who make it happen and those who wonder what happened."[8] Which of these three are you? There can be little hope without a large vision.

What We Do

A visionary possesses the ability to share his or her vision with the local church in such a way that members will want to fulfill the God-given dream. The vision determines "what we do" in the ministry. The "what we do" then directs the allocation of church resources. Never mistake "what we do" for "how we do it." Vision is about God's calling for the church—the "what we do." How we do it is about our values and personal preferences. We, the church, must let God's vision take precedence over our preference. When we do this, it is amazing how few conflicts we have with our resources.

The local church must be a place called hope, a place where a fallen King David would be welcomed, where a converted woman of the world like Mary Magdalene would find acceptance, and where a loving leader like the apostle John could feel comfortable sitting next to them. In short, the family of God consists of all kinds of people being accepted into the church. It does not focus on the *way* they came to the church but the *why*. That's when people find hope in cultural diversity. That's when the church becomes a place called hope.

If God is calling you to reach a culturally diverse community with the message of hope, now is the time to take a step of faith into the cities. Habakkuk 2:2–3 says, "Then the LORD answered me and said: 'Write the vision and make it plain on tablets, that he may run who reads it. For the vision is yet for an appointed time; but at the end it will speak, and it will not lie. Though it tarries, wait for it; because it will surely come, it will not tarry.'"

The Need for Hope

The need for a place called hope in the great urban canyons is greater today than at any time in American history. Scattered throughout our cities are the bleached bones of dreams that once had a proud and gallant beginning. Entrepreneurs are everywhere with their dreams. Money is made, buildings erected, people come and go, and a great deal of activity leads nowhere. But the question remains, "What is it all about?" In our world today, it's all about money. But in God's great churches, it's all about hope.

In the cities, you cannot rediscover hope without an awareness and respect for cultural diversity, blended music, and the desire to make a difference. Churches can rediscover hope through working in HIV prevention and AIDS victim care, working in partnership with Christian health services, developing a network with churches and supermarkets to donate food, sponsoring drug counseling centers, and hosting other outreach ministries. Other needs can be met by connecting with teen crisis pregnancy centers, working with other churches to develop youth organizations, and hosting open forums to discuss issues of the day. The only lasting hope for America is to see God at work in people's lives. We must lay aside prejudice and unneeded traditionalism to reach the millions of needy people in cities with the gospel of Jesus Christ.

Conclusion

It is a Sunday morning at our Miami-Dade location. I have just preached the Word, and God's Spirit has convicted lives. The front of the auditorium is packed with people in prayer. As I give the invitation, I notice a young woman kneeling at the altar. Her eyes are red from crying. She motions to me, and I go to her. She says, "Please, I want to be saved!" One of our counselors takes a Bible and shows her that Jesus Christ died to pay the penalty for her sins and to forgive her. For the first time in her life, this young woman has something she can grab hold of and hang on to, something she can count on. For the first time in her life, she has hope.

Multiple cultures are represented among those kneeling at the front of the church, but one thing is true for all of them. No matter what their heritage, their race, their nationality, or their culture, Jesus Christ gives them hope. The beat of diverse hearts, all sharing the love of Jesus Christ, proves to me once again that there is hope for the cities. But that hope lies not in government programs or private enterprise. It is possible to bring hope to cultural diversity, but that hope lies only in the Lord and His Word. That's why urban churches must be a place called hope for all who live in a diverse world of despair.

Chapter Notes

1. *Microsoft Encarta Encyclopedia, 1993–1997*, CD-ROM, s.v. "United States of America."

2. Ralph D. Winter and Steven C. Hawthorne, *Perspectives of the World Christian Movement* (Pasadena, Calif.: William Carey Library, 1992), B-35.

3. Ibid., B-37.

4. Tony Evans, *Let's Get to Know Each Other* (Nashville: Nelson, 1995), 2.

5. Henry Jacobsen, ed., *Facing Today's Problems* (Wheaton, Ill.: Scripture Press, 1970), 159.

6. Ibid.

7. George Barna, *The Power of Vision* (Ventura, Calif.: Regal, 1992), 17.

8. George Barna, *Turning Vision into Action* (Ventura, Calif.: Regal, 1996), 17.

Hope and the Battle with AIDS

Bill Pepper

MY NAME IS BILL PEPPER. I am a pastor, and I have AIDS.

Life is an unpredictable journey. Sometimes the road is smooth, and you sail along in comfort. Other times the road is filled with potholes, and the ride gets bumpy. And every once in a while a storm pounds the road so severely that it is all but washed out. That's when you become discouraged and confused, and hope is all but gone.

I remember the first time I said out loud, "I have AIDS." It was hard. If AIDS (Acquired Immune Deficiency Syndrome) sounds worse than HIV (Human Immunodeficiency Virus), that's because it is. HIV is a virus that causes AIDS, and AIDS causes death. The medical community has identified four stages of this illness. I am in the fourth and final stage.

Over the past twenty years, no other disease has caused more controversy, created more fear, and initiated more global hopelessness than has AIDS. It is a relentless virus that has the power to send every one of its victims to the grave.

This chapter is about my struggle with this dreaded disease, but it also demonstrates that AIDS is not the end. There is help, and there is hope. I have learned that hope is not something I do; it's something I have. Psalm 42:5 asks, "Why are you cast down, O my soul? And why are you disquieted within me? Hope in God, for I shall yet praise Him for the help of His countenance."

In this chapter I share my story of hope to show what it is like to live with AIDS, and what it is like for a Christian to live with AIDS. The physical, emotional, and spiritual trauma must be seen together; they cannot be separated. They also must be seen within the context of the love of my wife, my family, and my friends. Much of my strength has come from the wonderful folks at Grace Bible Church, the people I pastor, and special encouragers like a Jewish lady who helped me. More important than anything else is that, in my greatest trial, God proved Himself to be everything He promised in His Word. God is a God of hope.

My life is fuller and better because I have discovered that hope is a noun. It's what I have, not just what I do. W. H. Griffith Thomas once said, "The corn when green is upright, but when it is ripe it bends low."[1] Since I grew up on a farm, I understand this completely. God used AIDS in my life to bring about a harvest—a harvest of hope in Christ.

The American poet Robert Frost wrote, "Two roads diverged in a wood, and I, I took the one less traveled by, and that has made all the difference."[2] When it comes to AIDS, the road of spiritual and eternal hope is the road less traveled. If you or someone you know is HIV positive or has AIDS, invite them to come with me on the road of hope, the road that has made all the difference.

Life Before AIDS

I was a post-World War II baby, born on July 23, 1949. My folks farmed in Northeastern Pennsylvania. The family farm was a wonderful place to grow up, and the 1950s were good times in America. Our family produced bushels of unconditional love. Life was good. Life was carefree. AIDS was unknown.

In October of 1958, I trusted Jesus Christ as my personal Lord and Savior. Little did I realize on that autumn day what a difference Christ would make in my life.

The 1960s were turbulent years in America, but places like Berkeley, Haight-Asbury, and Saigon seemed far away from our little farm. I enjoyed high school and had a lot of great friends. Following graduation in 1967, I attended a community college for two years and studied architectural drafting. A young farm girl named Patti caught my eye, and I fell hopelessly in love. Soon we were married.

With a young wife to support, I returned to dairy farming. Within the next three years we had two children—a son, Tyler, and a daughter, Holly. We didn't have much money, but we were a million dollar family. We bought a productive little farm near my home, and that tied a nice bow on the whole package of our lives. I couldn't have been happier. What could be better than this—a wonderful wife, two lovely children, a nice family farm? I was living my dream. Life was good.

God's Call

I never expected God to soften my heart toward serving Him, but I felt Him calling me to the ministry. It wasn't something I wanted. I was growing as a Christian, but I was very content on my farm. As I did chores I kept my barn radio tuned to Christian radio station WPEL in Montrose, Pennsylvania. I listened daily to the broadcast teaching of Woodrow Kroll, who was at that time president of Practical Bible College in Binghamton, New York. The school had a fifteen-minute program. Every time I heard that man teach God's Word I wanted to learn more. God used the teaching of His Word to soften my heart toward serving Him. But give up the farm? After months of resisting, I finally yielded to the call of God on my life. My family and I moved to Practical Bible College to prepare for ministry.

I was a student at Practical when I first heard about AIDS on the evening news. I listened, but AIDS was something I'd never have to deal with. None of the people in my church would ever have AIDS. We Christians sometimes think that we can skirt the potholes on life's journey. The book of Job teaches us that we are not exempt from

I was physically exhausted; I was emotionally drained. This condition lasted for about six weeks. I don't remember how much weight I had lost by January 1, 1997, but for the first time in years I was thin enough to see my bones. I had almost no appetite. The loss of appetite was something new. I was the chocolate king; now I was never hungry.

By that Easter I was skinny. In the midst of all this physical change, my mind needed some rock-solid hope to grab hold of. So I was glad that Jesus never changes. I clung to Hebrews 13:8: "Jesus Christ is the same yesterday, today, and forever." My immutable Savior, my constant companion, my hope was there for me. The words to "Abide with Me," the tender hymn by Henry F. Lyte (1793–1847) often flooded my mind:

> Swift to its close ebbs out life's little day;
> Earth's joys grow dim, its glories pass away;
> Change and decay in all around I see;
> O Thou, who changest not, abide with me.

In late April I developed a dry-cough. With the dramatic weight loss and attendant problems, I decided to see another doctor. He diagnosed the cough as the result of allergies and said, "Get some over-the-counter medicine. You'll be okay." Buoyed by this reassurance, I didn't think much of the cough. It was like another small pothole on life's journey. I'd get over it. But I didn't.

The coughing continued. I was using cough drops like a junkie. On June 8, 1997, a Sunday morning, I woke up feeling unusually weak. Everything was in a fog. The title of my sermon for that Sunday was, "God Has a Plan for Your Life!" Little did I realize just how much I would need my own sermon, but I could not preach that morning.

The Chasm

By now my family doctor and I were on a first-name basis. I called him and he said, "If you feel you are in trouble, go to the emergency room." My associate pastor took the morning service, and Patti whisked me to the hospital. The people there didn't waste any time. Upon arrival a doctor gave me oxygen and took x-rays of my lungs. The diagnosis was PCP, pneumocystis carinii pneumonia.

My doctor suggested that I have an HIV test. I was stunned. An HIV test? What for? Patti and I held hands and prayed as we have never prayed before. We prayed with tears, in shock over the doctor's suggestion.

Good friends in the church, Roger and Patty, joined us at the hospital and did everything they could to encourage us. Roger read the book of Habakkuk to me, and my tears flowed when he came to chapter two verse four: "The just shall live by his faith." Habakkuk was a doubter, the Thomas of the Old Testament. Suddenly I was in their company. With my whole life being rocked, could I trust God with my prayers about HIV? Could I live by faith now that I'd entered the darkest, coldest winter of my life?

Habakkuk's doubts had turned to faith. Roger read chapter three, verses seventeen and eighteen: "Though the fig tree may not blossom, nor fruit be on the vines; though the labor of the olive may fail, and the fields yield no food; though the flock may be cut off from the fold, and there be no herd in the stalls—yet I will rejoice in the LORD, I will joy in the God of my salvation." Habakkuk had experienced a profound truth; when things aren't going our way, God is still good. It's an easy lesson, until you have to live it. I was a pastor. I had a good life. My family and our church family were wonderful people. And now this. If the tests didn't turn out the way I prayed they would, would I still call God good? Could God still be my hope, even if everything looked hopeless? Questions flooded my mind. Answers, however, did not.

It took two days to get the results from the HIV test. They seemed like an eternity. A dark cloud had spread over my blue skies, and I was getting weaker by the minute. My family rallied at my bedside. The prospects looked bleak, and I felt hope slipping away. I was alone when my doctor gave me the news.

Life with AIDS

"Bill, there's no easy way to tell you this. Your HIV test is positive. You have full-blown AIDS."

The doctor continued to talk, but I heard nothing else. My mind went numb. It was the most hopeless moment in my life. Finally, my doctor sat down in the chair beside me. He said he was sorry, and then he cursed God and started to cry. I said, "It's okay, Doc, everything will be just fine." He had no hope to offer me and nothing but disgust for a God who would allow this to happen to me. I was still in shock and not ready to respond to him. The doctor left the room.

I thought, *How will Patti take this news. What will become of her? Who will take care of her?* When she arrived, in my bravest voice I told her the news. Her response was something none of us could have predicted. With trembling voice she said, "Don't worry. I'm here. You won't have to die alone." Those words will echo in my mind until I draw my last breath.

Patti put her head on my chest and prayed out loud, thanking God for His love, His mercy, and His grace. When she finished praying, we didn't know what to do. We just held each other and wept. I'd been ill for the past year, but it felt like we had only now recognized the peril. The bridge was out, and we had just driven off the edge of the road into a bottomless chasm. We couldn't say it immediately, but we both knew it. My journey was over. Soon my life would be over too.

A Resignation to Die

I felt dirty in my despair. As soon as the numbness wore off, my mind was filled with all the usual questions about AIDS. "Can I give it to my family by hugging them or by holding their hands? Could they get AIDS by breathing the air in my room? Should they stay away from me?" Some of those questions now sound foolish, but the mind plays many tricks on you when you are hanging by a thread at the edge of despair.

After all the "what ifs," the fundamental question remained: How did I become HIV-positive in the first place? I was a pastor. I had never been unfaithful to my wife. I was not a drug-user. The typical means of transmitting the HIV virus were never a part of my life. How could this happen to me? The doctors questioned me and were able to discern the probable cause of my disease.

During the 1980s I was taking my children to a roller skating party. As I drove along a country road on this moonlit night we came upon the scene of a terrible accident. I told the kids, "Stay here in the car!" A young man was screaming for his three friends. I thought he was in shock, but later found out he was high on drugs. I made him sit on a bank, and I started looking for the others in this bloody scene. With flashlight in hand I found two in a ditch approximately fifty feet from the overturned car. Both were dead. An old man from a nearby farm soon appeared and said he would call for help. I looked frantically for the last victim.

I shined my flashlight under the crushed vehicle. There was a pool of blood but there was also a body. My instincts made me crawl underneath. The broken glass and twisted metal cut my hands. I tried to pull the person out, but when I did his head turned, and blood gushed out from the partially decapitated head. I was covered with blood. Soon others stopped to help and the emergency crew arrived. I remember how numb I was as I drove back home to get cleaned up and tend to my wounds. Later we learned that all four of these victims were drug users and companions of a known drug dealer. I had no idea what that would mean for me.

Throughout the months of sickness I had been puzzled by what was causing all my health problems. Now I knew. But somehow in my despair the Lord gave me peace. I learned the full meaning of Isaiah 26:3: "Thou wilt keep him in perfect peace, whose mind is stayed on thee: because he trusteth in thee" (KJV). The doctors gave me just six to fourteen days to live. I found out what my ailment was—just in time to die.

A Family United

I was taken to the PACT (Pittsburgh AIDS Center for Treatment) clinic at the University of Pittsburgh Medical Center via Med-I-Van. Many doctors examined me and talked with my family. Patti never left my side. Her support was incredible. My son, Tyler, and his wife, Kim, and their daughter, Lydia, were there. Our daughter, Holly, and her husband, Tim, and their daughters, Ivy and Alivia, stood by my bed. We all knew what was inevitable. We all felt helpless, waiting for me to die. I expected someone to quote Job 2:9: "Curse God and die!"

But we are a family who are prisoners of hope (Zech. 9:12). Instead of hopelessly giving up, my family gave me hope. They read the Bible to me, and we prayed together constantly. Sometimes the prayers were silent; sometimes out loud. They often cried with me. My family did the three most important things anyone can do for an HIV/AIDS patient—read Scripture, pray together, and cry together. Believe me, those three things helped me immeasurably in the earliest days of my nightmare.

Because of my enormous weight loss—the phase called the wasting-syndrome—I had lost all my fat reserves. When there is no more fat, the wasting-syndrome consumes muscle mass. One of the PACT doctors informed me that soon my main body system would shut down, and regardless of what machines, procedures, or medicine were available, they would be unable to save me. My immune system was so severely suppressed they had nothing to work with in my body. Bottom line? It was hopeless.

I hated to leave my precious family. I am a fighter by nature, but I had no energy left with which to fight this illness. It would soon win anyway. Strange, isn't it, how even we Christians put off things we should have done years before. Hurriedly I made a will, bought a cemetery plot, and made my funeral arrangements. I was resigned to the inevitable. It wouldn't be long now before I would be with Christ. I had learned enough about advanced AIDS to know that the doctors could give me no hope.

The Will to Live

Then one day Dr. Debra McMahon told us about some new drugs that the FDA (Federal Drug Administration) had approved just months earlier. They were called protease inhibitors. They had been proven to suppress the virus in some HIV/AIDS patients. If they worked in me, I might live six months. My children wanted me to try them. I refused. Why prolong the inevitable? I hung on to my belief that it would soon be over. But it's not over until God says it's over.

As a pastor, I had counseled many people who were terminally ill, urging them to fight their illness: "Never give up. God doesn't want you to give up." But what I had told others to do, I found myself unable to do. I didn't want to face the world as a person with AIDS. I knew what the Christian community would think. I knew my life and heart, but did they? How would people treat me? What would they whisper behind my back? Would they prefer not to be near me? Would they be afraid of contracting HIV from me? I now know how the lepers from biblical days felt. Unclean! Unclean!

There was only one island of safety: I found comfort in my Savior, Jesus Christ. I know this is hard to understand fully, but I actually felt Him holding me in His strong and caring arms. He held me tightly to His chest and I felt safe and secure. His abiding presence gave me peace.

My daughter, Holly, came to my hospital room alone. She stood at the foot of my bed, sobbing. "Dad," she said, "you just can't die, I'm not ready to let you go! I'm going to have another baby, and I want you to live long enough to hold it at least one time."

Suddenly a vibration of hope stirred within me. Should I try? Was there a glimmer of hope shining in my room? Was it possible that I could live through the night? Was there any reason to hope? Isn't it amazing how God brings the right people into our lives at just the right time? In my despair all I could think about was holding my unborn grandchild. You know what I've discovered about hope? Hope spreads. It multiplies. Christians everywhere began praying for God to do the impossible. If it were His will, I might be spared. Could I beat this thing? I didn't know, but I had to try.

Even with renewed hope, I was getting worse. For two days and two nights I felt my life slipping away. It was just about midnight on the second night that I took a turn for the worst. I had difficulty breathing. A kind and compassionate nurse stayed at my side until 5:30 that morning. My condition looked bleak, but about the time the light signaled the dawn outside, some light dawned inside me, too. I began to experience relief. My breathing wasn't normal, but it wasn't so labored either. I couldn't explain it, and neither could my doctors.

Several days later I received a letter from a dear lady in our church.

Linda said she woke up around midnight on the very night I was so ill. She prayed for me for almost an hour, then she went back to bed. But she couldn't sleep so she continued to pray. In fact, she prayed all night and didn't quit until—5:30. Then she felt like God was telling her that everything was okay. Linda didn't know how critical my condition was during those hours. She only knew that she needed to pray.

Later that morning when my doctor arrived she said, "Bill, you need to get back into life. Are you going to try this new medicine or not?" I said, "I'll give it a shot." It would have been so much easier to die. But now I was determined to hold on to life. My long night of despair was over. Hope was reborn.

Medicine—and More Medicine

My immune system had been so thoroughly destroyed that it reached the point where it could not recover. The permanent damage that occurred allowed many different types of illness and disease to infiltrate my body. I had developed everything except lymphatic cancer. As a result of these diseases, I took pills on top of pills. The nutritionist nagged me to eat, but I said, "How could I be hungry; every hour it's like I'm eating from a medication buffet."

I tolerated most of the medications quite well, but the protease inhibitors were a different story. I was so far gone that my doctors prescribed the maximum dosage. This medication is highly toxic, so I had to drink gallons of water with them. That in itself was a chore. Then once I worked my way up to the full dosage, I would be on these drugs the rest of my life. Building up to the maximum dosage took several weeks. At least I was alive.

Protease inhibitors are like cowboys riding through the blood stream, corralling the HIV into already infected cells. If the roundup is done effectively, the virus becomes undetectable. However, the virus is always trying to get out of infected cells to infect good cells. Not only does this nasty virus try to break out of the infected cells, it also makes new mutations of itself. From the first day of infection, HIV makes about a billion copies of itself every twenty-four hours. "It is absolutely imperative that you never miss a medication," my doctor said. The amount of medicine I was taking made me nauseous. The road to recovery appeared to be a million miles long. I was trapped in a long, hard winter.

Different combinations of drugs work best in different people. It's not unusual for the doctors to have difficulty finding the correct combination. My body rejected one type immediately, but within a week the proper combination for me was found. Often it can take months or even years to get this adjustment right. But time was a luxury I did not have. Again, God was so good to me. I managed to start the drug therapy quickly, and my body responded immediately. Hope continued to grow, even in winter.

Weakness, Dad's Cane, and Night Sweats

By this time I had lost ninety-six pounds. I looked like I had been a prisoner of war—a skeleton with skin. It took fifteen minutes for me to shave with an electric razor while seated in a chair. That chore was followed by a two-hour nap. All my muscle mass was gone. Since the days when I was young, Psalm 46:1 has been a special verse for me. Now it became my primary verse: "God is our refuge and strength, a very present help in trouble."

My sister and niece came to Pittsburgh and brought my father's cane to me. Dad had died of cancer in 1986. He had several canes in the later part of his life and now one of them was mine. Somehow that cane took me back to my boyhood days on the farm. It supported me physically when I walked, but it supported me emotionally, too. It was as if my dad were with me again. I even slept with that cane in the months that followed. It not only took me home, it brought me hope.

Sleeping wasn't easy. I was experiencing wrenching night sweats. You don't get much sleep when your bedding is changed two or three times each night. Because of some of the medications, I had almost constant fever, sometimes reaching 103 degrees. At times I had to be packed in ice. I can understand why Job wished he had died at birth, so that "I would have been carried from the womb to the grave" (Job 10:19). The struggle seemed futile and endless.

The Sidewalk Shuffle

Following my discharge from the hospital, I had to stay in Pittsburgh. Patti and I got an apartment in a predominately Jewish community. Each day I would sit at the window and watch an old Jewish woman care for the flowers that surrounded her house. When I was finally finished with all the IV medications, I decided (with the prompting of my doctors) to begin walking. I convinced Patti that I could walk outside by myself. So early one morning at around six, with Dad's cane in hand, I made my way outside in the cool summer air. She didn't know I knew, but Patti watched me from the window, holding her breath with each step. When I reached the sidewalk I glanced at the lovely flower garden across the street.

My walking gait was more like a shuffle than a walk. I noticed people jogging and power walking. They seemed swift as hares, and I felt a bit embarrassed, creeping like a turtle. A man jogged toward me, and when he got next to me I politely said, "Good morning." He turned his head away from me. I thought, *Somehow he knows I have AIDS, and he doesn't even want to acknowledge that I exist!* This rejection felt horrible and brought tears to my eyes.

I hadn't shuffled more than five more steps when a voice behind me said, "Good morning, beautiful day to be alive, isn't it." I looked slightly to my left as the old Jewish woman with the flowers gave me a nod. I responded with, "Oh, yes it is, it's a great day." Little did she know how much I needed that. It's amazing how God uses the little things of life in a very big way. That dear lady's simple greeting was used of God to strengthen the hope He had put within me. Her flowers brought me joy; her words brought me hope.

Going Public

Because I am a pastor and work with people all the time, the social workers and the team of doctors in Pittsburgh thought it would be unwise for me to go public with my disease. I knew they had my best interest at heart, but I could not keep my diagnosis private. I felt compelled to tell the world about the hope that God gave me in the midst of my darkest winter. We all know what most people suspect when they learn a person is HIV-positive or has AIDS, and many people harbor irrational fears concerning the disease. I had no idea how my church or my Christian friends would respond to the news.

We decided to compose a statement, and my dear friend, Dr. Chick Kiloski, would read it to my church. Chick pastored a church in Altoona, Pennsylvania, a neighboring town to Holidaysburg where I pastored. His daughter, Kim, is my daughter-in-law.

The response of folks at Grace Bible Church was overwhelming. First, they continued to pray and did everything they could to encourage us. Then they took an offering to help us with temporary expenses. The deacon board gave me a three-month sabbatical with pay. When we got home after three weeks in Pittsburgh, cards and letters filled with love and concern poured in. One day I received 121 cards. In the weeks that followed Patti and I received more than three thousand cards! Those were three thousand messages of hope. The ladies of the church provided all our meals. The men of the church mowed our lawn. Others gave us fresh produce weekly. Whatever our need, the body of Christ met it. Many AIDS patients are helped by a support group. I didn't need one. My support group was my church. Going public with AIDS gave them the opportunity to rally to my side and express hope in very tangible ways.

Cans of Creamed Corn and Cardinals

Eventually my appetite returned, but weight gain was slow. My muscle tissue was so depleted that my arms looked like single strands of spaghetti. It was difficult to lift anything, but I had to start rebuilding muscle. My daughter-in-law, Kim, suggested I use fifteen-ounce cans of creamed corn. I lay on the sofa with a can in each hand. After lifting the cans into the air three times I broke out in a sweat. The next day I pushed myself to four repetitions, then five. With each step of progress, hope strengthened. Some folks in the church bought me ten-pound weights, and soon I was lifting them. Slowly but steadily, I grew stronger with each passing day.

God continued to build my hope as He built my strength. Sometimes He would use the smallest things to strengthen hope. I asked Patti to fill the bird feeder. I had always enjoyed watching the birds come and eat. After several days I noticed a beautiful cardinal one morning at the feeder. I called Patti to come and look at this bird. It was a prettier red than I had ever seen before. To Patti it was just a cardinal, the same color as all the others, but not to me. The depth of red was more brilliant and more magnificent than I had ever seen before. A cardinal at the bird feeder was God's messenger to teach me that everything in life was becoming more precious again. Even everyday events had become marvelous moments of joy for me.

One day it rained, and I did something I've never before had the urge to do. I went outside, looked up, and just let the rain fall into my face. While enjoying this gift of God's hope I remembered that when I was a boy my mother asked me, "Don't you have enough sense to come in out of the rain?" On this day, I didn't *want* to come in out of the rain. This may have been my last chance to let the rain fall into my face. I wanted to enjoy it. AIDS changed my life, and a positive outcome of this disease is that I try to make every moment count. I take nothing for granted, especially my relationship with Christ.

Making a Difference

After three months of recovery I was eager to start preaching again. If God would just permit me to open His Word and minister to my people again, how thrilling that would be. I was scheduled to give it a try on the first Sunday of September. But in my eagerness, I surprised the church by starting a week early. Months before I had planned to deliver the sermon, "God Has a Plan for Your Life." Now the message was modified somewhat, because the preacher who delivered it was different from the one who had written it. Praise God that I had enough energy to get through the service. That in itself was a miracle, but God wasn't through with His miracles.

The next day a lady from the church called. Her son had been visiting for the weekend. He attended church with her and listened to my message. Following the service, he revealed to her that his wife had left him, and that he had come back to see his mother for one final time. He planned to return to his home to commit suicide. He added, "If God has a plan for Pastor Pepper's life, then I know He's got one for me!" He was going to try to work things out with his wife, and trust God to put their lives back together.

I'm so thankful that God uses His Word to repair broken people. I was so grateful that He was allowing me to make a difference in the lives of others. Life was good again.

Life with Hope

A few months later, Patti and I went to Glen Falls, New York, for the birth of my daughter, Holly's, baby—my "Job-experience grand-daughter." This was the baby for whom my daughter had so desperately wanted me to live. On January 28, 1998, I held in my arms, for the first time, Eliza Rae Tangen. Delicate and dainty, she was so special. I wanted to name her Hope, for that's what she brought to me. I held her close and told her "Jesus loves you." Then I said something I thought I'd never live to say. "I'm your granddad, and I love you, too." The whisper of hope that she had brought to me months before she had even been born was now full blown. God had done the impossible. I had survived full-blown AIDS. And He had given me full-blown *hope.*

> Behold, I have refined you, but not as silver; I have tested you
> in the furnace of affliction. (Isaiah 48:10)

Five months following treatment, my virus went into suppression. My CD4 (T-cell) count is now above 500, which is why I am experiencing such normal, strong health. I'm faithful at taking my medications, and with each dosage I ask the Lord to bless it—and me—with the miracle of life. I have lots of energy and a growing family. Granddaughter number five, Mara Faith Pepper, was born June 9, 1999. Whereas once I didn't have time to live, now I don't have time to die!

The Apostle of Hope

I am still the senior pastor at Grace Bible Church. But now I am more. I am the apostle of hope. I have the unique privilege of sharing my hope in Christ in a very special way. In October I led a man who has AIDS to Christ. He was in a nursing home and had no hope for the future. Now he does. Just last week I spoke on the phone to a young woman who has AIDS. She has two small children who are not

HIV-positive. This young mother is not a Christian; Patti and I plan to visit her. I'm involved in a research group at the University of Pittsburgh Medical Center. Recently I spoke to approximately five hundred students and medical personnel at a medical school seminar at the university. A Jewish lady was full of questions following the lecture, mostly about Jesus, my Messiah.

I often tell people, "Keep in mind that hope in the Bible is not a self-produced feeling of encouragement that is imaginary, nor is it wishful thinking. A Christian's hope is built on the solid foundation of the character of God and the Word of God. It is this hope that Job demonstrated when he said of God, "though He slay me, yet will I trust (hope) in Him" (Job 13:15).[3]

Medical science continues to make strategic breakthroughs, but will there ever be a cure for AIDS? Maybe not. I'm prepared for whatever God has in store for me. I am living with a God who saved me, with a family and church who love me, and with a noun that sustains me. That noun is hope. Someday I will likely die because of my weakened immune system. I don't know how many more miles I will travel on life's highway, but I've already seen the miracle of hope performed on my behalf. I have my Savior, Jesus Christ, to walk beside me and once again, life is good.

What AIDS Cannot Do

An unknown author wrote the following about cancer, but I have survived something even more deadly, and find these words to be true of AIDS as well:

> AIDS is limited.
> It cannot cripple love.
> It cannot shatter hope.
> It cannot corrode faith.
> It cannot eat away peace.
> It cannot destroy confidence.
> It cannot kill friendships.
> It cannot shut out memories.
> It cannot silence courage.

It cannot invade the soul.
It cannot reduce eternal life.
It cannot quench the Spirit.
It cannot lessen the power of the resurrection.

Today I face the future with hope. AIDS has not destroyed my life. I have discovered that AIDS is not the end. "For You are my hope, O Lord God: You are my trust from my youth" (Ps. 71:5).

My name is Bill Pepper. I am a pastor, and I have AIDS. But I have something even more tangible—I have *hope*.

Chapter Notes

1. W. H. Griffith Thomas, *St. Paul's Epistle to the Romans: A Devotional Commentary* (Grand Rapids: Eerdmans, 1946), 345.
2. Robert Frost, "The Road Not Taken," in *The Norton Anthology of American Literature,* ed. Nina Baym (New York: W. W. Norton, 1989), 1726.
3. Warren W. Wiersbe, *Meet Yourself in the Psalms* (Wheaton Illinois: Victor Books, 1984), 94-95.

Hope for the Troubled Heart

Woodrow Kroll

NO TWO WORDS IN THE ENGLISH language are more devastating than *No hope*. In his *Essays on Man*, the eighteenth-century English poet Alexander Pope said, "Hope springs eternal in the human breast."[1] But for some people, spring has turned to winter and grows bleaker by the day. For these people life is hopeless, and there's no way out.

Your fifteen-year-old daughter's room is ominously silent. You find her lifeless body draped across her bed, on the floor an empty pill bottle. She left behind a suicide note. She isn't popular, she doesn't look like the models in her teen magazines, and her relationship with her boyfriend is going from bad to worse. She suspects he's seeing someone else. She sees no reason to go on, and she ends her note with the words, *No hope*.

You're awakened out of a sound sleep at 3:10 A.M. You don't recognize the voice on the other end of the telephone. It's the hospital calling. Your son has been in a terrible automobile accident and is in surgery. You rush to the hospital emergency room only to be met by a physician who utters two words: *No hope.*

Your marriage is on the rocks. You and your husband have been drifting apart for a long time. Actually, you haven't really been husband and wife for months. He says he has to work late two nights a week, but his alibi is hardly convincing. One night when he comes home you confront him in order to bring some sense back into your marriage. His devastating reply is that he doesn't love you anymore, hasn't for years. His final response to your tearful pleas is, "No hope."

Maybe you feel like that ancient sage, Job. When everything in life had gone sour for him he said, "My days are swifter than a weaver's shuttle, and are spent without hope" (Job 7:6).

Finding Real Hope

If hope seems to be in short supply these days, maybe it's because we have lost the focus of eternal hope. Maybe it's time we looked for hope beyond ourselves. I know that doesn't sound politically correct, and it clearly doesn't have a New Age ring to it. But maybe for you it has a ring of truth.

Hope is not an emotion that wells up within when our circumstances are favorable. Hope is a concrete state of heart and mind when we are living in a dynamic relationship with God. Paul prayed that the "God of hope" would fill his Christian friends at Rome "with all joy and peace" (Rom. 15:13). That sounds like the kind of relationship we'd all like. What's more, that kind of relationship is possible. And it's tragic that today so many live without hope.

Living Without Hope

I think the greatest expression of hopelessness in ancient literature was penned by the apostle Paul to the Ephesian Christians. He was describing their life before they had trusted Christ Jesus as Savior. This apt description, found in Ephesians 2:12, says that "at that time you were without Christ, being aliens from the commonwealth of Israel and strangers from the covenants of promise, having *no hope* and without God in the world" (emphasis added).

Two expressions in Paul's words are inexorably linked: *without God* and *no hope.* As Gentiles, these people of Ephesus, on the western coast of Asia Minor (now Turkey), didn't have any of the privileges of being the chosen people of God. They were aliens from Israel's benefits and strangers to God's covenants. But even worse, as unbelievers, they were without hope because they were without a dynamic relationship with God. It's that simple: No God, no hope.

What's true for the ancient people of Ephesus is true for us today. No God, no hope. None of us has escaped this hopelessness. Read how inclusive the language is. "There is none righteous, no, not one" (Rom. 3:10). "There is none who does good, no, not one" (v. 12). "For all have sinned and fall short of the glory of God (v. 23). Hopelessness, then, is not just *our* problem; it's a universal problem, because sin is a universal problem. When people say "It's hopeless" and "I can't go on," they're right. Apart from God, all is hopeless. Sin has captured us all and made us hopeless cases.

God Brings Hope

But God doesn't buy the idea of hopelessness. "With God all things are possible" (Matt. 19:26). God is the God of hope, the God of the impossible. He can bring hope to you in the midst of your hopelessness. One of my favorite Christmas carols tell how.

When Phillips Brooks was pastor at Holy Trinity Church in Philadelphia he visited the Holy Land in 1865. He enjoyed a Christmas eve service at the Church of the Nativity in Bethlehem. Three years later he looked for a special Christmas carol for the children of the church to sing at the Christmas program. Recalling the peaceful village of Bethlehem he quickly penned the words to "O Little Town of Bethlehem."

If you are badgered by a sense of hopelessness, read carefully the first stanza of this wonderful Christmas hymn. You've sung it hundreds of times, but did you take notice of what it said?

> O little town of Bethlehem, how still we see thee lie!
> Above thy deep and dreamless sleep the silent stars go by;
> Yet in thy dark streets shineth the everlasting Light;
> *The hopes and fears of all the years are met in thee tonight.*

That night in the little town of Bethlehem an angel informed the shepherds, "For there is born to you this day in the city of David a Savior, who is Christ the Lord" (Luke 2:11). God met your fears with His hopes in the person of a baby, born in a stable and laid in a manger. The hope God brings to a hopeless world is His Son—Jesus Christ.

Faith Makes Hope Possible

In the book of Acts, the apostle Paul and his coworker Silas were imprisoned in the Greek city of Philippi for preaching the gospel. They were put into the inner prison and fastened in foot stocks to make sure they didn't escape. But suddenly, at midnight, a mighty earthquake struck, and the prison doors flew open. Their chains fell off, and they were free. It was the perfect opportunity to make their getaway. In fact, when the prison guard saw the devastation the earthquake had caused, he naturally assumed that all the prisoners had already made their escape. He decided to commit suicide rather than face the Roman authorities. The situation looked hopeless. He was doomed. But he failed to take into account that God is the God of the impossible. When he called for a torch to see if Paul and Silas had fled, to his surprise he saw them seated, a bit dusty and rattled from the earthquake, but there nonetheless. In the despair of hopelessness the jailer asked, "Sirs, what must I do to be saved?" and their classic answer was, "Believe on the Lord Jesus Christ, and you will be saved, you and your household" (Acts 16:31).

It is faith in Jesus Christ as Savior and Lord that fosters hope in the midst of hopelessness. If you do not trust what Jesus did at Calvary to be all that God required to pay the debt for your sin, I cannot offer you any hope. Life will be, as Macbeth said, "a tale, told by an idiot, full of sound and fury, signifying nothing." But faith fosters hope. Faith in Jesus to cleanse you from the hopelessness of your sin will produce "full assurance of hope until the end" (Heb. 6:11). Cleansing from sin does not come by any righteous things you can do for yourself (Titus 3:5), but "according to His mercy He saved us" and thus "having been justified by His grace we should become heirs according to the hope of eternal life" (v. 7).

When thirteenth-century Italian poet Dante Alighieri wrote his *Divine Comedy*, he depicted hell as a most terrible place. In *The Inferno's* description of hell, Dante said, "These words I saw inscribed in dark characters over a gateway, therefore I said: 'Master, their sense is dreadful to me.'" The words were *Abandon every hope, ye that enter.*[2]

Without faith in Jesus Christ as Savior, there is no hope of eternal life spent anywhere except in the inferno. But when Jesus Christ comes into your life, hope comes in too. If the Savior is kept at bay, kept outside of your life, you have also kept hope out of your life. The decision is yours. Make sure it's the right one.

Jesus Christ Gives Living Hope

Life is filled with challenges, nasty and nice. Even when you believe in Jesus Christ as Savior, those challenges continue. In fact, they may get even more nasty. You've read about some of them in the preceding chapters. But the same One who is your hope gives you hope. The apostle Peter praised God for this hope:

> Blessed be the God and Father of our Lord Jesus Christ, who according to His abundant mercy has begotten us again to a living hope through the resurrection of Jesus Christ from the dead, to an inheritance incorruptible and undefiled and that does not fade away, reserved in heaven for you, who are kept by the power of God through faith for salvation ready to be revealed in the last time. (1 Peter 1:3–5)

Jesus gives us a living hope, a hope that is now and forever alive. We have hope in this life because Jesus Christ is our Hope. That's present hope, concrete hope, the kind of hope that grows, even in the winter seasons of life.

When Things Are Going Our Way

King David was my kind of guy. When I need a shot in the arm, I usually read one or more of his psalms. He really knew how to pick you up. In Psalm 16:5–6 he said, "O Lord, You are the portion of my inheritance and my cup; You maintain my lot. The lines have fallen to me in pleasant places; yes, I have a good inheritance." Obviously David wrote this when things were going his way. He was on the top of his game. He came to the conclusion that the Lord Himself was his portion of the inheritance.

The word *portion* means a share or a part of something. When Joshua divided up the Promised Land among the tribes of Israel, each tribe, each family, each person got a portion. It was his share (see the last ten chapters of Joshua). The same was true when Israel defeated their bitter enemy Amalek and the soldiers scooped up the spoils of war (1 Sam. 15:21). It became their portion, their inheritance, their payment for fighting off the enemy and being victorious.

When the U.S. Women's Soccer team won the World Cup in 1999, the whole world (actually 91 million viewers) watched the match and held its breath. The United States and China fought to a zero to zero tie at the end of regulation time. It wasn't until Brandi Chastain booted a perfectly placed free kick into the net that the American jubilation began. Until that time, there was just a lot of nail biting. Each member of the team not only received the adoration of Americans everywhere and the respect of the world; they also received a lot of cash. It was their portion, their inheritance for winning the World Cup.

Imagine fighting a hard-fought spiritual battle during your life. You fight the Devil, tooth and nail. You withstand serious temptation. You do the right things and you wonder if it has been worth it. And then you stand on the raised dais to receive your share of the inheritance and you discover, much to your eternal glee, that your "portion" is the Lord Himself. He is the big prize, and you've won. God told Abraham, "I am your shield, your exceedingly great reward" (Gen. 15:1). That's what "The Lord is my portion," means. Jesus Christ is our reward. He gives us hope when things are going our way and "the lines have fallen in pleasant places."

When Things Aren't Going Our Way

But things don't always go our way. The lines sometimes look like spaghetti, and the places aren't always pleasant. We don't know which way is up. The sky is dark and prospects are dim. That's when we really need hope, and Jesus Christ specializes in giving us hope on those occasions.

Think back through the chapters you've just read. In almost every case, winter had taken hold of the author's heart. But Don McNeal found hope when he was embarrassed before millions of football fans in Super Bowl XVII. The whole world watched as he missed the tackle of his life. Michael Peck and his wife had two children, adopted eight children, and raised fifteen foster children. Together they discovered that they could love hard-to-love people and love them unconditionally because Jesus gave them hope. They would find it nowhere else. George Miller burrowed through family problems to discover hope, and came out the other end with a stronger family relationship. Don Hall suffered the death of one of his twin boys while serving God on the mission field, but he also discovered the God of hope during those difficult days. Carol Miller battled back from cancer, and God gave her the hope to minister to other victims' needs. Bill Pepper learned that hope sustains the believer when AIDS nearly took his life. And the list goes on.

Each of these chapters has been a story of hope, hope that grows even in the winter of the heart, hope that is a noun. Each person found Jesus Christ to be a real hope in their lives, not phantom hope. Any one of these people could have said with David, "I cry out to the LORD with my voice. . . . I pour out my complaint before Him; I declare before Him my trouble. When my spirit was overwhelmed within me. . . . Refuge has failed me. No one cares for my soul." Those are David's words in Psalm 142:1–4. But in the middle of that psalm something wonderful happens. David recovers hope: "You are my refuge, my portion in the land of the living. . . . Bring my soul out of prison, that I may praise Your name; . . . for You shall deal bountifully with me" (vv. 5–7).

When things aren't going our way, that's when we especially need to see Jesus Christ as our "portion," as David and the authors of this book did. That's what you need too. Discover the hope that only the Lord Jesus can give you. It will change your cry of despair into a shout of hope.

Hope During Life's Dark Times

Let's face it. All of us go through dark seasons. Each author in this book has experienced, in his or her own way, the darkest winter. But each one also experienced a concrete hope during those low times. It was when the dark times came that hope came. That's when they discovered that hope is something you have, not something you do. Hope is a noun.

When you experience one of the scenarios at the beginning of this chapter, when your whole world walks out the door and leaves you, when the report from the doctor is less than perfect, when people dear to you disappoint you, when dark times come—that's when you need hope the most.

John and Bobbi Bare went through dark times. John was a good man. He worked hard to provide for his family and was faithful in his local church. But years ago John's first wife suddenly left him and smashed his private and public world. His heartache was exponentially increased because John's wife left him for a woman. Bobbi didn't fare much better. After years of marriage, her husband also walked out on her. Ironically, Bobbi's husband left her for a man. Emotionally broken and spiritually bruised, John and Bobbi lived lives of sorrow and self-imposed shame for years. Then one day, God in His grace brought them together and gave each one hope. It was as if God said to them, "I love you both very much. I know how difficult your winter season has been. You have been faithful to Me, and I want you to experience all the joy of finding hope in each other." John and Bobbi were both victims of sinful spouses. Now they are "prisoners of hope" (Zech. 9:12), and the joy of the Lord is written all over their faces.

Never Give Up Hope

Victor Frankl, the Viennese psychiatrist who was long held in a Nazi concentration camp, once addressed an audience. He told them about his frightening experiences under Hitler's boot. But then he said, "Others gave up hope. I dreamed that someday I would be here, telling you how I survived the Nazi concentration camps. I've never been here before, never seen any of you before, never given this speech before. But in my dreams, in my dreams, I have stood before you and said these words a thousand times."[3]

Hope is a noun. It is concrete. Let your hope be firm concrete. When you pour cement for a footer you cannot build on it until the cement "sets up" or cures. Only when it is firm can you build a house on concrete. Hope is the same way. When hope is mushy or watered down, Satan can squeeze it into any mold he wants. But when it is firm, it is unbendable, made to last. Hebrews 3:6 counsels us to "hold fast the confidence and the rejoicing of the hope firm to the end." Firm to the end. That's a hope that gets you through life, whether times are good or bad. But it must be firm, it must be concrete. If it is not, your hope will be bent and plied, so as not to provide the support your life needs to build on.

Never give up hope, regardless of how cold the winter of your life may become. Psalm 42:5 asks, "Why are you cast down, O my soul? And why are you disquieted within me? Hope in God, for I shall yet praise Him for the help of His countenance." That's the confidence of hope that never gives up.

Gilbert Beenken said, "Other men see only a hopeless end, but the Christian rejoices in an endless hope." Hang in there with hope in Christ. If you hang in long enough, the concrete will cure and you will have a strong foundation upon which to build your life. "For You are my hope, O Lord God; You are my trust from my youth" (Ps. 71:5).

Living hope is something you can have—right now—because hope is a noun and Jesus deals in the concrete, not the abstract. Trust the Savior to give you a hope you can hold on to, not the hope you have to chase.

But the hope that Jesus Christ gives isn't just hope to live by. It's also hope to die by. If there is a time when we need the hope of the Lord, surely it is when we are facing the ultimate challenge of life—death.

Jesus Christ Gives Dying Hope

What kind of God would He be if He gave us hope throughout the good days and the dark days of life and then abandoned us when we needed Him the most? Not the God of the Bible. The consistent teaching of God's Word is that the God who brings hope throughout our lives does not abandon us at the end of our lives. "The wicked is driven away in his wickedness: but the righteous hath hope in his death" (Prov. 14:32 KJV). Those in the Old Testament didn't fully understand what that hope entailed, but it was concrete hope nonetheless.

The New Testament writers filled in the blanks. Paul said, "If in this life only we have hope in Christ, we are of all men the most pitiable" (1 Cor. 15:19). The hope that God gives begins at the cribside and continues to the graveside. If we enjoy hope in this temporal life and cannot enjoy the gift of God's hope in death, when we need that hope the most, we are to be pitied more than anybody. Temporal hope is not real hope; it's a Band-Aid© looking for a scrape.

Hope for a Murderess

In 1978, a woman who lived in rural North Carolina, Velma Barfield, was arrested for brutally murdering four people. As heinous as her crime was, it looms even more reprehensible because two of those victims were her fiancé and her own mother. She never denied her guilt. A victim of incest as a child and the abuser of prescription drugs as an adult, Barfield was sent to prison and placed in solitary confinement. There was no hope for her; she was irredeemable, or so everyone thought.

One night a guard tuned the radio to a Christian station. That night, Velma Barfield heard a radio speaker teach God's Word. She heard for the very first time that God loved her so much He sent His Son to die for her. That night, Velma Barfield's life was changed forever. She trusted Jesus Christ as Savior and became a new creature in Christ (2 Cor. 5:17). That night, for the first time in her life, Velma Barfield had hope.

Velma Barfield was the first woman in twenty-two years to be executed in the United States. She paid her debt to society, but she died knowing that Jesus Christ had paid her debt for sin. She learned that only God can give the kind of hope that lives beyond death. She faced her execution bravely because she had eternal hope.

With our hand in the hand of Jesus, we don't face death alone. The Lord Jesus Christ is our hope and gives us hope when we need it most.

Already Experienced

The kind of dying hope Jesus gives is the kind of hope that comes with experience. Talk about an advantage. It's like the difference between being a freshman football player in your first game and a senior who has played in two national championships.

Experience. There's nothing like it. And Jesus knows the way. He has walked it before. Place your hand in the hand of One who "was made a little lower than the angels, for the suffering of death crowned with glory and honor, that He, by the grace of God, might taste death for everyone" (Heb. 2:9). You can face your own death with hope if you face it with the One who faced His own shameful death with glory and honor. For when the mob was at its worst, crying "Crucify Him, crucify Him," Jesus was at His best, praying, "Father, forgive them, for they do not know what they do" (Luke 23:34).

If you have a choice between facing death with fear or facing it with hope, choose hope. Tap into the experience of Christ's death, and let Him walk you through that door to the future.

Death, Where Is *Your* Sting?

A scorpion without its stinger is just supper for some slightly deranged gourmet. A yellow jacket without its stinger is just a brightly colored bug. Without their stingers, these creatures are not to be feared. So, too, is death without its sting (1 Cor. 15:55).

God promised His people in the ancient days of Hosea, just before the fall of Israel in 722 B.C., "I will ransom them from the power of the grave; I will redeem them from death. O Death, I will be your plagues! O Grave, I will be your destruction!" (Hos. 13:14). What God promises in the Old Testament, He performs in the New Testament. In describing what it will be like when our bodies yield to the ground, the apostle Paul bubbles over, saying, "Then shall be brought to pass the saying that is written: 'Death is swallowed up in victory.' 'O Death, where is your sting? O Hades, where is your victory?' The sting of death is sin, and the strength of sin is the law. But thanks be to God, who gives us the victory through our Lord Jesus Christ" (1 Cor. 15:54-57). The God of hope is the God of victory.

Does death cause pain? Of course it does. Just look at the red eyes at a funeral home. So in what way has Jesus taken away the sting of death? If it were not for sin, death would have no sting. The Law of God and its stringent moral demands have been seriously and repeatedly violated by men and women of every generation. We know that we must pay a penalty for our sin and that penalty is death (Rom. 6:23) That's the sting. Men and women are afraid to die because they know they are sinners. Innately they realize that they are facing a day when God will square accounts.

The Christian, however, faces death with hope, knowing that our sin has already been paid for by the blood of Jesus at the cross. We are confident that "There is therefore now no condemnation to those who are in Christ Jesus" (Rom. 8:1). The scorpion still threatens us, but the stinger is gone.

I wouldn't want to face death without hope, but thank God I don't have to. And neither do you, if you face death with the certain knowledge that you have been born again. Jesus has taken the sting out of death and given us dying hope in it's place. Praise God!

Not the End

For most people death seems final. Death is the end; death is terminal. Not in the least. We face death with the confident hope that there is more to come. Death is not the end; death is like Chicago.

Because I live in Lincoln, Nebraska, which isn't on the way to anywhere, I have to fly somewhere to fly somewhere. That usually means flying to Chicago, sometimes as often as twice a week. When I pass through Chicago's O'Hare International Airport—one of the busiest airports in the world—I think of death. O'Hare is rarely my final destination. It's just a place where I change planes to go elsewhere. That's why I think death is like Chicago. Death is not the end. It is not my final destination. I'm only changing bodies there. I'm going on to heaven, and the body I'll be using on the other leg of my journey makes this one seem pathetic.

Have you seen the gravestone of Ben Franklin? He wrote the following epitaph for his tomb: "The Body of Benjamin Franklin, Printer, Like the Cover of an Old Book, Its Contents Torn Out, Stripped of Its Lettering and Gilding, Lies Here, Food for Worms. Yet the Work Itself shall not be Lost; for it will, as He Believed, Appear once More in a New and More Beautiful Edition, Corrected and Amended by The Author." That's what I'm looking for—a more beautiful edition.

No, the Christian faces death with hope knowing it's not the end. It's not all over at death. We're just changing planes. The destination is a much better place and with Jesus as the pilot, not only will we arrive in good condition and on time, we're even going to fly first class and enjoy the flight.

Dying hope is something you can have—right now—because hope is a noun. Nouns are things you have. Trust the Savior to give you a hope you can hold on to. When death comes, hold tightly to the confidence you have in Christ Jesus and you will hold tightly to concrete hope.

Jesus Christ Gives Resurrection Hope

The idea of resurrection, coming alive again after we have died, has been around for a long time. It's not uniquely a Christian doctrine. The Old Testament is filled with verses that allude to the resurrection of the body.

> And many of those who sleep in the dust of the earth shall awake, some to everlasting life, some to shame and everlasting contempt. (Daniel 12:2)

> Your dead shall live; together with my dead body they shall arise. Awake and sing, you who dwell in dust; for your dew is like the dew of herbs, and the earth shall cast out the dead. (Isaiah 26:19)

> He will swallow up death forever, and the Lord God will wipe away tears from all faces. (Isaiah 25:8)

This last verse sounds like the basis for 1 Corinthians 15:54—"Death is swallowed up in victory"—and Revelation 21:4—"And God will wipe away every tear from their eyes." In fact, it is.

Jesus gives us hope to handle the coldest winters of life. He gives us hope to face death. But when we die—and we all will unless the Lord returns first—He gives us hope that on the other side of death we will see Him in eternity. What does resurrection hope mean?

More Beyond Death

Resurrection hope confirms the validity of our dying hope. It is possible, I suppose, that dying hope is a crutch and that death really is the end. But God rewards dying hope with the hope of resurrection. Recall Job 19:25-27: "For I know that my Redeemer lives, and He shall stand at last on the earth; and after my skin is destroyed, this I know, that in my flesh I shall see God, whom I shall see for myself ." Job's confidence is striking. He has knowledge because he has hope.

When you're watching TV and it's time for a commercial, the station doesn't want you to bolt for the refrigerator. So it's not uncommon to hear something like, "Don't go away. There's more to come." That's what God says to all who have resurrection hope: "There's more to come." Resurrection hope, then, is not only the natural outgrowth of dying hope, it is confirmation of dying hope. Both say, "There's more to come."

Portugal is the westernmost country on the European continent. Its motto is *ne plus ultra,* "Nothing More Beyond." Ancient mariners leaving Portugal's ports would be warned not to sail too far west because there was nothing beyond the horizon. You can go that far and no further. The edge of the earth marked the outer limits. Christopher Columbus proved *plus ultra*—there is more beyond. Jesus Christ did the same in both the physical and spiritual realms.

Resurrection hope, coupled with dying hope, makes living hope even more concrete. They are all something we have, not something we do.

Not an Uncharted Course

Just as approaching death holding onto the Savior's hand provides great hope and strength, so it is with resurrection hope. We can face death with hope because Jesus already faced it and beat it. He laid the groundwork for us. That's true with resurrection hope, too. Jesus has already been over that ground and has blazed a trail for us to follow.

We know it is possible to be raised from the dead and never to die again because Jesus has already done it. Not only did He prove it can be done, He showed us how it's done. Jesus said, "Because I live, you will live also" (John 14:19). He is the firstfruits, which means there is more to follow. "But now Christ is risen from the dead, and has become the firstfruits of those who have fallen asleep [died]" (1 Cor. 15:20).

Have you ever stopped at a gas station for directions? It can be frustrating when you are not familiar with the area and a "local" gives you directions. "Go down the road to Culpepper's barn and take a right on route 63. After you pass the grain silo [of which there seem to be a million on this road], you'll see a fork in the road. Take it." It's almost impossible to follow directions like that. But what if the guy at the station said, "I've been over that road. Follow me. I'll take you there."

You can have resurrection hope in Jesus because He's been over the road before. He'll take you there; all you have to do is follow.

True Picture of Life and Death

It's impossible to adequately understand life and death without some understanding of resurrection. Many eastern countries, with their beliefs in reincarnation, will never break the cycle of poverty, disease, and hopelessness. Their thinking is cyclical instead of linear. If at first you don't succeed, be reincarnated and try, try again. But that's not how life works. Life is going somewhere; it is heading for a goal—that mansion over the hilltop. Resurrection gives us the only true picture of life and death.

Not only does death not end life; it doesn't end growth either. We just grow in a different time, a different space, a different dimension. We grow in glory. To some, death is a wall. But to the hope-filled Christian, Jesus has cracked the wall and given us a glimpse of what's on the other side.

A number of years ago I conducted the funeral of one of the dearest saints I have ever met—Annie Lott. When the family asked me to conduct the funeral service I was honored. I depicted death in much the same way that I have in these pages. I wanted the family to know that, not only was Annie alive, Annie was still on the move, still growing, still climbing higher to her Maker. I read this meaningful verse to conclude my message. I wish I knew who wrote it.

> Near a shady wall a rose once grew,
> Budded and blossomed in God's free light,
> Watered and fed by morning dew,
> Shedding its sweetness day and night.
> As it grew and blossomed fair and tall,
> Slowly rising to loftier height,
> It came to a crevice in the wall,
> Through which there shone a beam of light.
> Onward it crept with added strength,
> With never a thought of fear or pride,
> It followed the light through the crevice's length,
> And unfolded itself on the other side.
> Shall claim of death cause us to grieve,
> And make our courage faint and fall?
> No! Let us faith and hope receive,
> Because the rose still grows beyond the wall.

Resurrection hope is something you can have—right now—because hope is a noun. The resurrected Lord deals in the concrete, not the abstract. Trust Him to take you beyond the grave, all the way to Glory. It's a trip He's already made.

Jesus Christ Gives a Blessed Hope

This planet is becoming a scary place to live. On average, one person kills him- or herself every 17.1 minutes. Annually, there are 775,000 suicide attempts in the United States alone. More people die by suicide in the United States than by homicide.[4] In countries where people aren't killing themselves, the population is starving to death. In November 1996, a World Food Summit was held in Rome. It was attended by 185 countries and the European Community. Summit leaders said, "We consider it intolerable that more than 800 million people throughout the world and particularly in developing countries, do not have enough food to meet their basic nutritional needs."[5] And if they aren't starving to death, people are dying of disease at unprecedented rates. According to the World Health Organization and UNAIDS, seven out of ten people newly infected with HIV last year live in sub-Saharan Africa. An estimated 34 million people living in sub-Saharan Africa have been infected with HIV.[6] And many of them are children. Disease is destroying the continent.

A Climate of Violence

In the United States, some of the most hopeless news in the past few years concerns school violence, which seems to be escalating. On October 1, 1997, a sixteen-year-old boy in Pearl, Mississippi, is alleged to have killed his mother, then taken his gun to the high school, shooting nine students, two fatally. Two months to the day later, on December 1, three students were killed and five others wounded in the hallway at Heath High School in West Paducah, Kentucky.

On March 24, 1998, four girls and a teacher were shot to death and ten people wounded during a false fire alarm in Jonesboro, Arkansas, when two boys, eleven and thirteen, opened fire from the woods. One month to the day later a science teacher was shot to death in Edinboro, Pennsylvania, by a fourteen-year-old boy. May 19, 1998, three days before his graduation, an eighteen-year-old honors student opened fire in a high school parking lot in Fayetteville, Tennessee, killing a classmate who was dating his ex-girlfriend. Two days later two teens were killed and twenty others injured when a fifteen-year-old boy opened fire in a Springfield, Oregon, high school. And on April 20, 1999, two students at Columbine High School in Littleton, Colorado, shot twelve students and a teacher to death, wounding twenty-three others before killing themselves.[7]

To all of you who cling to the belief that man is evolving into something better and that utopia is coming, buy a paper. Turn on CNN. Get a clue. Things are getting worse, not better. The only salvation we have from a world becoming increasingly more violent is to be divinely airlifted out of here. That's God's plan. We call it the blessed hope—hope that is a noun.

Take a Bible Journey

Look in your Bible. Can you find where it says that we might not die? Begin in Genesis. Does anything there hint that we might not die? Likely not, especially in chapter five, which lists nine generations of Adam's family with this pertinent comment about eight of them: "and he died" (vv. 5, 8, 11, 14, 17, 20, 27, 31). The notable exception was Enoch who "walked with God; and he was not, for God took him" (v. 24). There is no promise in the Book of Beginnings that we will not die.

How about Exodus? Any hint in Exodus that we might not die? Not with the carnage of the plagues. How about Leviticus, Numbers, or Deuteronomy? Nowhere in the Pentateuch is there a hint that we may not die.

What about the historical books—Joshua, Judges, Ruth, the Samuels, Kings, Chronicles, Ezra, Nehemiah, or Esther? Try the poetic books of Job, Psalms, Proverbs, Ecclesiastes, and Song of Solomon. Then look at the major and minor prophets.

You can search the entire Old Testament, chapter by chapter, page by page, and you won't find any reference to the possibility that we might not die.

Now look through the Gospels—Matthew, Mark, Luke, and John. No mention of any blessed hope there. You can also search through Acts and Romans and you will not find a shred of teaching on the possibility that we may be taken from this earth without enduring the trauma of death.

Special Revelation

Finally we come to 1 Corinthians 15. Paul says, "Behold, I tell you a mystery: We shall not all sleep, but we shall all be changed—in a moment, in the twinkling of an eye, at the last trumpet. For the trumpet will sound, and the dead will be raised incorruptible, and we shall be changed" (vv. 51-52). Paul calls this a mystery because nobody knew about it before. It was hidden from all the previous writers of Scripture to be revealed specifically to Paul so that he could reveal it to us.

In 1 Thessalonians 4:13–18, the apostle comments,

> But I do not want you to be ignorant, brethren, concerning those who have fallen asleep, lest you sorrow as others *who have no hope* [hope is a possession]. For if we believe that Jesus died and rose again, even so God will bring with Him those who sleep in Jesus. For this we say to you by the word of the Lord, that we who are alive and remain until the coming of the Lord will by no means precede those who are asleep. For the Lord Himself will descend from heaven with a shout, with the voice of an archangel, and with the trumpet of God. And the dead in Christ will rise first. Then *we who are alive* and remain shall be caught up together with them in the clouds to meet the Lord in the air. And thus we shall always be with the Lord. Therefore comfort one another with these words. (emphasis added)

But there's more. The apostle challenged his friend, Titus, to deny ungodliness and worldly lusts and to live a godly life, all the while "looking for the blessed hope and glorious appearing of our great God and Savior Jesus Christ" (Titus 2:13). Paul had hope, a blessed hope that he might not die. He told Titus not to look for a crack in the ground but to look for a crack in the sky.

Special Encouragement

Knowing that Christ may return before we have to face death makes a positive impact on us.

It gives urgency and zeal to our service. D. L. Moody always preached as if Christ would return before he finished his sermon. He really believed that he would see his returning Lord before he saw death. If we all were prodded by this kind of hope, we would not only keep short accounts with God and live lives of purity (1 John 3:3), but we would take every opportunity God gives us to serve Him or to leave a witness with friends and family. If we really believed that every opportunity might be our last, then we'd live like we really believed it.

It gives us a better perspective on where history is headed. The nineteenth-century Bible scholar, Alexander Maclaren, said, "The primitive church thought more about the Second Coming of Jesus Christ than about death or heaven. The early Christians were looking, not for a cleft in the ground called a grave, but for a cleavage in the sky called Glory. They were watching, not for an undertaker, but for an uppertaker."[8] Believing that we have hope beyond the grave, and even a hope instead of the grave, gives us a whole new way of looking at where we as Christians are headed.

It gives us courage to hold hope as a noun. The twenty-first century will not be easy. Our technology will rapidly rise and, in the developed world, morality will just as rapidly fall. We will be wealthier and poorer at the same time. We will be raised on help but robbed of hope. That's why the blessed hope will become more important in the days to come. The courage to continue when we are discouraged is like the lopsided Little League baseball score. A man who happened by asked a boy in the outfield "What's the score?" The boy replied, "Eighteen to nothing, and we're behind." The man chuckled and said, "I'll bet you're discouraged, huh?" The little guy stared at him and questioned, "Why? We haven't gotten to bat yet." When you have hope, you know that things may be tough, but you haven't yet come to bat.

Got You Covered

When we belong to the Lord Jesus, when we are born again, when the blood of Christ has cleansed us from the penalty of our sin and we are on our way to heaven, we have a wonderful by-product of salvation. This by-product is a four-letter word called hope. The cross of Calvary is a place called hope. The One who suffered and died there for us is Christ Jesus, the hope of glory.

Are you sometimes baffled by the world around you? Do you think we are tripping headlong toward an indeterminate end? Does your world feel hopeless? If the answer is yes to any of these questions, I offer you the hope each author has written about in this book. This hope is real. It is eternal hope. It is living hope. It is dying hope. It is resurrection hope. It is the blessed hope. It is the hope that only

Jesus can give, the kind you can build a life on and feel secure in. When you find your hope in the Lord, you discover that hope is a noun. It's what you have as a possession when you have Jesus Christ as Savior. Whatever kind of hope you need, Jesus has got you covered. He can provide hope to the wealthy and the poor, the man and the woman, the Easterner and Westerner.

If your heart is troubled, grasp the hope that comes only in Jesus Christ, who said, "Let not your heart be troubled; you believe [hope] in God, believe [hope] also in Me" (John 14:1). For everyone, regardless of ethnic origin, religious affiliation, or cultural heritage, Jesus is hope. He is alive and real, and His hope is concrete. Take Him as your hope, and when you hold His hand you will hold hope in your hand. Hope is a noun, something to hold on to all the days of your life. Grab onto that hope today.

> My hope is in the Lord who gave Himself for me,
> And paid the price of all my sin at Calvary.
> No merit of my own His anger to suppress,
> My only hope is found in Jesus' righteousness.
> And now for me He stands before the Father's throne.
> He shows His wounded hands, and names me as His own.
> His grace has planned it all, 'tis mine but to believe,
> And recognize His work of love and Christ receive.
> For me He died, for me He lives, and everlasting
> Life and light He freely gives.
> — Norman J. Clayton, "My Hope Is in the Lord"

Chapter Notes

1. Alexander Pope, *An Essay on Man, 1734* (reprint, Menston, England: Scholar Press, 1969), 12.
2. Dante Alighieri, *The Divine Comedy,* translation and comment by John D. Sinclair (New York: Oxford University Press, 1961), I Inferno, Canto 3.
3. To read more of Victor Frankl's experiences in Nazi prison camps, see *From Death-Camp to Existentialism,* trans. Ilse Lasch (Boston: Beacon, 1959).

4. Statistics from American Association of Suicidology. http://www.suicidology.org/suicide_statistics.htm; INTERNET.

5. From FAO's World Food Summit report. http://www.fao.org/unfao/bodies/cfs/default.htm; INTERNET.

6. UNAIDS Fact Sheet. http://www.unaids.org/highband/fact/saepap98.html; INTERNET.

7. From an Associated Press wire story, 20 May 1999.

8. See Alexander Maclaren's full description of the Christian's "happy hope" in his *Expositions of Holy Scripture, Titus* (Chicago, Ill.: W. P. Blessing, n.d.), 158–71.